RENÉ

Peter Desbarats

RENÉ

A Canadian in Search of a Country

McClelland and Stewart

For Carla.

ISBN: 0-7710-2691-9

McClelland and Stewart Limited,
The Canadian Publishers,
25 Hollinger Road,
Toronto.
M4B 3G2

Printed and bound in Canada
by John Deyell Company

Contents

Acknowledgements

This book could not have been written without the encouragement and time provided by Bill Cunningham, Vice-President of News and Public Affairs of Global Television. I am indebted to him and to the network.

Pierre Cloutier, a young Montreal academic with a flair for journalism, conscientiously performed the drudgery of locating and assembling the journalistic record for me, as well as guiding me to other useful publications. He will recognize the very large share that he has in this book.

On his behalf, I would like to thank the newspaper librarians in Montreal who helped to assemble such a comprehensive biographical file. My own thanks go to the staff of the Parliamentary Library in Ottawa.

I was agreeably surprised by the readiness of most politicians to talk to me frankly about Lévesque, trusting in my own discretion. I hope that they will regard the book as useful.

Finally, I am grateful to René Lévesque for making himself available to a writer who consistently disagreed with the separatist option during the Sixties. When someone at a small party meeting in the Gaspé once asked Lévesque who I was, he replied briefly that I was "a strange kind of journalist." A suitable early biographer, I hope, for an unusual politician.

Introduction

René Lévesque arrives at a Montreal restaurant only fifteen minutes late, apologizing profusely. The man who kept cabinet ministers and political audiences waiting for hours in the Sixties, the nervous and harried Lévesque of those years, seems to have eased up, slowed down and filled out a little.

He's fifty-four years old. The youngest of his three children, his only daughter, is a rebellious twenty-year-old, almost as restless as her father was at that age. As he talks about her, he shakes his head with the bewilderment of all parents buffeted by the rush of their children into adulthood.

There's something else that he now talks about, briefly and without embarrassment: the fact that he hasn't lived with his wife for the past six years. Almost every Quebec journalist has been aware of Lévesque's erratic domestic life for years but few serious ones have ever written about it or, as a consequence, about his continuing strong attachment to his children.

Lévesque's children belong to a generation of French-Canadians whose political conservatism confounds their elders. For them, René Lévesque is an ancient warrior mumbling about forgotten battles. The opinion polls show that most of them will vote for his party but only as a matter of course, without any sense of rebellion.

Only outside Quebec does Lévesque still appear to be a revolutionary. Only in English Canada can he regain some of the excitement of the "quiet revolution" that shook Quebec in the Sixties.

However, even that is changing. A generation of English-speaking Canadians has grown accustomed to, even bored with the alarms and confusions of Quebec politics since the "revolution" began in 1960. While French-Canadians strive to comprehend the tangible achievements of the past sixteen years, the long struggle of the Sixties has produced in English Canada a tougher sense of self-reliance, and a feeling that the future of Quebec is best left to the Québécois.

If there is a single French-Canadian public figure whose life illuminates an entire generation, and reveals something of this future, it is René Lévesque.

Like Quebec itself, an old linguistic anomaly in North America, Lévesque's roots are in the countryside. He grew up in a society that had remained virtually static for almost two centuries. His home town in the Gaspé contained all the elements of the larger Quebec world—the stereotyped English-Canadian entrepreneurs and the French-Canadian parish priest, as well as the more subtle distinctions between the working class "Irish" of the Gaspé and educated French-Canadians like the lawyer Dominique Lévesque, René father.

Lévesque was educated by Roman Catholic priests, as were all French-Canadians of his generation who were privileged to go beyond elementary school. This traditional pattern was disrupted by the Second World War.

In French Canada, there was a long history of opposition to military service in overseas wars of the British Empire. Some of the opposition originated in the political struggle of French-Canadians to resist absorption by the English-speaking majority in Canada; but there was also a fear of letting young French-Canadians look at Quebec from a distance. The thousands who did serve overseas in this war never felt the same about the little Quebec battles over language and religion, after they returned.

Lévesque found his own way to wartime London and Europe, as a propagandist for the Americans, but the experience had the same effect. After such a dazzling exposure to world events and the scale of American power, it was years before he could see the concerns of his own people as significant.

His own growing importance in Quebec, as a television journalist, brought him back to his own people and their concerns. Explaining the world to the new television audience in Quebec made him see that audience afresh, made him think about farmers rocking before their TV screens beneath the fluorescent lights of their linoleum kitchens, and factory workers who went to American movies every week but desperately needed to have the news explained by one of their own.

Lévesque has always thought of explaining, interpreting, and teaching as the essence of journalism, and as his true vocation. Like all authentic political leaders, he has something highly personal to say to his people. His message created his style on the platform and shaped his political career. Understanding how he feels about Quebec is the only path to understanding him.

And the task is complex. He is both proud of the achievements of the past and ashamed at the price that French-Canadians have had to pay for survival. Hope for the future and fear of it, the national schizophrenia of Quebec, tear Lévesque apart. He loves this deformed society even as he rails against its weaknesses, It has survived, that is undeniable. Perhaps it has only started to live.

The first stirrings occurred in the early Sixties. For a few years, everything seemed possible in Quebec. The Roman Catholic Church was put into a corner and almost forgotten. New objectives transformed the school system, the civil service, public finance, labour unions and virtually all other Quebec institutions. There was an explosion of artistic energy as the new sense of achievement and national pride expressed itself in popular culture, particularly in music.

Amid all this, Lévesque was a new kind of Quebec politician. He was competent. He was honest. He worked incessantly. After he single-handedly nationalized the province's hydro-electric system in 1962, after only two years in politics, there was a feeling that he could do and become almost anything he desired.

The immediate effect of this burst of political creativity was as disappointing as it was unexpected. In 1966, a conservative political reaction threw Lévesque's party out of government and the whole province into uncertainty. The sense of direction that had seemed so clear for a few years, toward a capable and mature Quebec society, was lost overnight. Cynicism returned to political life as Lévesque, with a small number of friends in his old party, tried to discover what had gone wrong.

The answer, for some of them, produced a renewed commitment to Quebec, impractical as it seemed at the time. Only a few followed him in this direction. Most of Lévesque's colleagues of the early Sixties abandoned him then, submitting themselves to an assessment of Quebec's needs that seemed more realistic. Some went to Ottawa where the federal Liberals held power; others stayed with the Quebec Liberals until the party returned to power in 1970.

Most of them now, in 1976, appear to have been exhausted by the effort, and at the end of their careers. Only Lévesque still seems to look ahead to the future and to promise perhaps an even greater contribution than he has made in the past.

He has now been in politics for sixteen years. His political career began five years before Pierre Trudeau, Jean Marchand and Gérard Pelletier went into politics. Marchand and Pelletier have now given all they have to give. Of the "Three Wise Men" from Quebec who came to Ottawa in 1965, Prime Minister Trudeau alone remains powerful and at a decisive point in his own career. Lévesque is older in political life than Trudeau but it is Lévesque who now seems to contain the seed of new political life, and who may turn out to be the Canadian who completes the work that the four men started in the early Sixties.

The idea of René Lévesque negotiating the future of Canada with Pierre Trudeau is too far in the future to be anything but wildly speculative–but how potent that prospect is!

Should this ever happen, the two men may hardly recognize one another, remembering instead the early Sixties when they argued night after night about the future of Quebec: Lévesque the dynamic politician testing the limits of his new capability; Trudeau the aloof intellectual still unencumbered by concerns about political tactics. Now the Prime Minister has become the most calculating of politicians, wary and suspicious. It is Lévesque who explores the frontiers of new political territories.

Trudeau must defend the compromises that have kept Canadians together under his leadership; Lévesque can dazzle Canadians with an untarnished thesis–with the hope of a fresh start.

That's one way to look at Lévesque and Trudeau, at Quebec and Canada–but look a bit deeper. In the personalities of the two men, you can glimpse the social reformer who still struggles within the Prime Minister, and the grizzled political veteran who guides Lévesque from within.

Lévesque has his own compromises to defend. He was an integral part of a Quebec government that faltered in 1966 and almost deliberately threw itself out of office, as if it was afraid to face the full meaning and effects of its own success. Lévesque's reputation almost went down with that government; but instead of abandoning Quebec for federal politics, the higher bureaucracy, the corporate boardroom, or the coziness of academic life, Lévesque preferred the insecurity of a doubtful political adventure.

That decision says a great deal about him. There were a number of paths open to him in 1966, in Ottawa and Quebec, that promised status and financial security. He chose instead to create his own party while supporting himself and his family on his salary as an ordinary member of the National Assembly and later as a pensioner of the Assembly and a political columnist.

Money is not a powerful incentive for Lévesque. His severest critics say that without qualification.

It is just as clear that Lévesque has an appetite for polititical power; and when he has power, he doesn't share it easily. The path of his career is littered with bureaucrats and politicians who carry the scars of collisions with Lévesque and who regard him as a self-centred and ruthless politician.

What is at the centre?

It is fundamentally impossible to find the place, in Lévesque's career and perhaps in his heart, where the interests of Quebec stop in favour of Lévesque's own interests. He is a man possessed by a national ideal. In today's world this isn't an unusual phenomenon, but it is a rare thing in Quebec, and almost unknown in the rest of Canada.

Canada is still too large and too diverse for patriotism. That is why English-speaking Canadians work so hard at it. Quebec is still small enough, and the Québécois still enough of a family, for a patriot to love all of it, to create sentimental songs about it, and to make emotional political speeches about it. It's very personal.

Like Pierre Trudeau, like many politicians, Lévesque is a secretive man, with few close friends. None of these friends have any startling insights to offer about him. He seems to conceal himself as effectively in private as he reveals himself in public. His career is an emotional performance, both on the platform and in the "smoke-filled backrooms" of Lévesque's own personality.

The highs and lows of Lévesque's career stand out like a Himalayan range over the foothills and plains of more ordinary lives. Time and again, he has plummeted from the heights of achievement and optimism to the depths of disillusion. Lévesque doesn't just get discouraged when things go wrong. He dies for a while, and waits for some external event to resurrect him.

It's a recurring pattern. Lévesque has told so many people so many times that he's going to end it all, politically, that the threats no longer alarm anyone. Not then and not there.But there is an assumption among many people close to Lévesque that he will end his political career in an unexpected way at some point, before achieving a conventional kind of success.

Few people, envisage him as the eventual leader of an independent Quebec.

Whenever Lévesque has been lost in the valleys of self-doubt, he has despaired of Quebec. No polititician has ever exposed the flaws and delusions of French Canada more brutally. No politician in English-speaking Canada would dare to belittle the second-rate pettiness of this small nation, as Lévesque does in Quebec, or to treat its history as a record of misguided starts and predictable failures, just as no English-speaking Canadian politician offers to his people the promise of independent achievement that Lévesque holds out to Quebec.

English-speaking Canadians also hear Lévesque. There is enough dissatisfaction with their own national experience, enough yearning for a more complete future, to give his words resonance in other provinces. From a distance, English-Canadians can feel the attraction of his ideas and the force of his personality. They are excited and repelled by him.

Over time, they have also become accustomed to him. In fact, in a superficial way, Lévesque is more popular in English Canada now than he is in Quebec. His "separatism" is disliked as intensely as ever but Lévesque himself is regarded as a fresh, fascinating kind of politician. Not in Quebec, to the same extent. There, Lévesque's political ideas create less apprehension now but his personality has also become less exciting, a little shopworn.

For young French-Canadians, Lévesque is a figure from an "ancien régime." They are growing up in a Quebec that is, for better or worse, more separate from Canada than anyone would have believed possible in 1960. This has been the real "quiet revolution." One by one, major corporations have gradually separated their Canadian activities from their Quebec operations, leaving French-Canadians in charge of regional head offices in Montreal, the city that controlled half a continent in the nineteenth century.

With their own sphere of economic activity curtailed, with little participation in politics and none in the Quebec bureaucracy, the English-speaking people of Quebec no longer function as a creative element in Quebec society or as an effective link between Quebec and the rest of Canada.

More than they ever were, French-Canadians of Quebec are on their own today, as free as any of us are to decide their own future and to live with the consequences of their decisions.

Lévesque has contributed enormously to this, as a journalist, as a cabinet minister, and as a leader who gave political form to the vague ideas about independence that inspired Quebec in the Sixties. Now the concluding chapter is being written, perhaps with a surprise ending that no one could have foreseen when it started. Perhaps René Lévesque will be seen finally, by all Canadians, as a man who showed them how to live together.

Ottawa
July, 1976.

12

I
Five Wise Men at
the Crossroads

Around Gérard Pelletier's dining room table in the early hours of May 17, 1963, each man moved from the present toward the future wearing the past as a disguise.

André Laurendeau, Pelletier and Jean Marchand, who would have identified themselves then as Quebec nationalists, were destined to play important roles in Ottawa as definers and defenders of a new Canadian federalism.

Pierre Trudeau, the least "political" of the group in 1963 and a hostile critic of Quebec nationalism, was moving toward Canada's highest political office, where he would incorporate Laurendeau's work in a new definition of Canadian nationalism.

And René Lévesque, whose special field as a television commentator had been international affairs and United States' politics, and who had been regarded as having little interest in Quebec politics, was in the early stages of a political evolution that would bring him to the leadership of the first important independence party in Quebec history.

All the influential political ideas then circulating through Quebec were channelled into Pelletier's dining room that night. Like Quebec itself, the five men were moving, in different ways, through a period of swift change. Like all French-Canadians, they felt the excitement in the air in that spring of 1963.

It was the season for new departures in a society that had remained unusually static and defensive since it had been overwhelmed by British armies two centuries before.

In the early Sixties in Quebec, everything suddenly seemed possible. The walls that French-Canadians had raised and persistently reinforced to shield them from outside influences were being pierced by doors opening onto broad avenues leading toward bright horizons.

Two principle avenues were clearly visible.

One was the road taken by those Canadians Laurendeau once described as "the upholders of reconciliation" between French and English.

The other avenue was narrower and rougher. Only a small number of Canada's French-speaking minority had travelled on it in the past.

In 1952, looking back along this overgrown and almost abandoned trail, Laurendeau had written that "separatism, the splitting of Quebec from the rest of Canada, is a dream, a fantasy that we should abandon on leaving adolescence."

But only eight years later, the dream had become tangible in the first separatist political movement of real potential, the *Rassemblement pour l'indépendance nationale*, predecessor of the party that Lévesque would create in 1968 and that would become the official opposition in Quebec's National Assembly in 1973.

The two paths were theoretically on a collision course, but in 1963, most Canadians felt confident that there would never be a dangerous clash between Canadian federalism and Quebec separatism. That sense of security would be seriously undermined before the end of the decade.

II
Trudeau versus Lévesque:
The Beginning of Confrontation

May 16, 1963, was a warm, velvety evening.

It was the right moment to open the double kitchen doors of the grey stone house on Elm Avenue, to watch the tobacco smoke streaming through a tunnel of light into the dark garden, and to inhale, after the endless winter of smoke and talk in overheated rooms, the green smell of new growth.

Gérard Pelletier stood for a few moments on the back porch, savouring the sense of rebirth that compensates northern peoples for their hard winters. But it was too brief. The intensity of the late Canadian spring already seemed to be dissolving into the long, tropical nights of a Montreal summer.

Lighting another cigarette, he walked back through the kitchen to rejoin the four men seated around the remains of a late supper in his dining room.

René Lévesque was still talking.

The butt of a cigarette smouldered between his thin lips. He gestured absent-mindedly toward Pelletier for another, lit it from the remnant pinched between his thumb and forefinger, and inhaled quickly without interrupting the tempo of his argument.

His thin face glistened. In the overhead light of the dining room, the dark lines and sallow pouches made him look much older than his forty years. But he talked with the enthusiasm of a university student, not the deliberation that one might have expected from a senior member of the Quebec cabinet. And he talked. And talked.

Only Pierre Trudeau, the wealthy law professor from the University of Montreal, with the triangular, almost oriental face, was adept at locating the vulnerable spots in that seemingly impenetrable flow.

There had been some doubt, the previous autumn, that the Friday night meetings of the group would continue at all after Trudeau had goaded Lévesque almost to physical violence during an argument about the Quebec government's plan to borrow $300 million to nationalize the province's hydro-electric companies.

As Quebec's Minister of Natural Resources, Lévesque was the hero of nationalization – the central figure in the Quebec election of November, 1962, next to Premier Jean Lesage. Nationalization had provided the substance of the Liberal government's campaign slogan: *"Maître Chez Nous* – Masters in Our Own House."

Before the campaign, Lévesque had used Trudeau and the others in the group – labour leader Marchand and newspaper editors Pelletier and Laurendeau, to try out his arguments for nationalization.

Eventually he had convinced Pelletier, Marchand and Laurendeau that the hydro-electric takeover was a necessary reform at that stage of the political, social and economic transformation of Quebec that journalists had been referring to as the "quiet revolution." Only Trudeau had remained skeptical. Despite his socialist commitment to the new federal New Democratic Party he had argued that there were more productive ways to invest $300 million.

Nothing had made Lévesque angrier than Trudeau's claim that the takeover was motivated largely by nationalist sentiment and political tactics.

In his own mind, it was exactly the reverse. From the first stages of his commitment to nationalization in 1961, Lévesque had tried to base his approach on practical arguments. He was convinced that the plan made economic sense, and he had fought hard for it in the cabinet, at one point threatening to resign unless Premier Lesage allowed him to go ahead with it. During the nationalization struggle, it had been infuriating for Lévesque to encounter the cool, uncommitted skepticism of Pierre Trudeau.

Trudeau was one of the aristocrats of Quebec's highly structured society. His socialism had been acquired during a prolonged and comfortable education in the finest schools and universities of Quebec, Britain and France.

Lévesque, the son of a country lawyer, a drop-out from law school, had fought for his reputation in the competitive world of journalism, then, in 1960, staked everything on a political career.

Trudeau's casually ironic approach undermined Lévesque's belief in his own worth:

"A natural-born talent for getting slapped in the face," was Lévesque's description, in later years, of the future Prime Minister.

His relationship with Trudeau had deteriorated to that, or something very close to it, at the end of a long discussion on nationalization one evening in 1962 at Jean Marchand's apartment on St. Denis Street in the east end of Montreal.

Trudeau had insisted that the proposed takeover was expensive and unproductive. Lévesque had again reviewed his arguments for effective planning of power distribution in the province, the development of French-Canadian executive and technical expertise in a publicly-owned utility, and the recovery of taxes then being paid to the federal government by the private power companies.

But whenever Lévesque felt that he had conclusively proved his case, Trudeau sniffed his way back to the insinuation that it was all a costly exercise in nationalism in the classic Quebec pattern. Then he had started to analyse the political advantages. Wasn't nationalization merely bread and circuses for voters who were starting to look critically at the Lesage government after only two years in office?

Lévesque had exploded. He had told Trudeau that his ironic, Socratic pose was nothing but a joke. Trudeau had retorted that it was impossible to have a serious discussion with a small-fry party hack.

That session had broken up in disorder and it had taken all of Marchand's negotiating skill to bring them all together again.

The group really was Marchand's creation; and among its members, he had known Lévesque the longest.

The two had been at Laval University in Quebec City in the early Forties, Marchand to absorb the original culture of the yeasty "quiet revolution" in the School of Social Sciences, Lévesque to fritter away his time at law school. Most of their contacts, in those years, had been across a card table as they skipped lectures to play poker, blackjack and hearts.

They had not established regular contact again until 1959, when French-language television producers went on strike in Montreal against the state-owned Canadian Broadcasting Corporation. As leader of the *Confédération des syndicats nationaux*, (C.S.N.), Marchand had directed the strike from a suite of rooms in the Mount Royal Hotel only a few blocks from the CBC building. Lévesque's popularity as the CBC's leading news analyst had made him an important spokesman for the strikers.

Another regular visitor to Marchand's suite at the Mount Royal Hotel had been his C.S.N. colleague Gérard Pelletier who became editor of *La Presse* in 1961. During the long weeks of the strike, the conversation of the three men had turned often toward politics. It was then, for Marchand and Lévesque and to a lesser extent for Pelletier, that the idea of political careers began to take definite shape.

Marchand and Lévesque went so far as to make a pact to enter politics together. And in the following year, it had been in Marchand's hotel suite that Lévesque had made his decision, setting the pact aside. That same evening, he had started his political career alone by walking two blocks from the Mount Royal Hotel to the more elegant quarters of Liberal Leader Jean Lesage in the Windsor Hotel.

In the spring of 1962, as Lévesque had fought for nationalization against almost overwhelming odds in the cabinet and his own party, Marchand had been in Quebec City frequently as a member of the province's new economic planning council. Lévesque had suggested to him almost casually one day that he would welcome an opportunity to discuss nationalization and other issues with a small group outside his usual contacts in the party and bureaucracy.

Marchand invited Pelletier, who had worked on television with Lévesque before the 1959 strike; and Pelletier had suggested Trudeau, one of his associates on *Cité Libre*, a small but influential political magazine.

All three, in the late Fifties, had been leading members of a loose alliance of intellectuals and labour union leaders working to overthrow the conservative and corrupt regime of Quebec's Union Nationale government.

When Maurice Duplessis of the Union Nationale was Premier, André Laurendeau had been an editorial writer at *Le Devoir* in Montreal, the most intellectual of Quebec's daily newspapers and one of only two newspapers in the province that had dared to oppose the Duplessis government. By 1961, when he had accepted Marchand's invitation to meet informally with Lévesque, the rising star of the Quebec cabinet, Laurendeau had just been appointed to the editorship of *Le Devoir*.

Laurendeau was also beginning to be recognized across Canada in the early Sixties as a brilliant analyst of Quebec opinion. He was in the process of developing a concept of a bilingual and bicultural Canadian nationalism that was to become one of the dominant themes of the national debate about Canadian federalism as the decade progressed.

From the outset, the meetings of the group were informal and sporadic. As Trudeau described them: "There were no orders of the day, just the disorder of the night."

The timing of the meetings depended on Lévesque's ministerial schedule in Quebec City. Whenever he had settled on an appropriate night, usually a Friday, he would ask Marchand to round up the others. A few of the early sessions had been held at a small French restaurant in downtown Montreal, Chez Stein, but the usual place was Marchand's apartment on St. Denis Street. Later, as Pelletier settled into the Elm Avenue Westmount home that he had bought in the spring of 1962, this became one of the meeting places.

Long before that warm May night in 1963, as the conversation carried the group around Pelletier's dining room table into the early morning hours, relations among the five men had assumed certain patterns. Their responses to one another had become predictable. And perhaps there was a suspicion among the five men that evening that the group already had served its purpose.

From Lévesque's point of view, André Laurendeau was the most valuable member. It had been a great advantage, during the fight for nationalization in the cabinet and on the hustings, to have had regular access to an editor of Laurendeau's stature. The tall, dark-haired, aquiline journalist, who was to die only five years later in the middle of his work as co-chairman of the Royal Commission of Bilingualism and Biculturalism, had been a critic to whom Lévesque would listen. That was rare.

Lévesque remembers him as the most valued contact and consultant of his career in politics, and as an observer with a unique mixture of feeling and judgement for political situations. Even Lévesque's non-stop flow of argument used to falter before the pronouncements of Laurendeau, always serene and realistic, occasionally caustic. The editor of *Le Devoir* was already making incisive judgements about Lévesque in 1962 when he had turned to him, on one of those Friday nights, and inquired, "Monsieur Lévesque" – it was never just "René" or the informal "tu" between Laurendeau and Lévesque – "would you mind telling me which one of you has just spoken – the statesman or the star?"

By temperament, Jean Marchand was closest to Lévesque. Both men had spent part of their early years in Quebec City, where local society is older, more tightly-knit and more conservative than in Montreal. And they shared an emotional, intuitive approach to politics. It wasn't always necessary for them to reason the life out of a political decision.

However, by the spring of 1963, there already had been a fairly serious misunderstanding between them.

In the previous year, Marchand had still been thinking of adhering belatedly to the old pact with Lévesque and joining him in the Quebec cabinet. When the 1962 election had been announced in September, he was still under the impression that both Lévesque and Premier Lesage wanted him to run. At a meeting in the industrial city of Trois-Rivières, on the north shore of the St. Lawrence River between Quebec City and Montreal, he had told the executive committee of his labour federation that he intended to resign as president to contest the election, explaining it partly on the basis of his commitment to Lévesque. But when he had informed Lesage of this, the Premier had told him that Lévesque had changed his mind.

Lévesque has always vehemently denied this, claiming that the rejection came from Lesage and that he had been forced to go along with it. This has remained a source of misunderstanding between the two men.

The Liberals' reluctance to accept Marchand stemmed from the federal campaign of the previous June, when he had urged his union members to oppose the rightist Social Credit party in Quebec. After the Socreds unexpectedly won twenty-six of Quebec's seventy-five federal ridings, Quebec Liberals began to have second thoughts about the advantages of having Marchand on their side.

Marchand disliked not only the flavour of the decision but the way in which it was administered to him. He resented the fact that Lévesque had failed to warn him against committing himself, and that the humiliating rejection had had to come from Lesage. From then on, Marchand kept a wary eye on Lévesque.

Marchand and Lévesque were the most vocal members of the Friday night group. Gérard Pelletier, editor of Montreal's *La Presse*, the largest French-language daily in North America, was the one who was adept at setting out problems before the others and preventing the discussions from ranging too far afield.

The most detached participant was Trudeau. Other members of the group sometimes wondered if he was even following their conversation. Then the blue eyes over the high cheekbones would light up, and the professor would casually skim a barbed epigram at Lévesque, puncturing him in full flight and bringing him down to earth in a temper.

Lévesque respected Trudeau's intelligence and the breadth of his information; but his air of knowing all and imparting little was infuriating to the hard-pressed cabinet minister who was being forced to make decisions on the run, and who looked to the group for some indication of public reaction.

On that spring night in 1963, the future Prime Minister of Canada was the least important member of the group, as far as Lévesque was concerned. It was Laurendeau who seemed to tower above the others, not only because of Lévesque's personal regard for him but because of the importance that his ideas were beginning to assume for the future of Canada's French-speaking people.

III
The Emerging Crisis

At the beginning of the 1960s, André Laurendeau first broached the idea of a national inquiry into the divisions of language and culture between Canada's English-speaking majority and the French-speaking minority that represented, in the 1961 census, about 28 per cent of the total population of 19,000,000.

His suggestion had been flatly rejected by Prime Minister John Diefenbaker.

Diefenbaker was a prairie Conservative, proud of his "unhyphenated" Canadianism. In the first half of this century, in western Canada, an immigrant population of diverse origins had blended into a coherent if lumpy mixture that regarded itself as uniquely Canadian. That kind of Canadianism was Diefenbaker's model.

Lester B. Pearson, Diefenbaker's successor, had been more open to Laurendeau's proposal. Like most Canadians of Anglo-Saxon origin from Ontario, the largest and most developed of the English-speaking provinces, Pearson found it difficult to picture his own province without the accompanying massive triangle of Quebec on its eastern border. For more than a century, the dual political existences of Quebec and Ontario had given the people of both provinces an instinctive sense of linked destinies that Canadians in other provinces often found alien and presumptuous. This was Pearson's image of Canada, and it corresponded essentially to Laurendeau's.

On May 15, 1963, the day before Marchand's group met at Pelletier's home, Prime Minister Pearson had written to the ten provincial Premiers to propose Laurendeau's idea of a Royal Commission on Bilingualism and Biculturalism. The following day, the Speech-from-the-Throne opening the new Parliament in Ottawa contained references to the inquiry into "B'n'B," a popular abbreviation that became a catch-phrase of the Sixties. By the time Laurendeau reached Pelletier's home that evening, perhaps he had already given Pearson his commitment to serve as co-chairman of the commission with A. Davidson Dunton, a former Chairman of the Board of Governors of the Canadian Broadcasting Corporation.

Laurendeau's commitment illustrated both the pragmatic and speculative aspects of Quebec nationalism, both within individual French-Canadians and *la nation* as a whole.

Influenced by the Quebec nationalism of the Thirties and French-Canadian opposition to compulsory military service during the Second World War, Laurendeau in the early Forties had been a vocal defender of Quebec rights against the federal government. In 1941, Laurendeau had even criticized the Quebec government for accepting a constitutional amendment clearing the way for federal legislation to provide workers across Canada with insurance against unemployment.

As Laurendeau argued at the time, the federal program "would mean that reforms undertaken or needed to bring social life into closer conformity with Catholic ethics would come under the scrutiny of a Protestant majority...and for a long time set aside all hope of adjusting social legislation to family needs (the Anglo-Saxon outlook being geared more to the interests of the individual than to those of the family)."

Commenting on this position fifteen years later, Trudeau described Laurendeau's attitude as "rather startling...in view of the long-standing backwardness of Quebec's social policies.

"Self-government is an admirable aim, of course," wrote Trudeau, "provided a people really intend to govern themselves."

But Laurendeau's own analysis of French Canada's situation within the Canadian confederation was to grow more complex and questioning. By 1953, "having lived all my adult life among nationalists," Laurendeau had decided that the divisions and disillusionments of current nationalist movements were symptoms of the most serious crisis of Quebec nationalism in his own experience.

Attempting to diagnose this wavering of national purpose in Quebec, Laurendeau recognized that "first of all, the idea of a homeland is losing its force in the Western world...in Europe the homeland has demanded too many great sacrifices that led to the impoverishment of nations." Closer to home, French-Canadians were being forced to adapt to the fact that the historical British presence in Canada, political and economic, had quietly and efficiently been replaced by investment from the United States. Laurendeau warned French-Canadians in 1953 that they couldn't afford to ignore the political, economic or cultural effects of this massive American intervention in the economic life of Canada.

"Canadians are not so numerous or so rich," he wrote, "that they can afford to tear themselves to pieces or cordially hate each other so that they can risk one day wanting to throw themselves into the arms of their great giant neighbour that is so sure of its strength that it doesn't even dream of taking them."

The development that Laurendeau had identified as being of the utmost importance was that "our little world has undergone great changes within a universe in revolution." While Quebec nationalists had endlessly debated a narrow range of religious, social and political options, the "little world" of Quebec – conservative, pious, agricultural and isolated – had been drawn inexorably into the current of North American life in the twentieth century.

"It has taken half a century of existence to arrive at this result," Laurendeau wrote.

> For if the intellectuals and artists, with few exceptions, took refuge in a retrospective dream, hundreds of thousands of families were leading an urban life, looking for their daily livelihood and undergoing their own internal revolution.
>
> A change in vocation is a great upheaval for a people. They experience it profoundly, without admitting what is happening...
>
> In vain the people tries to reaffirm tradition, but slowly realizes it is speaking empty words. Then it begins to doubt itself, and has periods of despair followed by bursts of irrational faith...
>
> When tragedy strikes a people whose existence has already been precarious, it produces the sensation of falling into an abyss...

One of the few conclusions reached by Laurendeau by way of this depressing analysis was that "we are still very ignorant of the phenomena that take place around us and within us. . .research is necessary in all areas."

Eleven years after that was written, the federal government gave Laurendeau and his colleagues on the Royal Commission on Bilingualism and Biculturalism a mandate to undertake the most searching examination ever made of Canadian linguistic and cultural divisions.

By 1965, the work of the Commission would have broadened Laurendeau's diagnosis to national dimensions.

In a preliminary report to Parliament that year, the Commission stated that its members "have been driven to the conclusion that Canada, without being fully conscious of the fact, is passing through the greatest crisis in its history.

"The course of the crisis lies in the Province of Quebec," continued the report. "But, although a provincial crisis at the outset, it has become a Canadian crisis, because of the size and strategic importance of Quebec, and because it has invariably set off a series of chain reactions elsewhere."

Laurendeau's further development at this stage was reflected in the final paragraph of the report's preamble. Recognizing the dangers in probing these flaws in Canada's national personality, these scars of old defeats and forced alliances of the past, the Commissioners stated their conviction that "they are demonstrating a supreme confidence in Canada."

"It is in fact to say to the country," they concluded, "that you have faith in it and its future."

However, on that spring evening in 1963, Laurendeau had no idea that the work of the Commission would lead him to this conclusion. Nor could he have had any premonition that its main beneficiary would be the quiet, sardonic law professor seated across the table from him who would be elected Prime Minister in 1968, the year of Laurendeau's own death.

In 1963, Laurendeau might have selected Lévesque from the four men around the table as the one most likely to provide a sympathetic medium for his own ideas.

Only a few years before, Lévesque had discovered Quebec nationalism with all the enthusiasm of a late convert – perhaps a bit too much enthusiasm for Laurendeau's taste – while Trudeau had heaped scorn throughout the Fifties on Quebec nationalists of every description, including Laurendeau. Their interpretation of Quebec's cultural needs and Roman Catholic social doctrine, in Trudeau's opinion, had merely fostered authoritarianism and xenophobia and "helped to make it impossible for us to solve our problems."

"On the negative side," Trudeau had written in 1956, "it rejected all solutions that could be successful against our 'enemies': the English, the Protestants, the materialists, etc.

"And, on the positive side, it remained content with elaborating theoretical systems, devoid of any objective link with reality and often totally inapplicable in practice."

But in 1963, Trudeau's rejection of Quebec nationalism seemed to have little importance for the world of real politics.

There had been a brief possibility of a political career for Trudeau before the federal election of April, 1963, when Marchand had met Liberal Leader Pearson in Montreal. Marchand had come away from this meeting persuaded that Pearson would agree to his two conditions for becoming a Liberal candidate: that a Pearson government would not accept nuclear weapons from the United States, and that both Pelletier and Trudeau would be acceptable as Liberal candidates. But a second meeting with Pearson in Quebec City revealed that both assumptions were wrong.

In Pearson's list of priorities, the commitment to accept nuclear warheads from the United States was essential, the candidacies of Marchand, Pelletier and Trudeau were not.

In April, 1963, the month of the federal election, Trudeau's *Cité Libre* magazine described Liberal policy as a nefarious scheme to "sell Canada down the river in return for American campaign funds." The article strengthened the assumption among his friends that Trudeau would slip further into political obscurity within the law faculty at the University of Montreal.

IV
The Introduction of Violence

In the spring of 1963, for the first time in the history of Canada, persistent and organized urban terrorism became a conventional part of the political scene.

Young guerrillas began to operate in Montreal and other Quebec centres, pulling down the statue of a colonial British general, throwing Molotov cocktails at federal buildings, and planting crude dynamite bombs.

Their activities were an imponderable new element in the delicate web of traditional relations between English and French.

The first victim claimed by the terrorist group, the *Front de libération du Québec*, was a sixty-five-year-old night watchman employed at an army recruiting centre in downtown Montreal. He died when a ten-stick dynamite bomb exploded in his hands as he was trying to remove it from a garbage container in an alley behind the recruiting centre.

The next and up to that time, most serious attack by the F.L.Q. started shortly after midnight of May 16. Four young French-Canadians – three twenty-year-olds and an eighteen-year-old – drove a battered Volkswagen from the east end of Montreal to the wealthy English-speaking municipality of Westmount on the south slope of Mount Royal near the centre of the city. While this city-within-a-city of 25,000 people settled down for the night beneath the watchful eyes of its own police force, the young men in the Volkswagen deposited five bombs in five mailboxes. At the same time, a nineteen-year-old French-Canadian, operating alone or with unknown accomplices, completed his circuit of five mailboxes in another part of Westmount before boarding a late bus and heading east toward the French-speaking districts of Montreal.

On Elm Avenue in Westmount, the five French-Canadians in their late thirties and early forties continued to debate the future of Quebec while the five in their teens and early twenties were transforming the entire district into a minefield controlled by crude timing devices set for 3.00 a.m.

Surrounded by bombs in bright red mailboxes bearing Her Britannic Majesty's golden crowns, Lévesque's main concern at the moment was that everyone had run out of cigarettes.

It was after 2.00 a.m. and Trudeau and Marchand, the early-risers of the group, had already left in Trudeau's car. Accustomed to the schedule of his morning newspaper, Laurendeau was willing, as usual, to talk with Lévesque until dawn. Pelletier was trying to decide whether he would sleep for a few hours after the others left or drive downtown to the *La Presse* office to check the early edition. He often did this after the late night sessions.

As Lévesque clawed desperately through his pockets for cigarettes and rasped out arguments in a voice that turned syllables into wheezes and consonants into coughs, the warm night beyond the kitchen doors was disturbed by a muffled report. Lévesque's monologue continued but Laurendeau raised his head suspiciously. Lévesque rejected his suggestion that it might have been a bomb and plunged ahead with his argument, interrupting himself only long enough to curse the fact that all the cigarettes in the universe seemed to have disappeared.

In a few minutes, there was another roar that rattled the windows.

Laurendeau started to insist that bombs were exploding nearby. Lévesque impatiently said something about underground blasting for the city's new subway and was just picking up the threads of his argument again when a third explosion shook the house. This brought Pelletier's wife downstairs. Police sirens could now be heard in the distance.

The Pelletiers, Laurendeau and Lévesque piled into Pelletier's car and drove toward the sound of the sirens, Lévesque still grumbling about not being able to find any cigarettes.

Soon they happened on the scene of one of the explosions. A few dazed men and women in dressing-gowns were edging from doorways near a streetcorner where the front of a small restaurant had been heavily damaged. The first thing that Lévesque and the others noticed, as they drove past, were the packs of cigarettes lying among the shattered glass. Lévesque groaned in frustration.

By this time they had heard another explosion only a short distance away. On one of the upper avenues above Sherbrooke Street, where Westmount climbs toward the mansions of Summit Circle, they came across a large crowd at the scene of an explosion near a church. By now Lévesque was worrying that a bystander might identify him. Any connection between the bombings and the "radical" of the Quebec cabinet could have been dangerous for him. Pelletier parked his car some distance from the crowd, leaving Lévesque with his wife while he and Laurendeau went to investigate.

As they walked toward the scene of the explosion, Pelletier recalled that one of his associates at *La Presse* had informed him recently about loose talk in the news room, something about exploding bombs along Sherbrooke Street.

Most of his younger reporters were sympathetic to separatism and cultivated contacts in the *Rassemblement pour l'indépendance nationale,* as well as among more extreme groups. Strange faces drifted through the editorial corridors of the newspaper from time to time.

All at once, Pelletier realized that he was staring at one of those faces, pale and bearded, across the empty space where the mailbox had stood. My God, he thought to himself, he's come to check the work of his friends.

As the two men returned to the car where his wife waited with Lévesque, Pelletier noticed something that had escaped his attention a few minutes before. He had parked his car beside another mailbox.

It was the mailbox, he still insists to this day, that contained the bomb that exploded the next morning in the hands of an army explosives expert, maiming him for life.

V
Hydro-Québec: The Power Struggle

Marchand's group of 1962 and 1963 is like a commonplace artifact, a pen or a notebook, that eventually seems significant because someone important once used it. Picturing the five men together now brings the whole period to life. We turn the faded image over and over in our minds and new aspects continue to appear – portents that were hidden from the five men at the time.

To them, the conversations were commonplace, the same topics and the same human types that they encountered almost every day. Lévesque and the others now find it hard to remember much about them. At the time, he regarded them as a relatively minor part of the political career that had absorbed him so suddenly and completely.

The subject that obsessed him then was his ambitious program of hydro-electric nationalization. It was his first serious political challenge. He knew that success or failure would determine at least his immediate political future.

The history of Lévesque's nationalization achievement is a strategic vantage point for a first look at Lévesque as a political visionary and a political craftsman; and the crucial moment occurred on September 4, 1962, at an informal meeting of the Quebec cabinet at Lac-à-l'Epaule.

After only two years in office, the Lesage cabinet was showing signs of disintegration and lack of direction.

Lévesque was threatening to resign if he failed to get an early decision on nationalization. The Minister of Youth, Paul Gérin-Lajoie, proposed to bring Quebec's antiquated educational system out from under the skirts of the Roman Catholic clergy, a proposal which alarmed more conservative ministers. And on Monday evening, September 4, 1962, Premier Jean Lesage was well into one of his most difficult moods – opinionated, pompous and overbearing – as the cabinet and a few Liberal party officials gathered after the Labour Day weekend for a political discussion at the government rest house at Lac-à-l'Epaule, north of Quebec City.

As the drinking continued during the evening, the atmosphere became poisonous. Isolated groups of ministers plotted sullenly in various parts of the guest house. The morale of the cabinet had reached its lowest point since the election victory of 1960.

Out of this mood of desperation, on the grey day after, came the unexpected decision to nationalize Quebec's hydro-electric industry, and to make this the key issue of an early election.

The crucial inspiration came neither from Lévesque nor Lesage but from Georges-Emile Lapalme, the brilliant, moody and unpredictable former leader of the Quebec Liberal party.

Lesage fastened on it at once as the solution to his immediate problems.

It was a chance to close the door on the interminable debates in the cabinet, and to go to the people with a simple statement. Lesage made that statement at a fund-raising dinner on October 1, in Montreal, shortly after the election was called: "The people of Quebec *versus* the electrical trust."

"He who is for the people of Quebec is against the trust," he proclaimed, "and he who is for the trust is against the people of Quebec."

Everyone in the province knew what that meant.

The "trust" was Quebec shorthand for the financial centre on St. James Street, the great houses along The Boulevard in Westmount and the private schools in the west end of the city that were copies of British public schools. It meant afternoon tea and hot cheese rolls in the Château Frontenac in Quebec City and lunch at the Mount Stephen and the other business clubs of the Montreal Anglostocracy. It was the kilted piper skirling the customers out of Ogilvy's department store at the end of the day, the coming-out parties at the Ritz, and all the other pleasant and comfortable aspects of English-speaking life in Quebec in 1962.

The "people" referred to by Premier Lesage were the French-Canadians who clerked in the banks and financial houses, delivered the mail and laundry and milk in Westmount, sent their skimpy kids to old schools among the tenements of east end Montreal, and who talked hockey and politics all night beneath the fluorescent tubes of cheap taverns smelling of stale beer and piss.

Everyone also knew that the situation wasn't quite as simple as Lesage's rallying-cry.

The French-Canadians themselves over the years had produced a succession of political "negro kings," leaders more than willing to extend their well-greased palms to work hand-in-glove with the English.

And not all of the "English" were wealthy, Anglo-Saxon and Protestant. In the previous century, when open rebellion had broken out against the British, Quebecers of Irish-Catholic origin had been among the leaders of the unsuccessful revolution. Some of their descendants were now in Westmount but many still lived in such working class districts as Verdun, St.-Henri, Ahuntsic and St.-Léonard among the Italians, Greeks, Portuguese, Germans and other members of the great non-French urban mass that French-Canadians referred to simply as "les autres" – all the rest.

The decision to buy out the private power companies reflected the complexity of Quebec society.

On September 19, 1962, when Premier Lesage unexpectedly asked for the dissolution of the Quebec parliament and an early election, he said that the government had decided "to ask the people of Quebec for a decisive mandate to bring about the unification of the electric power system in the province.

"It is for the people of Quebec to decide, freely and proudly," continued his formal statement, "whether they wish to take into their hands the most important of all the keys to a progressive economy."

Despite the hortatory language of the Premier's statement and the usual rhetoric of the "quiet revolution," it really required quite a stretch of the imagination to see the takeover as revolutionary.

The hydro-electric network in the neighbouring province of Ontario had been owned by the provincial government for forty years. The provinces of Manitoba and Saskatchewan in western Canada also had state-owned power utilities. Even the conservative Social Credit government of British Columbia had recently nationalized the power utility in that province.

But it was undoubtedly the most ambitious economic decision ever taken by a Quebec government.

Eleven privately-owned utilities would be involved, including the giant Aluminium and Shawinigan groups. Together, the eleven utilities produced more than half of the province's electricity. The cost was estimated to be more than $600 million.

After the takeover, the province's publicly-owned utility, Hydro-Québec, would own, on behalf of Quebec's 5,259,000 people, power generating capacity of 13,000,000 horsepower. This was a per capita wealth of hydro-electric power unsurpassed by any country in the world. Undeveloped hydro-electric sites in northern Quebec, on the Labrador-Quebec border, and south of Hudson Bay promised to maintain a surplus of the "white energy" in Quebec for decades.

Nationalization provided the slogan of the 1962 Quebec election: "*Maître Chez Nous* – Masters in Our Own House." But even the slogan had a tarnished origin. It was coined at a party at the Liberals' Reform Club in Quebec City on the day that the election had been announced. At the height of the celebration a drunk contractor, still bloated on the patronage of the old Union Nationale government but sniffing now at the Liberal trough, had thrown his arm about Premier Lesage's shoulder and roared, "It's about time we were the bosses in our own place...*maître chez nous.*"

The phrase was still ringing in Lesage's head the next morning when he telephoned his chief campaign strategist in Montreal to ask: "*Maître chez nous!* What do you think of it?"

It was exactly what he had wanted to say, a few months earlier, when he had been visited by a delegation from the financial houses on St. James Street. Lévesque had already been talking publicly about nationalization and the businessmen had wanted to warn the Premier. A scheme of that magnitude, they had said, would make it extremely difficult in future for the province to borrow money for other purposes.

Along the civil service grapevine in Quebec, it was rumoured that Lesage had virtually thrown them out of his office, shouting that the era of "negro kings" in Quebec had ended.

For a time, the story even topped the one about Lévesque's interview with representatives of one of the power utilities, when he had become so enraged that he had put his fist through the glass top of his desk.

"Maître Chez Nous!"

Long before the British redcoats had defeated the French grenadiers at Quebec, the Frenchmen of the new world identified themselves as a distinctive and exploited people in relation to the state authorities, the religious orders and the commercial interests in France. Conquest by the British had merely replaced one colonial power with another.

Eventually the French-Canadians had gained important political, religious and social rights from the British authorities but their economic development had been hindered by isolation from their traditional markets and sources of capital in France and its colonial empire. The business activity of Quebec had fallen into the hands of immigrants from Quebec's new "mother country" and from the former British colonies to the south who had chosen to remain under the Crown after the American War of Independence.

By the nineteenth century, the French-Canadian community's economic position had become so inferior that some of its intellectuals had begun to think of it more as a reflection of divine will than a natural condition.

"We have the privilege to be entrusted with this social priesthood, granted only to select peoples," Monseigneur L.-A. Paquet had said in his 1902 Saint-Jean-Baptiste Day "Sermon on the Vocation of the

French Race in America," sometimes popularly called "the French-Canadian's daily prayer book."

"Our mission is less to handle capital than to stimulate ideas; less to light the furnaces of factories than to maintain and spread far and wide, the glowing fires of religion and thought...

"While our rivals are struggling for...the power that stems from industry and finance," said Mgr Paquet, "our aspirations shall above all aim to uphold the honour of the doctrine and to gain the palms of apostleship."

This philosophy had encouraged a remarkable degree of smug conservatism in Quebec's society – farmers, small tradesmen and craftsmen dominated by a religious and lay elite educated in the liberal professions. Only after decades of industrialization, when Quebec society was irrevocably urban, had French-Canadian thinkers started to appreciate the shortcomings and blind spots of their traditional outlook.

"What remains to us?" the Mayor of Montreal, Jean Drapeau, had asked in 1959. "Agriculture, small-scale manufacturing, a small portion of banking, of retail trade and construction. For the rest, we are more and more employees...of large English-Canadian, English and American companies. We are tending more and more to become a proletarian people."

The social geography of Montreal reflected this economic dichotomy strikingly. The favoured western suburbs were populated mainly by English-speaking Canadians who lived at least as well as their compatriots in Toronto, Winnipeg or Vancouver. These western suburbs provided the executive class for the downtown offices. The crowded central districts and monotonous new suburbs at the east end of Montreal island, both populated by French-speaking Canadians, provided the work force.

Familiar as this pattern was to French-Canadians, they were shocked by the 1961 census. That census discriminated more clearly between language groups than previous surveys, and revealed that as a rule unilingual English-speaking Montrealers earned higher salaries than bilingual French-Canadians of equal education.

But by 1961, French-Canadians' passive acceptance of economic inequality had largely disappeared. It was being replaced by a new philosophy that saw the state – the government of Quebec, the most important institution controlled by French-Canadians – as a primary means of giving Quebecers a larger share in the ownership and direction of their own economy.

"It's time to act," Premier Lesage had told representatives of the mining industry in the spring of 1961. "I can assure you that economic colonialism is no longer acceptable to the people of Quebec."

In outline, this was the historical setting and contemporary mood when René Lévesque first began to study Quebec's hydro-electric system in the spring of 1961. All the elements were present for the kind of spontaneous political combustion that occurred between then and the election of November, 1962, although the bringing together of many of these elements was accidental.

The first cabinet list that Lesage had revealed to his closest associates in the days following the 1960 election had assigned two portfolios to Lévesque: the Ministry of Public Works, which he was given immediately, and the eventual direction of a new Ministry of Natural Resources. In the first distribution of cabinet jobs, hydraulic resources had been added to Lévesque's responsibilities in line with Lesage's intention to place him eventually in charge of all natural resource development.

Neither assignment appears to have been dictated by weighty considerations.

Lévesque's recent recruitment to politics and his clean public image had influenced Lesage's decision to place him initially in Public Works, a department identified as a prime source of patronage under the former government. One of Levesque's first tasks there had been to institute an improved system of public tenders for roads and other government projects.

Natural resource development had been one of many program areas discussed by Lesage and Lévesque before the 1960 election; but there had been no specific talk of nationalization before the Natural Resources portfolio had been formally given to Lévesque on March 28, 1961.

Nor had nationalization been mentioned by Lévesque in the summer of 1960 when he had persuaded a young Quebec economist, Michel Bélanger, to leave a federal job in Ottawa to become his assistant deputy minister. Lévesque had told Bélanger only that, amid the confusion in his new office, there were requests for action on a number of immediate hydro-electric problems such as renegotiation of water rights with the Shawinigan group and extension of power lines for a new pulp plant in a region of the Gaspé served by one of the smaller private utilities.

During the department's subsequent study of the jumble of private utilities and electrical cooperatives in the Gaspé peninsula, the notion of unifying the whole system had begun to emerge. By the fall of 1961, some of the basic studies had been completed. Lévesque had then begun to discuss full-scale nationalization with a few close advisors.

Lévesque kept abreast of the developing file in the department, formulating his own approach as the practical arguments in favour of nationalization accumulated. By the end of 1961, he was saying publicly that hydro-electric power should be developed and distributed by a state utility but that the expansion of Hydro-Québec, the publicly-owned utility created in the Forties with a distribution network limited to the Montreal area, would be carried out in a "reasonable and co-ordinated" way.

Behind the scenes, Lévesque started to acquire allies for the fight that loomed ahead. One of the most powerful was Louis-Philippe Pigeon, legal advisor and "lay confessor" to Lesage who had been involved several decades earlier in the creation of Hydro-Québec. When Lévesque discovered that Lesage was failing to show his reports to Pigeon, perhaps to protect himself from further pressure, he arranged to brief the wily old lawyer himself.

On February 12, 1972, Lévesque had come out publicly in favour of a single state-owned power utility covering the entire province. The question was being discussed by cabinet at this time and there had been a unanimous vote approving the principal of nationalization but reserving judgement on its feasibility. Lesage then agreed to establish a special committee to examine the practical aspects.

Several weeks later, though, Lesage had decided that there wouldn't be a committee after all.

Until the September 1962 meeting at Lac-à-l'Epaule, the attitude of Premier Lesage toward nationalization remained enigmatic. His early reaction to pressure from the financial barons of St. James Street encouraged Lévesque. But the cancellation of the feasibility committee seemed to point in the opposite direction. It began to look as if the favourable vote in the cabinet on the principle of nationalization, without a commitment to further action, had been simply a delaying tactic.

In fact, the Premier had been genuinely concerned about the province's ability to finance the takeover. With his experience as a corporation lawyer and as a federal cabinet minister before assuming the leadership of the Quebec Liberals in 1958, Lesage was more capable than Lévesque of grasping the financial implications of nationalization. His decision in 1960 to keep the provincial treasurer's portfolio in his own hands gave him a close and up-to-date picture of the province's economy as well as economic trends on a wider front.

Lesage also had George Marler at his right hand. A former leader of the Quebec Liberal party who had switched to federal politics in 1954, Marler had had hopes of becoming Finance Minister at Ottawa before both he and the Liberal government were defeated in 1958. He had then worked for the national Liberal party in Ottawa before deciding, in 1960, to return to his notarial office in Montreal. That September, Lesage asked him to accept an appointment as Government Leader in the Legislative Council.

The existence of this upper house in Quebec's parliament, a remnant of British colonial administration abolished in 1966, had enabled Lesage to bring Marler into his cabinet without routing him through the electoral process.

As Minister without Portfolio, Marler had special responsibility for administering the finances of the province. It was Marler who "sat on the cash box" of Quebec, as he was fond of saying, when Lesage was on one of his grand tours overseas or in the other Canadian provinces.

Marler was also the last heir of a long tradition of English-speaking influence at the highest political level in Quebec.

After the relatively brief period of British colonial rule following the conquest, this influence had made itself felt behind the scenes, where the nationalist rhetoric of Quebec politicians confronted the economic realities of North America.

Marler's brief venture into the spotlight as a Quebec party leader in the Forties had shown him the limits of ambition for an English-speaking Quebecer, no matter how fluently bilingual. On his return to Quebec in 1960, he had been ready to work quietly in the old tradition, serving the province conscientiously in Quebec while maintaining his contacts in legal and business circles in Montreal.

Marler was the antithesis of Lévesque. He was always punctual for the morning Treasury Board meetings that preceded cabinet sessions. Lévesque rarely would get up early enough to reach the cabinet meetings on time.

Where Marler was strongest, Lévesque was weak. When he joined the government in 1960, Lévesque had nothing more than a political journalist's skimpy familiarity with economics and government finance. Despite his ability to absorb information quickly and synthesize complex subjects, these continued to be areas where Lévesque was forced to rely on the competence of others, and his advisors usually were academic economists or civil servants. Neither his social background, his work as a journalist, nor his political career had ever enabled Lévesque to gain the contacts in business and financial circles that Marler took for granted.

The isolation of the two men from one another, as they sat at the cabinet table in Quebec City, exemplified the divided nature of the Quebec community.

Some time after Lévesque took over the Natural Resources portfolio in 1961, Marler received a visit from a friend who was associated with one of the private power companies and who expressed grave apprehension that nationalization was in the cards. Marler informed him that it was unlikely. Financing such a gigantic takeover, Marler said, would simply be too difficult for Quebec. Right up to the time of the meeting at Lac-à-l'Epaule, Marler was certain that this would dominate Lesage's calculations.

But unknown to Marler, Lesage had launched his own inquiries in a number of directions. Although he was careful to state publicly that Lévesque's February 12 commitment to nationalization was only an expression of personal opinion by one of his ministers, he had treated the question as a serious issue for himself and his government. His refusal to appoint the feasibility committee had not been simply to delay action; by then, his own investigation of the scheme was well underway.

Lesage started with an initial sounding of reaction among a few leading men in financial circles in Montreal and New York. After the "negro king" episode, the Montreal financial community's response was cautious. They had told Lesage that if it could be shown that nationalization was desired by a majority of Quebecers, they would go along with the scheme even if they continued to disapprove of it in principle.

By the end of February, Lesage followed up this line of inquiry by summoning one of his 1960 campaign strategists to Quebec for a private lunch at the Garrison Club.

In that campaign, the Liberals had been the first political party in Quebec to use large-scale motivational research as a basic element of their election planning. Now Lesage wanted to know how the techniques of the 1959 survey could be used to predict public reaction to nationalization. If the survey were undertaken, he warned, it would have to be done in such a way as to disguise this purpose even from those who would be in charge of analyzing the findings.

The party strategist told Lesage that it would be politically useful in any case to follow up the 1959 survey with another, and that he could insert the essential questions on nationalization himself without arousing suspicion. Because it would require at least six months to complete the survey, Lesage had authorized it immediately.

The survey in fact took somewhat longer. Answers to the critical questions on nationalization had been unavailable when the meeting was held at Lac-à-l'Epaule the following September. Perhaps if Lesage had the results by then, he might not have been so eager to plunge headlong into an early election.

The party strategist had come away from the Garrison Club luncheon persuaded that the Premier had already decided that nationalization was inevitable. But in the months that followed, others received conflicting impressions. Senior bureaucrats working on the takeover proposal were still hearing, in the summer of 1962, that Lesage was giving assurances to the power companies that total nationalization would never occur.

Lévesque had intensified his public campaign for nationalization throughout the spring and summer of 1962.

For the most part, his arguments were practical. He claimed that it was simply inefficient to continue the province's mixed hydro-electric system. The mixed system included publicly-owned Hydro-Québec and forty-six privately-owned producers of electricity, including the three giants of the industry, the Shawinigan group, the Aluminium group and Gatineau Power Company, as well as forty-eight cooperatives and thirty-four municipalities, each with their own distribution networks. This system had created lack of coordination in investments and development of new resources, unproductive duplication of facilities, and slow progress toward creating a rational structure of rates that would promote industrial decentralization.

While some of these points were debatable, there was no argument about the desirability of retaining in Quebec the $15,000,000 that the private companies paid annually in taxes to the federal government. Lévesque frequently alluded to this money as a kind of subsidy that Quebecers were contributing, through Ottawa, to provinces where the power utilities were already owned by the state.

There was little that the power companies were able to say to counteract the effect of these arguments. And even if they had won the statistical debates, it would not have mattered. The most important argument in Lévesque's case was not the cost of electricity but the national pride of French-Canadians.

At Shawinigan Water and Power and its subsidiary, Shawinigan Engineering, only about 20 of the 175 engineers on staff were French-Canadians. Admittedly there had been some improvement since 1944 when Hydro-Québec had taken over Montreal Light, Heat and Power and discovered only three French-Canadians among the private utility's senior executives, but the record at Shawinigan was far from satisfactory when compared with Hydro-Québec where 190 of the public utility's 243 engineers were French-Canadians in 1962.

Officials at Shawinigan and the other private companies defended themselves by pointing out that Quebec universities had started producing graduates in electrical engineering only in 1943. But in 1962, it was no longer acceptable in Quebec to justify inequities by referring to history.

French-Canadians themselves still had to struggle against the effects of several centuries of economic inferiority as they contemplated Lévesque's proposal.

"But does Hydro-Québec have enough experience to administer a province-wide system?" a French-speaking journalist had asked in the spring of 1962.

"The fact that a question like that can be asked," Lévesque answered, "reveals once again our terrible inferiority complex: we aren't able to do it, we don't have what it takes, we're not made for such undertakings...

"But think about it calmly and carefully. For eighteen years, French-Canadians have been running Hydro-Québec and they are doing just as well today as anyone else...*aussi bien aujourd'hui que tous les 'gentlemen' des compagnies!*"

Lévesque continued: "This area is the only important sector of our economy where we have trained people who are capable of taking over the whole thing.

"The only thing that we have to fear, as Roosevelt once said, is fear itself."

Lévesque also had to defend himself against claims, repeated in the House of Commons by a Conservative member from Quebec, that he was "another Castro." After years of being educated by the Union Nationale government and the Roman Catholic Church to see Communists behind every progressive movement in the province, most French-Canadians in the early Sixties still twitched nervously whenever anyone was accused of being Red.

Lévesque tried to place himself somewhere between total socialism and "pseudo-miraculous free enterprise," as he often described it, but he was conscious of the special position of the state in an economy where much of the effective power was in the hands of outsiders. He frequently cited statistics showing that French-Canadians, representing 85 per cent of Quebec's population, controlled only 15 per cent of its economic activity.

"The key to progress in this area is the state," he said, "but it's necessary to be pragmatic and not to apply, a priori, a single ideology to all situations."

His opponents weren't always as willing to make the same distinctions. In October, 1962, the business executives who made up the membership of the Canadian Club of Montreal invited an American, F.J. McDiarmid, of Fort Wayne, Indiana, to address one of their regular luncheon meetings. Mr. McDiarmid, vice-president of the Lincoln National Life Insurance Company, was considered to be qualified to discuss Quebec affairs because he had been born in Canada and because his firm was reported to have about $4,000,000 invested in some of the private power companies in Quebec.

"You have a politician up here who talks like his name is Robespierre and acts as if the aristocrats are to be lined up for the guillotine," Mr. McDiarmid told the Canadian Club. "He is harming the investment climate. I think this man should be told."

Within the cabinet, Lévesque continued to fight against Marler's assumption that it would eventually prove impossible to finance the takeover. After months of discussion, Lapalme had been won over. His conversion came late one night when a close friend, another lawyer, had telephoned his room in Quebec's Château Frontenac hotel to inquire about the progress of Lévesque's scheme.

"One of the largest banking houses in Boston is asking me to get information for them," he had confided to Lapalme. "They want something more precise about the amount of money that's going to be required but as far as I can tell, they think the whole thing is quite feasible."

In Lévesque's eyes, things were moving at a snail's pace. As Premier Lesage had continued to show few signs of reaching a decision on the issue, and had gone out of his way on a few occasions to reassure investors that "the rights of capital will not be endangered" in Quebec, Lévesque began to indicate to his friends in the cabinet that his future in politics depended on an early favourable decision.

In July of 1962, Quebec newspapers had published speculation about Lévesque's dissatisfaction. Some of the more extreme stories had him leaving the cabinet to create a new political party with Montreal's Mayor Jean Drapeau.

The most authoritative political column written from Quebec City at that time, by Richard Daignault and Dominique Clift in *La Presse,* referred to "uncertainty" about Lévesque's future and stated that "few political observers believe that Lévesque would agree to remain in the cabinet if the Prime Minister was not in agreement on nationalization."

Lévesque allowed almost two weeks to go by before saying that the rumours of his resignation were "ridiculous...without foundation."

In the meantime, the *Gazette* of Montreal reported that opposition to nationalization was still strong among government supporters. Journalist Robert McKenzie quoted an unidentified "prominent Liberal" as saying: "Nationalization of all the private companies would cost $800,000,000 and it wouldn't win us a single vote."

McKenzie further observed: "What Mr. Lévesque would do if he lost the nationalization battle is still difficult to predict...

"Some believe he would set out immediately to organize a new party, seeking to attract a broad cross-section of the province's present political forces under a nationalistic banner."

If Lévesque really had been thinking about other political options at that time, he did not let it interfere with his campaign within the cabinet for nationalization.

An important addition to his arsenal of arguments had come in August through Maurice Sauvé, a former organizer and publicist for the Quebec Liberals elected to the House of Commons in the federal election of June, 1962. Sauvé served as a vital link between the Liberal administrations in Quebec and Ottawa up to the time of Pierre Trudeau's entry into federal politics with Marchand and Pelletier.

Earlier that summer, when Lesage indicated to Sauvé that he might be in favour of nationalization if he could be convinced that it could be financed, Sauvé had suggested getting an opinion from an objective expert. He had proposed Douglas Fullerton, an Ottawa economist who had worked on the Royal Commission on Canada's Economic Prospects and who, later in the decade would become chairman of the National Capital Commission in Ottawa.

Fullerton was an old friend of Sauvé's and well known to many other Quebec Liberals. He had already met Lévesque through Sauvé the previous spring to discuss his new book about the Canadian bond market and in particular, his research on provincial government financing.

Fullerton's memorandum for Lesage, as he later recalled, said in essence that "the dough will be there as long as you don't screw it up." But before he gave the memorandum to Lesage, Sauvé had brought Fullerton and Lévesque together.

Lévesque arrived at the Sauvé home in Outremont – French-speaking Montreal's relatively modest version of Westmount, on the opposite side of Mount Royal – only an hour late for dinner. After eating, he and Fullerton discussed the takeover for about three hours. Lévesque was still talking as he left the house, looking back over his shoulder at Fullerton standing on the front porch, and he tumbled into a shallow excavation that city workers had prepared for a new sidewalk. And he was still talking as the others helped him back to the house for minor repairs.

The ostensible reason for their meeting was to permit Lévesque to give the economist a letter authorizing him officially to undertake the memorandum for his department. But the meeting also gave Lévesque the benefit of Fullerton's work at a critical time, only a few days before the meeting at Lac-à-l'Epaule.

VI
Winner Takes All at Lac-à-l'Epaule

Maurice Sauvé would never have given Fullerton's memorandum to Lévesque if he had known that nationalization was to become the crucial question at the Lac-à-l'Epaule meeting only a week later.

At that time, like most Liberals, Sauvé was expecting the next Quebec election to take place in 1964, after the government had completed a term of average length. When he gave Fullerton's paper to Lévesque, he had been under the impression that Lévesque agreed with this schedule and was willing to promote nationalization slowly within the party and cabinet until it emerged as the obvious theme for the 1964 election.

With Lesage still hesitant on the issue and other programs beginning to take up more of the government's attention, particularly reforms in education, Sauvé had felt that the Quebec government had enough on its plate for the time being but that nationalization would be needed as an election issue in another few years.

Perhaps Lévesque even agreed with this analysis up to a point. At the same time, however, he had pointedly started to clear out his desk in the Department of Natural Resources and to hint to some of his closest associates that his usefulness in the cabinet was coming to an end.

But he also found time, the day before going to Lac-à-l'Epaule, to have a long discussion with Dr. Roger Brault, a prominent and wealthy Quebec gynaecologist who was then president of the Quebec Liberal Federation. Brault, a close friend of the Premier's, had been designated as chairman of the sessions at Lac-à-l'Epaule. Later that day, Lévesque told a few of his senior people in the department that Brault had been won over to nationalization and that his attitude might be decisive in the following two days.

The confusion that apparently existed in his own mind as he drove north to Lac-à-l'Epaule on September 3 was shared by everyone else in the cabinet.

Many ministers had grievances of their own which they regarded as far more important than Lévesque's dream of spending $600,000,000 to buy a hydro-electric system that was already in place and functioning perfectly well. No one, perhaps not even Lévesque himself, expected that nationalization would become, the next day, not only the pivot of their discussions but the dominant issue of a completely unexpected election campaign.

After the embittered drinking and grumbling of the first evening at Lac-à-l'Epaule, the members of the cabinet were in a surly mood as they gathered after breakfast the next morning.

For some time, their discussions were simply a somewhat more formal replay of the previous evening. When it was Lévesque's turn to talk about his own department, his discussion of nationalization fell flat. Marler, after a sleepless night with a bad cold, was even more miserable than the others that morning, and contented himself with a routine review of the financial arguments against nationalization.

The meeting bogged down in an atmosphere of discouragement and futility. After only two years, all the ringing slogans of the "quiet revolution" sounded hollow.

The easy excitement of criticizing the conservatism and corruption of the previous government was over. Brave speech-making about planned reforms was also beginning to wear thin. The time for practical decisions had arrived and they had to be taken not in the congenial intellectual company of an evening at Jean Marchand's apartment but in the cabinet room of a provincial government operating with restricted powers within a federal system.

The decisions also had to reckon politically with the suspicious conservatism that had shielded the French-Canadians from outside influence for two centuries. And they had to stand up to the shrewd financial analysis of men like George Marler who recognized the provinces' position within an economy that was largely beyond the Quebec government's control but in which the goodwill of major financial and business institutions was vital to the survival of the Quebec Liberal party.

Not all the decision-makers at Lac-à-l'Epaule were heroes of the "quiet revolution." Many of the rank-and-file cabinet members still had vivid memories of the emotional response that Quebecers had given to the conservative nationalism of Maurice Duplessis. They felt that Lévesque and some of the younger members of the party had forgotten that Duplessis had died little more than three years before, and that the premature death less than a year later of his picked successor, the capable

Paul Sauvé, had seemed to many Liberals almost to be an act of divine intervention in their favour. Sauvé's death and not Lévesque's arrival on the political scene, according to these men, had been the decisive factor in the Liberal party's victory.

These men resented Lévesque's sudden rise to influence. They feared his ability to carry his favourite issues to the public. Time and again, they had urged Lesage to muzzle Lévesque before it was too late.

"When Lévesque wasn't present at cabinet meetings," recalled Georges-Emile Lapalme in his memoirs, "Lesage, encouraged by his supporters, would promise to put an end to the campaign of this Liberal prima donna.

"But when Lévesque finally arrived at cabinet toward noon, after we had been in session since nine, the arrival of the member for Laurier would silence all the belligerent threats of the leader who had just been saying that he would cut him to ribbons."

At Lac-à-l'Epaule, Lesage appeared to be behaving even more evasively than usual as Lévesque and Marler finished their desultory debate. Then he turned to Lapalme.

"Well, Georges, are you in favour of René's thesis," he asked, "and if you are, what do you say to an immediate election on it?"

Suddenly the discussion became charged with significance. Everyone there knew that Lapalme had been persuaded to support nationalization by Lévesque; they also knew the history of Lapalme's relationship with Lesage and how it would complicate the response that Lapalme would now have to make.

Instead of retiring gracefully after he handed over the party leadership to Lesage in 1958, at a time when the Liberals seemed to have no chance of winning the next election, Lapalme had stayed on to watch the deaths of two Union Nationale Premiers pave the way for a Liberal victory that might just as easily have occurred under his own leadership.

At the height of the party's victory celebration in 1960, his reactions had been contradictory. It had been shortly after midnight when Lapalme, elected in Outremont, was able to reach Lesage's home in Quebec on the telephone. The first words that he had said were, "I want to resign." Maurice Sauvé, Lesage and other Liberals who were at the celebration in the Premier-elect's home had had to plead with him to at least discuss it with them the next day before saying anything publicly.

Lapalme's reaction to the election had taken shape earlier in the evening as he wandered through the crowded festive rooms of the Liberals' Reform Club in Montreal. Within a few hours, as news of the unexpected victory spread through the city, the club and the party had changed. It was no longer a quiet and congenial place for political discussion among friends united by the seriousness and hopelessness of their fight against a corrupt government. The Reform Club had become the government club, already invaded by contractors, small businessmen, party organizers and political hacks from its own ranks and others making their way from the wreckage of the old government.

Finding it difficult to accept the twists of fate that had barred him from the Premier's office, Lapalme now had to adapt to changes that success was forcing on his party. Although he finally decided not to resign, Lapalme was still dithering over the question of accepting a cabinet post three days after the election.

"I've got problems with Georges," Lesage complained to one of his associates. "He wants everything and nothing."

He had finally agreed to become the Attorney-General in the first Lesage cabinet. But relations between the two men became more and more difficult and he resigned from the cabinet in 1963.

Lesage's patience with Lapalme had worn thin by the summer of 1962 but at Lac-à-l'Epaule, his political instinct made him turn to the former leader at the critical moment, perhaps to receive the answer that he knew beforehand that Lapalme would have to give.

The answer was yes and yes: an affirmative decision on full-scale nationalization, and an election as soon as possible. Lesage drew out a pocket calendar and began thinking aloud about dates. His pen came down decisively on November 14.

The double decision was announced two weeks after the Lac-à-l'Epaule meeting, taking the power companies, most Liberals, the opposition parties and the public completely by surprise.

On this occasion, despite his reputation among Quebec journalists as the leakiest source in the cabinet, even Lévesque kept silent. Not a whisper of speculation had been printed. The only thing that Lévesque had told reporters on his return from Lac-à-l'Epaule was that he had won $30 playing poker with the other ministers and that he had given George Marler a lift to Quebec and had dropped him among the millionaires at the Garrison Club before going to his own dinner in a modest restaurant.

Marler never quite forgave Lévesque for that gibe. But the next day, when he read about it, he was thinking about a more serious subject: the possibility of his own resignation from the cabinet.

Lac-à-l'Epaule had done nothing to change his opinion about the difficulties involved in financing the power takeover.

From Quebec, Marler drove east to his summer home at Métis on the south shore of the St. Lawrence River, a favourite resort of wealthy English-speaking Montrealers for more than a century. He mulled for a week over the probable consequences of the decision and its effects, in financial circles, on the reputation of both the province and himself. Finally, without having reached any specific conclusions, he decided to accept Lesage's assurances that financing the takeover would not be an insuperable problem.

Whether or not Lesage actually had firm assurances about financing before his election announcement on September 19, uncertainty about this aspect of the takeover soon disappeared. When the decision to nationalize became final, one of the most important, irascible and individualistic figures of the financial world along St. James Street, the late Douglas Chapman, the President of Ames and Company, took it upon himself to fly to New York. He returned to give Lesage commitments from Metropolitan Life and Prudential to take $100,000,000 each of the Hydro-Québec bonds that would be issued to finance the nationalization.

It never became necessary, as it turned out, to rely on such heavy single commitments. More than forty institutions in the United States eventually were involved in providing funds for the $300,000,000 Hydro-Québec borrowing that Premier Lesage announced the following January, calling it not only the biggest loan negotiated by Canadians in the United States but the biggest ever drawn by foreigners on the U.S. market since the First World War.

The Lac-à-l'Epaule decision breathed new life into the cabinet and its leader. Lesage soon went into the hospital for a three-day check-up and emerged in fighting trim.

Publicly identified as the victor at Lac-à-l'Epaule, Lévesque prepared to take the case for nationalization to the public, lugging along the chalk and blackboard that had been familiar parts of the studio set during his years as a television commentator.

All the niggling problems of the "quiet revolution" that had bogged down the cabinet were swept away in the grandeur of a simple combat: the people *versus* the electrical trusts.

VII
The 1962 Election: Flawed Triumph

"We have arrived at the moment of truth," Lévesque said during the campaign.

By using the state to give French-Canadians control of their own economy, and by viewing economic development as a help rather than a threat to cultural survival, French-Canadians would be able to break the vicious circle of the past where economic weakness had encouraged a cultural isolation that in turn had made it increasingly difficult to achieve economic equality.

In this historical context, the decision to nationalize Quebec's hydro-electric system was sound. But the concurrent decision at Lac-à-l'Epaule to use nationalization to justify an early election was debatable. It revealed the weakness rather than the essential strength of the Lesage administration, as well as of Quebec society in general.

It comforted the Liberal politicians. To fight large-scale battles with simple slogans made them feel revolutionary, even if their grand reform was one that should have occurred years before. But the 1962 campaign also delayed progress by interrupting the orderly process of administration for yet another round of self-congratulatory nationalist Quebec rhetoric.

In his own mind, the question of the legitimacy of the 1962 election has continued to bother Lévesque ever since. His own insistence on nationalization was the main factor in bringing about the election, but the election also gave Lesage an escape from the real problems that faced his cabinet in 1962. As events were to show, the escape was temporary. The victory that Lévesque won at Lac-à-l'Epaule was to be a costly one for him and the party.

Weaknesses in the decision made themselves felt even during the campaign.

For their own reasons, neither Lesage nor Lévesque had paid sufficient attention to the Liberal party apparatus in Quebec since the 1960 election. Lesage, by temperament, belonged to the old Quebec school where party members were treated as troops to be summoned into action for election campaigns, then left in the barracks during peacetime. As far as Lévesque was concerned, most rank-and-file Liberals were interested only in post-election plunder. Why else were they there? Lévesque had never been an ordinary party member himself and couldn't understand why anyone else would want to be, unless there was money in it.

Under Lapalme, the Quebec Liberals had amassed a considerable pool of intellectual talent. During the Fifties, the conservatism and anti-intellectualism of the Duplessis government had driven many Quebec intellectuals toward the Liberal party although a small number, like Pierre Trudeau, had found refuge in Quebec's minuscule branch of the C.C.F. party.

"As a French-Canadian, I was very near to resigning from my own race in those years, sending my kids to an English-language school and, in effect, changing sides," recalled a lawyer who was a central figure in three Liberal campaigns of the Sixties.

"But I thought – perhaps there's a last hope. That was my attitude when I agreed to do some work for the party."

By the time Lesage had taken over the party in 1958, its policy committee, made up mainly of young lawyers, academics and journalists, about forty people in all, had discussed and formulated most of the ideas that the Liberals were to implement during the Sixties. Starting with the motivational surveys of 1959, this committee gave the party the first modern, coordinated electoral campaign that the province had ever seen.

The members of the committee intended to continue as a "permanent thinkers' group" after the 1960 campaign, but Lesage gave them little encouragement. An intellectual pressure group that could dominate the party apparatus, stir up trouble at annual conventions, and foment dissension in his cabinet was exactly what Lesage did not want. This attitude had become so clear that, about a month before Lac-a-l'Epaule, the members of the 1960 campaign "brains trust" voted to disband their committee, at the same time advising Lesage that it was dangerous for the party not to have something like their group functioning within its ranks.

The head of the policy committee, Montreal lawyer Claude Ducharme, had requested an appointment with Lesage to notify him of this decision to disband. When he had received word that the Premier would meet him at the Windsor Hotel on a Saturday in September, he assumed that it was in response to this request. Unknown to him, Lac-à-l'Epaule had taken place a week before. Without giving Ducharme a chance to say a word, Lesage informed him that an election would be announced within a few days. Mentally ripping up the statement that he had prepared, Ducharme set to work with Lesage on the new campaign.

His initial advisory report to Lesage was cautious. By that time, the preliminary results of the 1962 motivational survey had shown that nationalization wasn't as big an issue in the minds of Quebecers as Lévesque might have imagined. The proportion of respondents to the survey who were in favour of it was less than 60 per cent, despite the intensive campaign that Lévesque had been waging. Some of Ducharme's experts were seriously concerned about sustaining a two-month electoral campaign on this single issue.

But Lévesque's enthusiasm was contagious, in the party and on the platform. He quickly emerged, next to Lesage, as the star of an election where success seemed a foregone conclusion.

The Liberals did win a comfortable victory on November 14, 1962, but hardly by the margin that most of them had anticipated. The government increased its standing in the ninety-five seat Quebec legislature from fifty-one to sixty-three seats while the Union Nationale declined from forty-three to thirty-one seats. But the Liberals' percentage of the total vote rose by a mere 5 per cent, to 56.5 per cent while the Union Nationale, with 43 per cent, declined by only 3.6 per cent.

The strongest Liberal support had come from the wealthiest areas of the province, particularly from the ridings in Montreal and its suburbs where traditional English-speaking support for the Liberals had combined with the votes of a growing French-speaking middle class. In the poorer regions of Quebec east of Montreal, the Liberals had merely exchanged ridings with the Union Nationale, and there had been many instances where the majorities of Liberal members had decreased since 1960. Nationalization of electrical utilities had not impressed many low-income French Canadians as strongly as had Union Nationale promises to bring in a minimum wage of a dollar an hour, to reduce taxes on low incomes and to assist the poor with free health insurance.

"Mr. Lesage got no sweep," cautioned the Montreal *Star* on the morrow of the election.

He has been served notice that a very substantial minority of the province opposes his policies...

This means that the great surge of the last two years should be slowed down. The framework of reform has been established and endorsed. The next few years should be spent in filling in that framework.

The breakneck pace of the years from 1960 to 1962 cannot be maintained.

VIII
A New Kind of Politician

Despite the weaknesses hidden in the cabinet's decision at Lac-à-l'Epaule and the doubts about the "quiet revolution" harboured by a large segment of the Quebec population, Lévesque emerged from the 1962 election with a reputation that could have taken him wherever he wanted to go in Canadian politics.

His personal appeal crossed many of the economic, social and cultural barriers of Quebec and Canadian society. Although he was still viewed with a mixture of admiration and suspicion in the backwoods of Quebec, the province's French-speaking middle class had adopted him as a liberal humanitarian whose Quebec nationalism appeared to be as pragmatic as its own. For these urban French-Canadians, the old philosophy of "the language and the faith" had little relevance. Lévesque provided a useful new creed for the French-Canadians in factories and the executive offices of large corporations when he said that language and culture were not the means of survival for the French-Canadian community but objectives to be reached through economic development.

"The means are economic," he stated, "and only the state can enable French-Canadians to become masters of their own economy."

Some English-speaking businessmen by this time perceived the pragmatism behind much of Lévesque's rhetoric.

After the 1962 election, the nationalization of the private electrical utilities was achieved swiftly and relatively painlessly by the careful preparation of a successful takeover bid. By the spring of 1963, an issue that had lurked under the surface of Quebec politics for more than three decades was resolved in what *Le Devoir* termed an "elegant victory" for both the Prime Minister and his Minister of Natural Resources.

"Even before the last chapter of the electrical battle is written, Lévesque has taken his place as a leading force in what English Canada is becoming accustomed to calling Quebec's 'Quiet Revolution,'" wrote the Montreal *Gazette's* Robert McKenzie, in January, 1963.

"The man nobody believed could be a politician has given everyone a telling demonstration of how political power can mould French Canada's future."

In McKenzie's opinion, Lévesque, after less than three years in politics, had become "an extremely plausible future leader of the Quebec Liberal party and Premier of the province," although he added that this was a prospect "that die-hard conservative elements in his own party are the first to view with some anxiety."

Lévesque was also gaining a reputation among those Europeans whose curiosity about Canadian affairs was being aroused in 1963 by the unexpected activity of political terrorists in a country that most of them had regarded as a placid El Dorado. British readers of *The Economist* were advised in the spring of 1963 to keep an eye on Lévesque as the most powerful man in the Quebec cabinet, next to Premier Lesage, and to discount the lingering suspicions of some businessmen in Montreal and Toronto that Lévesque was a dangerous socialist. In *The Economist's* opinion, Lévesque was nothing more than "a technocrat of the left who expressed sensible ideas about economic expansion and the role of the public sector."

The final verdict of *The Economist* was: "If René Lévesque is a Red, then General de Gaulle is a communist."

In the summer of 1963, when conservative and clerical opposition in Quebec forced Paul Gérin-Lajoie to moderate his drive to create the province's first Ministry of Education, Lévesque's stature within the cabinet became even more apparent.

"At the beginning of the Liberal regime," wrote Richard Daignault and Dominique Clift in *La Presse,* "Gerin-Lajoie appeared to be the heir apparent to Lesage.

> His grand charter of education for the province signified the beginning of a new era. But that hasn't lasted long. After the opening fanfare, he had to face the daily administration of an educational system – a task that consumes the prestige of a man relatively quickly.

Surprisingly enough – in particular, it came as a nasty surprise to Gérin-Lajoie – Lévesque sided with Lesage in the decision to postpone the legislation that symbolized Quebec's progress toward replacing its church-dominated educational system with schools financed and controlled by the state.

"Since the nationalization of electricity," stated Daignault and Clift, "one has been able to see a closer and closer alliance between the Premier and René Lévesque.

"In his personal relations with the Premier, Lévesque has always remained extremely loyal. When the Premier has had a difficult and unpopular measure to bring ahead, it is almost always Lévesque who has gone to bat for it.

"But the closer Lévesque gets to Lesage," warned the columnists, "the farther he moves away from the image that made him a popular hero."

Another early warning came in June, 1963, from the new editor of *Le Devoir*, Claude Ryan, a thoughtful and systematic observer who was instinctively disturbed by the fact that Lévesque "speaks and acts non-stop, like an inexhaustible machine."

Ryan said that Lévesque, aided by his "extraordinary intuition" and the "instinct that helps him to identify popular expectations," had "introduced a new element into public life and had obtained astonishing successes in a short time, thanks to a deep sympathy with public opinion.

"But Mr. Lévesque has also arrived at a stage," continued Ryan, "where he is going to have to formulate his political and economic objectives in a clearer and more coherent fashion."

In view of Lévesque's importance for the economic future of Quebec and the future of Canada, Ryan suggested, more than "frankness and spontaneity" were required in this case. Lévesque would also have to develop a conceptual framework for his ideas.

"This progression from raw instinct to careful thought has not yet occurred," he concluded.

But in the spring of 1963, it was this very atmosphere of politician-in-the-making that created excitement around Lévesque. "I feel that I'm in full evolution," he stated at this time. "My viewpoint changes from one month to the next."

Four years later, Lévesque told a journalist that his basic decision for Quebec independence had been taken in 1963.

"I became convinced then that independence was the inevitable denouement to the process in motion," he said.

To an outside observer, nothing could have been less obvious in 1963. Lévesque seemed to be moving then in many directions simultaneously. Around the table in Pelletier's home that summer, he stood out as a figure of great, but undefined political potential. It was not unrealistic at that time to speculate about his chances of becoming Premier of Quebec, perhaps even Prime Minister of Canada. His chances appeared to be in most respects better than those of the law professor, Pierre Trudeau, who sat at the same table.

Lévesque had travelled a long way from the small Gaspé town that gave him his first, indelible impressions of Canada; and it seemed to be only the beginning of an unusually creative political career.

IX
Young René: Peace and War

Lévesque's childhood in Quebec's Gaspé peninsula was secure, almost idyllic and typically Canadian in its main influences.

New Carlisle, where he was born on August 24, 1922, is a beautiful, tree-shaded community of about a thousand people on the gentle south shore of the peninsula. Although it is flanked by the paper mill towns and fishing villages of the Gaspé coast, New Carlisle exists graciously without any visible means of support. No mills spew acrid smoke across its lawns; no fishing wharves clutter up its shoreline. Even today, the stores along its main street, part of the main highway encircling the peninsula, look small and old-fashioned. Tourists have to drive through to the larger adjoining French-speaking community of Paspébiac before they find shopping centres, motels and restaurants scattered sloppily along the highway.

Unlike most rural communities in Quebec, and unlike its immediate neighbours along the highway, New Carlisle is primarily English-speaking. It is one of a small number of communities around the coastline of the Gaspé peninsula where English-speaking people established themselves in the eighteenth and nineteenth centuries, looking out across the sea toward the coastlines of New Brunswick and Prince Edward Island rather than inland to the interior of Quebec.

The families of many of these English-speaking townspeople came originally from the Channel Islands. They bore the French names of their Norman ancestors although the French language had disappeared generations before. One of René Lévesque's first grade-school sweethearts in New Carlisle was an English-speaking Gaspésian whose family name was Legrand.

Lévesque's parents were part of a much later movement of French-speaking people to the Gaspé. They came to New Carlisle from a town on the northern coast of the peninsula, Rivière-du-Loup, where the administrative and cultural links are with Quebec City further up the St. Lawrence River.

Although his parents were French-speaking and his father had to struggle to improve his English after he joined the New Carlisle law office of John Hall Kelly, an Irish-Canadian lawyer and entrepreneur, René grew up speaking both languages. No stigma was attached to speaking English in the Lévesque household. In fact, the exposure of their children to English was regarded by René's parents as one of the advantages of living in the town. English was deliberately introduced into family activities. Often his father would bring home *The Standard,* an English-language weekly newspaper supplement from Montreal, and members of the family would compete in solving the crossword puzzle.

English was the language of the streets in New Carlisle. Children in the local Catholic school were taught in both languages, usually by English-speaking teachers of Irish-Catholic origin who "taught both languages badly," according to Lévesque's recollection.

There is a temptation now to go back to New Carlisle and study it in the light of Lévesque's career. The town, with its self-contained English-speaking community and its French-speaking minority, presents itself almost too quickly as a microcosm of Canada. The position of Lévesque's father in John Hall Kelly's prosperous law practice, earning an adequate but modest living while Kelly wheeled and dealed through the region, seems to symbolize the whole economic relationship between English and French in Quebec.

But Lévesque himself left New Carlisle at the age of fourteen, after his father's death, without having drawn any such parallels. He thought of his father then, and has thought of him ever since, as a cultivated and widely-read man with a sense of his own value, and without feelings of inferiority in relation to his own English-speaking neighbours.

René's father, Dominique Lévesque, had a secure position within the elite of New Carlisle. He owned one of the first automobiles in the town; he was one of the first to string an antenna beside his house to bring in distant radio stations, those broadcast in French from Montreal and the more powerful stations from the United States.

There was no disgrace in being less wealthy than John Hall Kelly. Dominique Lévesque shared this distinction with almost everyone else in the Gaspé, regardless of language. It was Kelly who stood as the godfather of Dominique's first child, happily unaware that the squawling René in his arms would one day shout "bandit, profiteer" at his memory.

René Lévesque remembers the town on the Bay of Chaleurs, with the hills of the wooded peninsula rolling up gently behind it, as a "paradise for kids." Language was rarely a source of serious trouble between the

French-speaking "pea-soupers" and the English "crawfish," particularly for a youngster who could slang away in both.

However, there were long-term disadvantages to this everyday bilingualism, which were easily perceived by someone as well-read as Dominique Lévesque. He soon decided to take his oldest son out of the inadequate school at New Carlisle and send him to a French-language boarding school at Gaspé, a small town on the tip of the Gaspé peninsula, 115 miles to the east. René was eleven years old when he came under the care of the Jesuit fathers who had been sent from Montreal in 1926 to staff the new Gaspé school.

"I began discovering then that there was such a thing as French Canada and I began to learn about its problems," he recalled many years later. "It was quite a shock for a boy from New Carlisle."

In 1933, Montreal was the centre of a strong nationalist movement that had been nourished by the economic troubles of the Depression. Unemployment in the larger cities, the emigration of thousands of French-Canadians from Quebec to seek work in the mill towns of New England, and the search for national purpose as industrialization changed the face of Quebec were among the factors that contributed to the rise of a political reform movement called *l'Action libérale nationale*. It grew rapidly in the Thirties, helped to defeat a corrupt Liberal government in Quebec and then itself fell prey to the conservatism and corruption inherent in the Quebec politics of the day.

During this time, the Montreal priest-historian, Lionel Groulx, became the nationalist guru of French-Canadian intellectuals as he envisioned "a day of wholesome retaliation when it will be possible for us to say to ourselves, as others do: 'I have a land of my own; I have a soul of my own; I have a future of my own.' "

Some of this fervour was transmitted to Lévesque at the Gaspé school before his mother, after the death of his father, moved the household from New Carlisle to Quebec City, where René's education was continued at a local French-language college and the University of Laval.

Before his last summer holiday in New Carlisle, his father had obtained a job for him at the radio station owned by the local doctor. The young student translated news reports and advertisements from English into French in the back room of the white frame house, on New Carlisle's main street, which still contains the studios of station CHNC. When the station's announcer fell ill during the summer, the thirteen-year-old translator had gone on the air for the first time, and stayed on.

Later, as he continued his education in Quebec City, Lévesque worked for station CKCV. In the summer of 1942, he left the privately-owned station for CBV, the Quebec City outlet of the state-owned Canadian Broadcasting Corporation.

At the Gaspé school and later at the Jesuit college in Quebec City, Lévesque was known as a brilliant student with a remarkably retentive memory.

One of his former teachers at Gaspé claimed years later that the young Lévesque, on his arrival at the school, immediately asked to be shown to the library. One of his two brothers, Fernand, recalls a party where everyone was asked to recite a poem and where his oldest brother dazzled everyone – and, incidentally, rescued Fernand from a dreaded ordeal – by reciting the works of Victor Hugo from memory for more than an hour.

At the college in Quebec City, in 1939, Lévesque wrote an essay that stands today as an uncanny adolescent portrait of the future man. It was entitled "The Spirit of Sport in Life" and it contained a discussion of political idealism and pragmatism that would serve as a touchstone at every stage of Lévesque's future career. Almost forty years later, it still rings true. Lévesque constantly plays variations on the same theme.

"A spoiled idealism can be just as dangerous as the lack of idealism," he wrote. "There are, for example, those hazy thinkers, the so-called inspiration of so-called patriotic movements (don't worry, I'm not going to mention any names...)

"Resounding sentences, fiery exhortations...and then, nothing; no action, no reality; nothing but a lot of talk, sincere, I suppose, but ineffective all the same."

There was such a thing as "practical idealism," concluded the young student, that expressed itself in "tangible projects"; it bore little relation to ideologies that "drum on the tom-toms of patriotism."

This was a comparison, and a test, that Lévesque was to apply to political objectives throughout his life.

Scholastic success came easily to Lévesque until he reached university. Like many bright students who learn everything except diligence in the early years of their education, he began to falter before the difficulty and dullness of law school. Before the end of his third year at Laval, Lévesque was an indifferent student who skipped lectures, played cards and spent an inordinate amount of time at the movies.

Toward the end of 1943, the twenty-one-year-old law student faced the prospect of failing his courses and being drafted into the Canadian Army. To forestall this, Lévesque travelled to Montreal and to New York where he managed to obtain an interview with Pierre Lazareff, a prominent journalist and Jewish refugee from Paris who was then in charge of the French-language service of the United States Office of War Information. Lévesque's combination of bilingualism, brashness and radio experience impressed Lazareff. He offered him an immediate assignment overseas and early in 1944, Lévesque sailed from Montreal. He remained with the Office of War Information until the end of the following year.

"Anything to get overseas," Lévesque later recalled, "but not in His Majesty's uniform."

Before he left, he paid a visit to his former professors at the Jesuit college in Quebec. One of them later recalled that Lévesque had arrived at eight o'clock in the evening and that it was after midnight when he escorted him to the front door. There was a light burning in the college's reception room; a young woman stood up as the two men approached; and Lévesque introduced his fiancée, Louise L'Heureux, daughter of the editor of the Quebec City daily *l'Action Catholique*.

"René, don't tell me that she arrived with you!" the priest said.

"Well," shrugged the young man, "she brought a book along."

With an American uniform and the "simulated" rank of junior lieutenant, Lévesque worked in the London radio studios of the Office of War Information, writing scripts and reading reports aimed at French-speaking listeners in Belgium and northern France. In November, 1944, he sent home a clipping from *The Star* of London describing his work on the night of the U.S. election. The Star's headline – "Europe Listens to Freedom via London Radio" – was followed by this report:

> Three young Americans, speaking from London, today fought a major action in the Allies' psychological warfare against Hitler. They are announcers of the American Broadcasting Station in Europe, who kept a sleepless vigil to ensure that Germany, the countries still occupied, and those recently liberated, should have a supreme example of a great nation exercising its democratic right. Each was typical of millions of their countrymen fighting the battle of freedom.
>
> Eldest was Tys Teowey, aged 34, of Dutch ancestry, who spoke in English, and the youngest was Rene Levesque, 22, who originally came from Canada and who spoke the French of his forefathers.

Lévesque enjoyed London, even in wartime. He found the British "not very talkative or brilliant but obliging and polite." Standing among the crowd at Hyde Park Corner, he was astonished to hear "a Hindu with a long beard discoursing on the obvious decadence of the British Empire!" This struck Lévesque as the "summum of free speech," as he wrote to his mother.

The year after the invasion of Europe, Lévesque was sent to the continent to report on the advance of the U.S. forces and to act as liaison between American and French officers. In the spring of 1945, he was assigned as senior correspondent to the U.S. Seventh Army which incorporated elements of the new French First Army for the attack on the Rhine.

The closing months of the war took Lévesque through Alsace, southern Germany, Bavaria and Austria, and provided the most memorable episodes of his wartime career. He was with the first Americans to reach the infamous concentration camp at Dachau near Munich, encountering among the horrors of "a world turned upside-down," as he later remembered, a French prisoner from Britanny who had lived in Montreal before the war.

He was among the first correspondents to reach the château of Itter in Austria, where the Germans had kept such distinguished prisoners as Paul Reynaud, the last French President before the surrender to the Germans in 1940; Edouard Daladier, Prime Minister and Defence Minister of France during the same period; and General Maxime Weygand, commander-in-chief of the French forces before the surrender. In this exotic setting, wandering at will with his microphone among these historic personages, Lévesque achieved a degree of journalistic frustration that he has never quite forgotten. All the distinguished French statesmen and generals informed him, politely, that their recollections were being saved for the eventual publishers of their memoirs.

That was the final chapter of Lévesque's wartime experiences with the French, and it was typical. In London, he had decided that his French colleagues in the U.S. information service "weren't worth saying very much about...if they don't have something better than that in France, I don't think she'll ever overcome her problems."

Lévesque was preparing for a Pacific assignment when the atomic bomb brought the war with Japan to an abrupt end. Early in 1946, he was back in Montreal.

X
Lévesque Discovers TV:
Quebec Discovers Lévesque

On his return to Quebec, Lévesque thought seriously of using his war-time contacts with American correspondents to find a job with one of the radio networks in the United States. But it was simpler in 1946 to accept an immediate offer to join the French-language section of the new International Service started by the Canadian Broadcasting Corporation in Montreal in 1943. One of the reasons was the persistent laryngitis that had afflicted him since the previous winter in Europe. Lévesque's radio voice was an almost toneless rasp from 1945 until it made a dramatic recovery in 1960.

"Fortunately, the International Service was more interested in my kind of experience than in hiring a glamorous radio type," Lévesque recalled.

Within a few years, he became one of the top journalists at the CBC, specializing in international affairs and U.S. politics.

"The experiences of the war had opened up the world to me," he said later. "I had never had any contact with anything outside Quebec, except through books.

"I became so impressed about the important issues in the world that Quebec's problems seemed trivial. The war made me an internationalist, which is a very easy thing to be."

In later years, Lévesque talked scornfully about this period of "fake internationalism." But it was during this time, first on radio and later on television, that he learned the basic techniques of synthesizing a complex situation and communicating its essence to a mass audience in terms that are understandable and relevant.

In 1951, he was sent by Radio-Canada, as the French side of the CBC was called, to cover Canada's military involvement in the Korean War. This time, the sense of adventure that had enthralled the young correspondent in Europe was replaced by foreboding as Levesque watched

North American troops, including the "Van Doos" of Quebec – the Royal 22nd Regiment – battle communist forces in a relatively undeveloped country. Korea started him on the road to pacifism.

In 1953, he went to England to cover the coronation of Queen Elizabeth. Two years later, he was in the Soviet Union with Lester B. Pearson, then Minister of External Affairs and later Prime Minister of Canada.

His television career began in earnest in 1956 when he became the star of a news analysis show called "Point de Mire" – a mixture of commentary, documentary film and interviews by Lévesque that made him overnight the most talked-about journalist in Quebec.

The early Fifties was a time of rapidly widening horizons in Quebec and Lévesque seemed to know everything that was taking place everywhere and to be able to explain it to everyone.

When the French-language television service of the CBC started in Quebec in 1952 it shattered forever the cultural isolation of French-Canadians, particularly in small communities.

Before television, French-Canadian culture was restricted mainly to an elite who had attended the few good colleges of Quebec, read the better newspapers and magazines of opinion, and purchased the works of French-Canadian novelists, poets and historians. And while these intellectuals had talked, written and fretted about the purity of their culture, most French-Canadians had absorbed a popular culture supplied largely from American sources. English-language films from Hollywood dominated the Quebec movie circuits; disc jockeys played U.S. hits on French-language radio stations; and in the larger communities at least, U.S. magazines far outnumbered Canadian publications.

Within a few decades, television helped to broaden Quebec's cultural base dramatically. Forced to rely on its own resources for French-language programming, the CBC soon produced a complete range of television productions in its Montreal studios, which became the largest French-language television production centre in the world.

Variety programs created a new generation of French-Canadian entertainers as well as a new public to applaud them. Quebec fan magazines, focusing on the TV stars, began to crowd U.S. publications from the news-stands. French-language films, produced in Quebec as well as imported from France, replaced American and British movies in the cinemas in French-speaking districts.

By the Sixties, it was more possible than it ever had been for a French-Canadian, even in Montreal, to live almost entirely in French and, through television, to acquire a broad outlook on the world – a world that now came to him in his own language, not as an imported product packaged in a strange language and controlled by outsiders.

Lévesque was at the centre of this cultural development. From the early days of television in Montreal, it became apparent that this wispy man with the sandpaper voice was made to order for the new medium. Even the voice was a distinctive asset. The Levesque wheeze explaining world events within a cloud of cigarette smoke and chalk dust before a blackboard in the TV studio became a familiar performance in homes where newspaper reading traditionally started at the sports pages and finished at the comics.

Lévesque was one of the few journalists at Radio-Canada who came to television from radio rather than from newspapers. He was always ready to speak before a microphone, but writing articles was, for a long time, an alien discipline that he undertook reluctantly. Even in the studio, he preferred to write the opening and closing lines of his script in longhand on sheets of foolscap, then improvise the rest. His sense of timing was so instinctive that he could improvise voice-over narration for film sequences on television as precisely as if he were reading from a carefully timed script.

Lévesque's preference for the extemporaneous performance on television gave some people the impression that he was a slapdash worker. But the content of his shows, both commentary and interviews, usually showed that he had briefed himself thoroughly. He would devour so much research material before every program that a few key sentences, written in the studio during rehearsal, were enough to trigger a flow of lively and informative commentary.

His appetite for newspapers and magazines was insatiable. Another journalist, recalling an assignment with him in New York, remembers Lévesque fidgeting through the first part of an early Bergman film, obviously impatient with the slow pace. Finally he bolted from the theatre, and his colleague found him later sitting on his bed in the hotel in a nest of newspapers and periodicals.

"He could discuss the most complex subjects on television in a way that gave him tremendous popularity with very simple people," recalled one of his former colleagues at Radio-Canada.

"I remember someone turning from Lévesque's show on the screen one night and saying, 'Why the hell am I watching this man talking about politics someplace in the Middle East?'

"The secret was that you felt intelligent when you listened to him."

In the studio, Lévesque functioned with the certainty of a professional, and with a growing awareness of his own stature.

"He was basically a prima donna," said a former associate.

When you were working a show with him, he didn't pull all the covers over to his side, but neither did anyone interfere with his portion of the program.

There was only one producer, Claude Sylvestre, who could work smoothly with him. If there was a problem, Sylvestre would come into the studio from the control room and say, 'Okay, René, you can swear for five minutes now, and then we'll discuss it.'

He had a very short temper if a producer tried to cut his material. We were doing a half-hour show, and every Sunday night, Lévesque would have a festival of swearing. He would shout that they gave two and a half hours on television to a hockey game, how could he be expected to explain the world in 28 minutes and 30 seconds!

XI
The 1959 Strike:
From Studio to Platform

Television first introduced René Lévesque to the Quebec public; then it introduced him to politics. When seventy-four French-language radio and television producers voted to strike against Radio-Canada on December 29, 1958, they did more than bring Lévesque's show, "Point de Mire," to a temporary halt. They gave him his first opportunity to become an actor rather than a spectator at a political event, to make news rather than to report it. He seized the opportunity eagerly and from then on, although he returned to his program for a few months after the strike, he was a politician in search of a party.

At issue in the strike was the producers' right to form a union, against management's insistence on including the producers within its own ranks, elevating them safely above union activity. That was the starting point. Soon the scope of relevant issues expanded to include the position of Radio-Canada within the Canadian Broadcasting Corporation, and the attitude of English-speaking politicians in Ottawa to a conflict that affected only French-Canadians.

Before the sixty-nine-day strike was resolved, it had come to symbolize many of the grievances held by French-Canadians at that time. It was Lévesque's baptism of fire in the politics of Quebec nationalism. He dove right in, and discovered his natural element.

It was a belated discovery. At university, the nationalist movements of the day had brushed past Lévesque without marked effect. The years of the Second World War and his career with the CBC's International Service had further insulated him from the local preoccupations of many Quebec intellectuals. The written journalism that he produced during this period consisted mainly of film criticism for a small but respected weekly newspaper.

In 1958, shortly before the producers' strike, a Quebec politician who dealt with Lévesque at the federal Liberals' leadership convention was struck by his isolation from Canadian affairs. The politician, who briefed the new federal leader, Lester Pearson, before his television interview with Lévesque, claimed years later that Lévesque showed little interest at that time even in Quebec politics.

The strike suddenly changed that. Lévesque himself has always identified it as a decisive event that focused his thoughts on the place that Quebec and French-Canadians occupy in Canada. Two developments during the strike made a particularly strong impression on him: the unsympathetic attitude of Prime Minister John Diefenbaker's Conservative government in Ottawa, and the failure of English-speaking producers in the state-owned broadcasting system to feel that the strike also involved them.

"I never quite got over it," Lévesque has said.

Something happened during that strike.

The whole bloody French network became virtually non-existent, and nobody cared. Here Radio-Canada was supposed to be so vital a part of the CBC – it was so important to broadcast in French. But Ottawa didn't give a damn.

And the non-Quebec labour unions tried to stab us in the back...

I learned then that French was really very secondary in the rest of Canada's mind, certainly in Ottawa's.

The strike also brought Lévesque together again with his old poker partner from Laval University, Jean Marchand, who was then leader of a confederation of Catholic trade unions in Quebec. André Laurendeau was another who was sympathetic to the strike from the start. Laurendeau and Lévesque found themselves fighting the same battle side-by-side in the columns of Laurendeau's newspaper, Le Devoir. Lévesque was one of sixty-six Radio-Canada writers and performers who signed a letter supporting the strike a week after it began.

Many of these artists took part in a benefit show called "Difficulties Are Temporary" that opened on January 12, 1959, at a Montreal theatre and ran for three months. Lévesque's popularity with audiences at these performances surprised the other entertainers; and a journalist who saw him on stage wrote that "his following is obviously much larger than any of us had believed."

The Diefenbaker government had expected the strike to last a few days, and kept hoping that it could stay out of it. Its refusal to intervene was seen by the strikers as scornful disinterest rather than benevolent neutrality.

"Once again, we have to face up to the tragedy of being French-Canadian," wrote André Laurendeau in Le Devoir three weeks into the strike. "We're not masters of our own institutions and we don't find, outside of Quebec, in times of crisis, the kind of solidarity that should be the basis of Canadian unity."

A few days later, Lévesque presented Laurendeau to one of the nightly audiences at the Comédie Canadienne, where the "Difficulties. . ." show was playing, and the editor of *Le Devoir* read one of his editorials to them. On January 23, Laurendeau opened his editorial page to Lévesque, who wrote, "We're not going to crawl back!"

Lévesque and Jean Marchand were among the leaders of a march of 1,500 Quebec workers on Parliament Hill at the end of January. On March 2, they were among twenty-eight people who were arrested during a noisy demonstration outside the Radio-Canada building in Montreal. Everyone was released four hours later as newspapers were appearing with photographs of the diminutive Lévesque struggling in the arms of gigantic policemen. The Montreal *Star* published an editorial the next day – "CBC Deadlock and Rowdyism" – that so enraged Lévesque that he sent a long rebuttal to *Le Devoir*, in English. It was published there, for the benefit of "les autres," on March 7, only a few hours before Radio-Canada signed an agreement with the producers' association. It showed how far Lévesque had travelled during the strike, and in what direction.

He wrote at the conclusion of his article:

Many, many weeks back, some people said that a racial cry was being raised, when it was advanced that a prolonged strike could mean ruin or at least serious damage to a valuable public property of French Canada. So a lot of us stopped saying that truth as we saw it. Now most of the damage has been done. CBC's higher-ups have run the gamut from corporate irresponsibility to anonymous viciousness. Cabinet ministers have stood up in the House like knights in incredible armors of denseness, small-town vanity and brutal indifference. Some of us, maybe a lot of us, will come out of this permanently disgusted with a certain ideal called National Unity. Never before have we felt that apart from pleas every four years in painful *political French*, National Unity is something designed almost exclusively to keep negligible minorities nice and quiet.

Never before have we felt that our affairs are bound to be either tragically or comically mismanaged, as long as they remain in the hands of men who have no understanding of them and make it quite clear that they don't consider such lack as any kind of personal flaw. Some of us, and maybe many, come out of this with a tired and unworthy feeling that if such a strike had happened on English CBC, it would – as the Hon. George Nowlan said, and on this occasion not erroneously – have lasted no more than half an hour. To this day, ours has lasted 66 days. Of such signal advantages is the privilege of being French made up in this country!

Laurendeau's verdict, after the strike, was more elegant in style but equally pessimistic. The crisis had shown him "two parallel solitudes, a stronger one that leads and a weaker one that can't do anything but rebel."

In a 1972 CBC documentary, Lévesque recalled that Laurendeau had said to him during the strike, "You don't even realize it, but you've started in a political direction that can take you a long distance."

Lévesque remembered saying to him, "Perhaps. I don't know. I haven't the faintest idea."

Of the three, Laurendeau, Marchand and Lévesque, only Lévesque followed the logic of the 1958 producers' strike to its ultimate conclusion. It wasn't a development that he foresaw in 1958, just as no one could have foreseen the strike itself or his own role in it. It was, as Laurendeau seems to have perceived, something that happened within Lévesque himself. He was as powerless to resist it as Quebec itself was to hold back the tide of the "quiet revolution" that was about to engulf it.

XII
The Lévesque Style:
Quoting the Unquotable

Lévesque returned to "Point de Mire" after the strike but his days at Radio-Canada were numbered. He returned briefly to radio with a privately-owned station in Montreal before accepting the Quebec Liberals' invitation to become a candidate in the 1960 election.

When he decided to enter politics, Lévesque brought more than his television reputation with him. That attracted crowds to his meetings, but it was his ability to synthesize complex situations and his genius for improvisation that made him a political star in his first campaign.

His abilities also made him highly controversial as soon as the Liberals' 1960 victory shot him into the provincial cabinet without any political experience. His quick responses to political issues, offhand and disarmingly frank, or apparently so, soon created endless conflicts between himself and other members of the government.

The problem was compounded by Lévesque's difficulty in deciding whether he was a journalist dabbling in politics or a politician who still tried his hand at journalism from time to time. His political colleagues found it to be a poisonous combination, but Lévesque's old friends in Quebec's Press Gallery loved it. They tended for a long time to treat him as one of their own and Lévesque often seemed to share this view, even when cabinet secrecy and solidarity were involved.

This arrangement provided news for the journalists and a remarkably sympathetic press for Lévesque. A careful reading of articles about Lévesque in Quebec newspapers of the Sixties illustrates exactly what happens when journalists encounter a politician who embodies and expresses many of their own delusions and ideals. There was virtually no critical reporting of Lévesque.

French-language journalists continually made allowances for him, rarely taking his remarks out of context and carefully avoiding the temptation to crucify him on a single careless phrase.

English-language journalists didn't always attempt to be so sympathetic. They sometimes took Lévesque at his word, or thought that they had; and they frequently discovered that the *camaraderie* of journalism disappeared if Lévesque felt that he had been stung by their reports.

One incident in the 1962 campaign for hydro-electric nationalization illustrated this neatly. The worst suspicions of *The Gazette's* readers in English-speaking Quebec were confirmed by a report on a Lévesque speech under the headline: "Quebec Eyes 'Formulae' for Pulp and Mines." The story claimed that Lévesque had "suggested the possibility that mining and pulp interests may be next in Quebec's 'economic liberation' plans." It quoted him as saying, "We will have to find other formulae for the mining and pulp industries where French-Canadians don't really exist either."

Lévesque held a special press conference the following day to accuse *The Gazette* of wrenching his words out of context. Outlining his economic policy once again, he stated that the French-speaking majority in Quebec, representing 80 per cent of the province's population, had long been composed of "second-class citizens." Giving Quebecers a greater share in the "tasks and profits" of economic development was an objective that Canadians of both languages should support. They should "look with suspicion particularly on hypocritical efforts to caricature this policy and to make it seem more or less than it actually is."

Throughout his career, Lévesque's journalistic style of expression frustrated those who tried to define his basic political philosophy. As I wrote in 1964,

> When René Lévesque is speaking, there isn't much time to think. Ideas flash like computer lights. Impromptu phrases tear through sentences like tracer bullets.
>
> It's heady stuff to listen to, difficult to report. No other politician makes a journalist more aware of the difficulties of communication, the weaknesses and dangers inherent in the so-called 'straight news story.'

Claude Ryan in *Le Devoir* in 1963:

> The classical system of expression, which consists of placing one sentence after another, is too orthodox and too slow for him.
>
> He starts out a sentence, suddenly begins a second one, then pauses on a third idea and finally returns – when you imagined that he had forgotten all about it – to his initial theme.

"René Lévesque speaks so often that he doesn't have time to edit his texts," explained Michel Roy in *Le Devoir* in 1964,

> and he often has to improvise the larger part of his speeches in the course of a meeting.
> He uses striking images and epithets. Every sentence resembles a slogan. But taken out of context, the slogans twist his thought.
> For a reporter, it's an enormous job. He has to re-organize the speaker's thoughts, like a puzzle where the whole picture doesn't appear until the last piece is in place. Under these conditions, it's difficult for a journalist to summarize accurately not only the words and sentences of the minister but his thoughts.

Robert McKenzie, the *Gazette's* political correspondent in Quebec, found Lévesque to be "one of the hardest Quebec politicians to cover."

"The mixture of humour and emotion in his speeches is almost impossible to convey in a few lines of print," he wrote," and often the stark quotations that are left give a false impression of what he has said."

By the spring of 1964, relations between Lévesque and Quebec's English-language media had deteriorated to the point where Lévesque refused to allow certain radio stations to tape a debate between himself and Douglas Fisher, the New Democratic Party Member of Parliament and newspaper columnist from the Lakehead.

"Several stations in Montreal which broadcast in English," wrote Fisher after the incident, "seem to feel that he is the main threat to the right and proper future of Quebec, especially of the English minority. He believes they have used, with deliberate intent, taped remarks of his in such a way that he appears dangerous, unreasonable and vindictive to the English-speaking community."

Like other journalists, Fisher found it easier to describe Levesque's platform manner than to analyse exactly what the Quebec minister had said.

"His magnetism to an audience is as evident as John Diefenbaker's," he wrote. "One wonders 'how' and 'why'?

> Mr. Lévesque is as short as Tommy Douglas (then national leader of Fisher's New Democratic Party) although he appears weightier because his suits are looser and less spruce or jaunty. He is not quite bald. His skull is fashioned in sallow planes...like Yul Brynner, the nakedness has force and virility, not an effect of age or peacefulness.

Describing how Lévesque could establish rapport with an audience, even a critical one, Fisher told of a woman turning to her neighbour during an uproarious Lévesque speech to an English-speaking audience in Montreal, and saying: "Why are we laughing? He's insulting us!"

The quicksilver quality of Lévesque's pronouncements created suspicion among not only the province's English-speaking minority but also his colleagues in the cabinet. There was something unnerving about having the reputation of your party, not to mention your own political image, so closely tied to a politician who boasted about being "*en pleine évolution*" toward an unknown political destination.

"He doesn't have any political theory," said Jean Marchand in 1962, "and that makes him both forceful and unpredictable. His attention is fixed on realities and problems, not on the theories of various parties."

Lévesque himself had said, "I will never be a politician."

Robert McKenzie of *The Gazette* observed:

At close range, it becomes obvious that the labels of 'socialist' and 'leftist' – not to speak of such electoral mud-slinging as 'Quebec Castro' and 'Lenin without a beard' – miss one point badly.

That is Rene Lévesque's practical approach to problems as they arise. He is a pragmatist. The only other 'ism' that can be suitably tagged to his name is 'nationalism.'

In the Sixties, no other 'ism' was more potent or created more apprehension among English-speaking Canadians.

Most Canadians favoured, at least in principle, the economic objectives of Lévesque and the Lesage government. This created the kind of positive Lévesque image that a reporter for one of the Newfoundland newspapers reflected after a visit to Quebec in 1963: "This wiry, balding, admirably articulate hero of Quebec's young intellectuals may well go down in history as the man who turned his people away from the sterile forms of nationalism..."

But Lévesque didn't stop there. A few months later, for instance, he was on Pierre Berton's interview show telling a national audience that "I certainly wouldn't cry very long" if Quebec should separate.

"Confederation to most French-Canadians has no sentimental pull," he told Berton.

"It was a bargain...and the bargain was not very good and if it is not changed in some deep and profound ways – well, it's like a couple; if you can't sleep together, you might as well have separate beds."

He used the same imagery before a Toronto audience in 1963 when he said, "It is urgent for you to come to grips with the fact that we are uncomfortable in bed, while you snore comfortably on."

"Time is precious," he told an alumni dinner at the University of Toronto.

"In four or five years, unless there is a new Canada, Quebec will secede."

Lévesque described himself on that occasion as "first a Québécois, and second – with rather growing doubt – a Canadian."

Phrases like this bounced wildly across English-speaking Canada whenever Lévesque opened his mouth. Denials, clarifications and interpretations would echo after them. It kept English-speaking Canadians nervous and irritated; many of them suspected that Lévesque knew exactly what he was doing, even if they didn't know exactly what he was saying; but for years, trying to pin him down was as frustrating as trying to nail a ball of mercury with a hammer.

Lévesque always professed to be mystified by the confusion. From his point of view, it was quite clear: something new was happening to Quebec, something new was happening to him, and the process was more important than the result, at least for the time being.

XIII
Political Début:
Harnessing the Star

Lévesque never liked to be called a politician.

It was a title that carried perhaps less respect in Quebec than in other parts of Canada. French-Canadians elected to Ottawa had always been branded as sell-outs by Quebec nationalists. The corruption of Quebec politics, nourished by English-speaking businessmen for their own purposes, had tarnished the reputations of many of those who had been elected to the provincial legislature.

Despite the prevailing cynicism, French-Canadian politicians both in Ottawa and Quebec City had effected many changes in the lives of their own people since Confederation. And Lévesque owed more than he usually acknowledged to the succession of political hacks who preceded him, and to the inglorious compromises that had brought Quebec to a point of political self-ignition by 1960, when he happened to arrive on the scene.

After the Second World War, the role of all provincial governments was enhanced by the growth of activities within their jurisdiction such as education, health services, welfare and natural resource management. Quebec politicians were particularly alert to these changes and sensitive to federal attempts to encroach on these fields.

While the Duplessis regime of the Fifties failed to implement what Lévesque would have regarded as an adequate program of economic development, it did formulate a clear idea of its own political authority. Much of this was negative, in response to federal initiatives. Moreover, it was costly, as for example when the Quebec government refused to recognize Ottawa's right to make direct grants to Quebec universities. But Duplessis' defence of provincial "autonomy" did advance the concept of a parallel rather than subservient level of provincial government, a concept that had particular meaning in the Quebec "homeland" of French-Canadians.

The role of the Quebec government as the supreme political institution of the French-Canadian national state, however imperfect and limited, was discussed intensively within the Quebec Liberal party during the Fifties. In response to Duplessis' defensive definition of Quebec autonomy, the Liberals under Georges-Emile Lapalme drew up a program of positive measures. In education, for example, they were willing to go against a conservative Roman Catholic tradition of church-controlled schools to formulate a coherent philosophy of public education. Their analysis of Quebec's economic weaknesses had brought them to accept the principle of state participation in many activities formerly reserved for private enterprise.

The development of this new Liberal philosophy was a long, slow process. In the early Fifties, the party was no more democratic in its structure than the Union Nationale. It had no annual convention, no continuing grass-roots organization and no intellectual wing. In fact, the founding convention of the Quebec Liberal Federation was held only in 1955.

Although the Liberals lost ground to the Union Nationale in the 1956 election, long-term reform of the party was well underway. The reform reflected hidden currents of thought in Quebec society that were eroding popular support for the Union Nationale government beneath its facade of electoral impregnability. The pages of the party's weekly newspaper "La Reforme," increasing in circulation from 5,000 to 45,000 copies during the late Fifties, reflected the lively discussions within the party's policy committee.

So many ideas were circulating within the Liberal party when the Union Nationale government called the 1960 election that the challenge of condensing them into a conventional election platform almost overwhelmed the party in the first few days of the campaign. Working with the Liberal record in the legislature, resolutions adopted by the annual conventions, the reports of the policy committee and the results of the 1959 motivational survey, the party's election strategy committee had produced a document that was impressive but totally impractical. After several days of chaotic meetings in Montreal's Windsor Hotel, Lesage turned in despair to Lapalme and asked him to draft a program for the campaign.

Lévesque had been shown various drafts of the party's program when Lesage persuaded him to become a Liberal candidate. In this indirect way, Lévesque might have had some influence on the program, as he was led to believe. There were many others in the party who later claimed ownership of certain parts of the program. But the document used in the campaign was the one that Lapalme eventually agreed to produce. He drafted it during two days of isolation in a room at the Windsor while Lesage waited nervously in his suite on another floor.

The main burden of the 1960 campaign was shared by Lesage, Lapalme, Gérin-Lajoie and Lévesque. Lévesque was invaluable because his popular style helped to moderate the rather pompous image projected by Lesage, particularly before large audiences.

"There were many people who looked at Lesage and said, 'Well, he's just the old style,'" remembered one of the strategists of the party's 1960 campaign. "Lévesque consolidated a positive image with people like that, mainly intellectuals, who were against the Union Nationale but cool to the Liberals."

After the 1960 election, Lévesque started to develop his own concept of the role of the Quebec state. It was embodied specifically in the nationalization issue of the 1962 campaign. Between 1960 and the 1966 election, no Quebec politician spoke more often or more effectively about the French-Canadians' new potential for political self-realization through the government in Quebec. Other members of the cabinet, in particular Gérin-Lajoie, were as deeply involved in exploring the limits of action for the Quebec government but none was as closely identified with this political adventure in the public mind as Lévesque.

On the platform, quivering with energy and exhaustion, chain-smoking, lighting up a new idea from the glowing tip of an earlier one after only a few mental puffs on it, optimistic and fearful at the same time about the future, Lévesque *was* Quebec.

If they sometimes responded to the "grand seigneur" style of Lesage, confirming the judgement of a Quebec economist who had written in 1945 that "French Canadians like to be ruled," the Québécois of the Sixties identified strongly with Lévesque's pragmatic and irreverent individualism. They respected Lesage, but they loved the snotty little underdog who was able to make them laugh and cry about themselves, and dream about their future.

Lévesque preached the dream with all the enthusiasm of a late convert. It had come down to him from generations of Quebec politicians whom he dismissed as corrupt hacks, but it was Lévesque's great gift to make the concept of "the state of Quebec" seem like the special creation of the Sixties rather than the result of a long, slow and not always heroic sequence of political decisions.

The role of prophet for the new state suited Lévesque. He always looked ahead with excitement and optimism; it was only the past that disappointed him.

There was something infinitely sad, for Lévesque, about the history of the French-Canadians. He saw them, among the new nations of the Sixties, as "the last and oldest of the colonial peoples." Only the discovery of a new political vocation, he believed, could restore the vitality of this stubborn remnant of an eighteenth century European empire.

XIV
Quebec Nationalism: Fresh Starts and Stale Hopes

"At the present time," said René Lévesque in 1962, "there is no more devouring interest for me than the interests of five or six million French-Canadians.

"I've always been proud of being French-Canadian. We've been stuck in the mud for a long time, and much of it was of our own making. But what's important is that we shouldn't slide back into the mud."

"Mud" was the translation selected by the editors of the English-language press in Montreal. "Merde" was the term used by Lévesque. French-Canadians, he was saying, had put up with a lot of crap over the years. Now that they were finally digging themselves out of the particular dungheap that history had assigned to them, the past had to be completely forgotten. It was now unthinkable that French-Canadians, having glimpsed daylight and sniffed the open air, should ever again return to the cozy, suffocating warmth of their own decayed ambitions.

Defeat and despair were, for Lévesque, the major themes of French-Canadian history.

His own generation had matured in the corrupt and cynical atmosphere of Maurice Duplessis' Union Nationale government. Deliverance became thinkable only after Duplessis' death in 1959. The instinctive rejection of their own heritage by many French-Canadians of Lévesque's generation sprang from this immediate past. Lévesque called it a generation that had been "cursed" and "damned" by Duplessis' fourteen years in office after the Second World War.

Duplessis stood at the forefront of villains in Lévesque's pessimistic view of Quebec history but preceding him loomed a succession of betrayals and failures beginning with the abandonment by France after the British soldiers had conquered Quebec in 1759.

In the opinion of modern French-Canadian historians, the people of

New France were already a distinctive national group when they fell under British rule.

"This nation, though small, had fought valiantly to maintain the Empire that had given it birth and upon which its future prosperity depended," wrote historian Michel Brunet.

Despite its courage and energy, it had been forced to yield to superior numbers.

These 65,000 settlers – peasants, craftsmen, merchants, and priests – had been brutally and much too prematurely severed from their metropolis. They nevertheless retained, to a certain extent, the illusion that they were continuing the work of France in America. For them, Canada had not disappeared. It was the country they had always known, the realm founded by their ancestors, the native soil they had defended from invaders. Canada was, in a word, their homeland.

Before the end of the eighteenth century, the American Revolution increased the flow of English-speaking people into this homeland. Loyalists from the new republic to the south joined new arrivals from Britain in the streets of Montreal and Quebec.

The American Revolution also provided the first test of loyalty for French-Canadians. In 1774, in an "Address to the Inhabitants of the Province of Quebec," the Continental Congress urged them to abandon their British masters and "seize the opportunity presented to you by Providence itself."

"You are a small people compared to those who with open arms invite you into fellowship" proclaimed the Congress. "A moment's reflection should convince you which will be most for your interest and happiness, to have all the rest of North America your unalterable friends, or your inveterate enemies. The injuries of Boston have roused and associated every colony, from Nova Scotia to Georgia. Your province is the only link that is wanting to complete the bright strong chain of union."

The French-Canadians were in 1774 the first to face "the Canadian choice between dollars and distinctiveness." Their memories of old French and Indian wars against the *"Bastonnais,"* as well as the Quebec clergy's fear of assimilation by a Protestant and Anglo-Saxon society, were enough to keep most of them on the sidelines two years later when American forces captured Montreal and attempted to occupy Quebec City.

American soldiers soon withdrew from Quebec but American political ideals continued to influence French-Canadians. By 1837, frustrated by Britain's slow response to their demands for democratic reform, some French-Canadians began to dream of *"une nation canadienne,"* a sovereign French-speaking state in North America.

Led by Louis-Joseph Papineau, an aristocratic seigneur of the old school, these *"Patriotes"* launched a confused and ineffective armed rebellion against the British in 1837. It was put down ruthlessly by British troops, English-Canadian volunteers, and French-Canadians who identified their own interests with those of the established power.

In the wreckage of the rebellion, according to Lord Durham, a contemporary observer, the French-Canadians "brood in sullen silence over the memory of their fallen countrymen, of their burnt villages, of their ruined property, of their extinguished ascendancy, of their humbled nationality." Against the government and the British, they appeared to maintain "an indiscriminating and eternal animosity."

One of the veterans of Papineau's rebellion, George-Etienne Cartier, led French-Canadians into Confederation in 1867 in collaboration with John A. Macdonald, Canada's first Prime Minister. But the very creation of Canada, regarded as a great positive achievement by English-speaking Canadians, is treated by many historians of French Canada as yet another crisis. Cartier himself proposed it to his compatriots as a lesser-of-two-evils: "We must either have a confederation of British North America or be absorbed by the American union."

The contemporary Quebec nationalist interpretation of Confederation is that it established, "once and for all, political and economic inequality between French and English Canadians – it made us permanent subjects."

However, the federal constitution also created a new level of government to administer the various provinces. In Quebec, this placed education and other important social services for the first time within the hands of the province's French-speaking majority. And this meant, as interpreted by Michel Brunet and other nationalist historians, that "progressively, successive generations of French-Canadian leaders over the last century have totally changed their outlook and their frame of reference."

"They no longer consider themselves as the spokesmen of a minority group whose future in North America depends on the goodwill of English-speaking Canadians who, incidentally, treat them most of the time just as the British Americans did," Brunet has written. "They now act as the legitimate representatives of a nationality that can re-negotiate with English Canada the terms on which the union of Canada can be maintained.

"The new leaders of Quebec have learned that good government in Ottawa by the English-Canadian majority is no substitute for self-government in a territory where they have a democratic right to majority rule."

Only two years after Confederation, the rebellion of French-speaking Roman Catholic Métis in the territories west of Ontario produced another crisis within French-Canada. The absorption of the western territories by Ottawa, and the opposition of their inhabitants led by the visionary Louis Riel, forced the French-Canadians to confront the realities of political power within the new confederation. English-speaking Canadians saw the westward expansion as a fulfilment of their own destiny; for Canada's French-speaking minority, it was yet another example of English-Canada's drive to dominate and assimilate.

From this crisis came Honoré Mercier, a Premier of Quebec who mourned the execution of Riel by the Macdonald government as "a blow at the heart of our race."

"Riel, our brother, is dead," said Mercier, "the victim of his devotion to the cause of the Métis, of whom he was the leader, victim of fanaticism and treason."

Mercier's "Parti National" won a sweeping victory in the Quebec election of 1886 but the federal Liberal party already had recruited the French-Canadian who was to embody his people's alternate response to English-Canada.

"Our country is Canada, it is the whole of what is covered by the British flag on the American continent," said Wilfrid Laurier in 1885, the year of the second and final rebellion led by Riel in Saskatchewan, and eleven years before Laurier became the first French-Canadian Prime Minister of Canada.

> Cannot we believe that in the supreme battle on the Plains of Abraham, when the fate of arms turned against us, cannot we believe that it entered into the designs of Providence that the two races, enemies up to that time, should henceforth live in peace and harmony?

Laurier's era in Ottawa, from 1896 to 1911, saw the rise of Henri Bourassa in Quebec. In response to the British imperialism that involved Canada in the South African war and prepared the way for its participation in the wars of 1914-18 and 1939-45, Bourassa's nationalism envisaged a Canadian nation that would be a politically and economically independent unit of the British Empire. Bourassa's ideal subsequently became the accepted Canadian model; at the time, it seemed traitorous to a majority of English-speaking Canadians who regarded their own attachment to the "Mother Country" as an essential element of Canada's national identity.

In the final year of the 1914-18 war, French-Canadian opposition to compulsory military service sent crowds into the streets of Quebec shouting *"Vive la révolution!"* In the Quebec legislature in 1918, the possibility of separation from Canada was debated officially for the first time under a motion put forward unsuccessfully by a Liberal backbencher, J.-N. Francoeur: "That this House is of (the) opinion that the Province of

Quebec would be disposed to accept the breaking of the Confederation Pact of 1867 if, in the other provinces, it is believed that she is an obstacle to the union, progress and development of Canada."

The 1939-45 war created similar tensions when Quebec, in opposition to the rest of Canada, voted overwhelmingly (72 per cent) against military conscription while the rest of the country approved it by a four-to-one ratio.

This succession of political crises reflected basic and persistent maladjustments between the French-Canadian community and the English-speaking society that surrounded and infiltrated it. In 1956, Pierre Trudeau described the French-Canadians historically as "a people vanquished, occupied, leaderless, kept aside from business life and away from the cities, gradually reduced to a minority role and deprived of influence in a country which, after all, it had discovered, explored, and settled..." In response to this, according to Trudeau, French-Canadians had evolved "a system of self-defence ...against an English, Protestant, democratic, materialistic, business-minded, and later industrial environment" that "glorified every contrary tendency, and made a cult of the French language, Catholicism, authoritarianism, idealism, the rural way of life, including later, the myth of a 'return to the land.'"

Trying to make the best of a bad world became a hopeless and often self-destructive crusade for generations of French-Canadian intellectuals.

"In their anxiety to obtain nothing but the best for French-Canadians," wrote Trudeau in 1956, "they developed a social outlook impossible to put into practice, and which, to all intents and purposes, left the people without effective intellectual guidance."

One by one, the blueprints for brave new worlds were taken up, eagerly discussed, occasionally attempted and always discarded.

During the Twenties and Thirties, while French-Canadians were streaming into the cities to work in factories, and emigrating to the United States, their intellectuals were promoting schemes to settle them as farmers in remote and unproductive regions of the province. While the popular culture of North America dominated the growing cities, the intellectuals still talked about French Canada's spiritual and cultural vocation. Against this powerful chorus, with its religious undertones, the voices of those who tried to look realistically at the economic position of French-Canadians were lost. Proposals to reform education to take account of the technical and business trends in North America were stubbornly advanced, even in the nineteenth century, and just as resolutely opposed by the dominant hierarchy of orthodox thinkers.

The process became self-perpetuating. As each new utopia was explored and rejected, it stimulated another cycle of introspection. In the

Thirties, influenced by events in Europe and shaken by economic difficulties at home, the nationalists began to look for messiahs who could provide final solutions.

"Who will be the national leader?" asked the historian Groulx in 1934.

> Who will prove to be a de Valera, a Mussolini, whose policies may be disputed but who, over a ten-year period, psychologically made a new Ireland and a new Italy, just as Dollfuss and Salazar are building a new Austria and a new Portugal?
>
> It is, alas, necessary to recognize that no such national leader is in sight. Will we ever have one?...
>
> Let us, with humble hearts, ask Providence for this leader without whom no people can forge their destiny...

The same instinct turned many French-Canadians during the Thirties toward corporatism, a form of representative government where legislators represent certain groups in society – business interests, labour unions, teachers, farmers, and so forth – rather than being elected directly by the people.

"In fact, our corporatism was conceived in terms of an elite which might use it to discipline popular forces and to preserve its authority over the organized masses," wrote Trudeau in 1956, drawing attention to the fact that "almost half a century of theoretical corporatism" had produced "practically no organization in existence whose administrative structure comes close at all to the model described by the theorists."

The end result of all this intellectual and political activity, measured against professed objectives, was insignificant. This led sociologist Léon Dion to write in 1957 about the "pessimistic neo-nationalism" of that time, and to put forward a suggestion that was plainly heretical in the context of traditional nationalist thought in Quebec:

> Could the failure of the neo-nationalists be explained by the fact that they were mistaken about the reality of the French-Canadian national object, since it has to be defined today with reference to all of Canada and not just to French Canada?
>
> Indications of a new Canadian nationalism, which is sometimes called Canadianism, are seen here and there...
>
> The French-Canadian ethnic group is in no worse a position than other peoples. Following the proper methods in the situation, they also can legitimately search for the best means of using the cultural tools which they share with English Canadians, or even with foreign peoples, to the best profit of their own culture. Everywhere the emphasis is on the re-evaluation and re-creation of societies. Everywhere there are 'fundamental' problems and 'crucial' areas.

So there is nothing abnormal about the position of the French-Canadian ethnic group. The abnormal part might be that this group sees in the Conquest of 1760 an irremediable cause for its present situation and, believing in the uselessness of searching for solutions, it waits for death.

Dion's verdict on neo-nationalism is no harsher than the fate that history has meted out to the leading political exponents of French-Canadian nationalism.

Mercier's ringing cry of 1889 that "this province of Quebec is Catholic and French, and it will remain Catholic and French" has failed to age well, except as an exotic curiosity. Mercier himself, three years after this pronouncement, was thrown out of office following a series of scandals, and died a bankrupt.

When Henri Bourassa died in 1952 at the age of eighty-four, he had lived long enough to experience the special limbo that French-Canada reserves for once-popular nationalist spokesmen, where the sound of cheering crowds echoes in an eerie and almost total silence. Once described by one of Laurier's friends as "too forceful without sufficient reason," Bourassa in the Thirties "slowly lost his prominence as a radical in French-Canadian society as other men of very different ilk took his place in the limelight." Among them were the precursors of the modern separatists, men like Lionel Groulx who had worked closely with Bourassa in their younger years but whose nationalism brought them into opposition to him during the Twenties. Eventually, to Bourassa, "separatism came to appear nearly as dangerous as the dreaded imperialism which he had fought so long," according to one of his biographers, Casey Murrow.

Groulx himself, although he died only in 1969, already appears today to have slipped into irrelevance. His Catholicism and his advocacy of too many lost causes during the Twenties and Thirties rendered him useless to the leaders of the "quiet revolution" of the Sixties.

This succession of nationalist political leaders and theorists in Quebec reveals little continuity of political thought or action. The irony of Papineau's career, as perceived by historian Mason Wade, was that "as Papineau became more radical and increased his demands for the French-Canadian nation, he began to lose his support among those very people." Mercier, Bourassa and Groulx lost their popular following long before their political ambitions died. There were never enough disciples to continue and elaborate the master's work. Each new generation of nationalists seemed to think that its predecessors had been almost as mistaken and misguided as those other French-Canadians who had collaborated with their English-speaking compatriots.

Lévesque's career has followed this pattern. On rare occasions, when he has been interviewed about his early years, he has paid tribute in passing to the influence that Groulx exerted on Lévesque's generation of students. Little more than that. None of Groulx's ideas or writings find their way into Lévesque's speeches. It is almost as if, as far as Lévesque is concerned, the thousands of books and pamphlets that have been produced by Quebec nationalists over the years had never been written.

Speaking to a venerable nationalist association in Montreal in 1964, Lévesque blamed both the dominant Quebec elite and the nationalists of the past for the fact that Quebec had entered the Sixties without a modern economic philosophy.

"Our elites scorned or disregarded the economic role of the state," he said.

> In their eyes, the state had only one role: to act as a kind of insurance company and supplier of technical services to the large corporations. It was a colonial regime, supported by negro-kings, which sustained an economic system where Quebec was absent.

> The nationalists in the past enclosed themselves in an economic conservatism that was absolutely absurd in a country like ours.

XV
The Cabinet Shaker

Remembering how Lévesque had fidgeted during the formal swearing-in ceremony for the new cabinet on July 5, 1960, a Press Gallery journalist recalled several years later that "one already knew that Lévesque, in the cabinet, would be like Quebec in Confederation: not like the others."

Rumours about Lévesque's restlessness in the cabinet began to appear little more than a year after the 1962 election. In January, 1964, the Quebec newspaper *Le Soleil* criticized Lévesque for referring to the federal Liberal government as a "monster" of centralized authority. *Le Soleil* predicted that Premier Lesage would be "too realistic to fall into the crypto-separatism of Lévesque's thoughtless statements." Lévesque's "sentimental and irresponsible declarations," according to the newspaper, wouldn't solve the financial problems of the province that Lesage had discussed recently in Ottawa with Prime Minister Pearson.

This theme was expanded a few days later in the Union Nationale periodical *Le Temps*. According to this partisan view, *Le Soleil's* comment probably had been inspired by Premier Lesage himself "who might have given certain newspapers precise orders along these lines: it's essential to destroy René Lévesque before he publicly denounces the Liberal party."

Le Temps claimed that Lévesque had told a friend at Radio-Canada that he would retire from politics and return to journalism within six months.

"The 1960 marriage of reason between Lesage and Lévesque is almost finished," concluded the Union Nationale newspaper.

The divorce announcement was premature. There was dissension among Quebec Liberals in 1964 but it focused, in large part, on an internal struggle between Liberals who wanted to maintain a single Liberal federation in the province and others, notably Lévesque, who wanted to split the party into federal and provincial organizations.

Historically, the Liberals of Quebec had been proud to affirm: *"Rouge à Québec, et rouge à Ottawa."* When the question of dividing the parties came to a head in 1964, traditionalists among Liberals in both capitals accused the "radicals" in the Quebec cabinet and the party's political committee of separatist tendencies. Junior members of the Pearson cabinet such as Yvon Dupuis, appointed after the federal Liberals won a minority victory in April, 1963, were allowed to voice these suspicions publicly.

Despite the opposition of most federal Liberals, the "old guard" around Lesage, and the Premier himself at the outset, the decision was taken to split the party. Lesage not only supported Lévesque's position at the critical moment but seemed to go out of his way subsequently to affirm Lévesque's leading role in the cabinet. During the spring of 1964, in the face of rumours of dissension, he pointedly included Lévesque in the Quebec delegation to a federal-provincial conference in Ottawa.

A year later, however, rumours of trouble between Lévesque and Lesage were circulating again. This time, the authoritative Daignault-Clift column from Quebec hinted that "a showdown...may be shaping up."

The apparent issue was a typical Lévesque speech accusing the Toronto-based Noranda mining group, operating in a number of Quebec regions, of "medieval and backward" employee relations. Noranda replied by buying newspaper space to reprint an article from a Quebec weekly newspaper reporting that Lévesque intended to nationalize its mining operations.

As Daignault and Clift explained to their readers, Lévesque's immediate objective was only the creation of a state corporation to carry out mineral exploration in Quebec. They doubted that this alone was enough to cause a serious rift in the cabinet. They wrote:

> The Lesage-Lévesque showdown seems to be over something else, and it is probably over the question of Lévesque's popularity with the voters, particularly with the trade union movement which he has been courting for many years.
>
> Lesage may be tired of trying to manoeuvre a cabinet that has many strong personalities in it...
>
> In his efforts to bring unity to the cabinet, Lesage seems to have picked on Lévesque first, because of his tremendous pull with the electorate. Some people say that if Lesage pursues his present course, Lévesque will leave.

Only a few months after this, Lévesque came closer to the point of departure than at any time since the 1962 nationalization debate in the cabinet. Seriously alarmed this time, a small group of his senior bureaucrats booked a suite at Quebec City's Holiday Inn, invited the minister to meet them there and "put the pressure on," according to Lévesque's own recollection.

The spokesmen for the group were Michel Bélanger, Lévesque's deputy minister of Natural Resources who later became president of the Montreal Stock Exchange and now heads the Banque Provinciale du Canada, and Eric Gourdeau, the director of the office that Lévesque had created to administer the province's growing activities in northern Quebec. Both men had been recruited by Lévesque personally in 1960 and now they told him, plainly, that his resignation wasn't justified.

This personal approach influenced Lévesque more than policy arguments.

In 1962, he had coolly condoned and perhaps even encouraged newspaper reports of his impending resignation as part of his effort to push hydro-electric nationalization through the cabinet. Again in 1965, he pointedly told journalists that party loyalty wasn't high on his list of political virtues. But loyalty to individuals within a cabinet, party or bureaucracy was another matter. He has said:

> I felt tied to the guys I was working with, because ultimately it's within a series of personal relationships that you use what you have to try to get a certain result.
>
> You get the same feeling in the cabinet, because there's always a split. There are men who are on your wavelength and others whom you just have to live with. This is the basic loyalty that I've always felt, more than this wishy-washy thing called party loyalty.

Personal relationships, political alliances and individual ambitions started to tear apart the Lesage cabinet after the 1962 election. At the centre of every storm, alongside Lévesque, was Eric Kierans. The former businessman and economist had been appointed Minister of Revenue in August, 1963, and then had won a seat in the legislature in a by-election the next month.

This "imaginative Irish bastard," as Lévesque once called him, was a new type of English-speaking politician in Quebec despite his blue-ribbon credentials as a former director of McGill University's commerce department and former president of the Montreal Stock Exchange. What many French-Canadians didn't realize when he was appointed to the cabinet was that Kierans was already known in business and academic circles in English-speaking Montreal as a creative innovator and something of a rebel. Members of the Stock Exchange were still recovering from Kierans' assault on their ban against Jewish brokers when he entered the government. It wasn't long before Kierans was tangling in the cabinet with George Marler, whom most French-speaking ministers had always regarded as an authoritative spokesman for English-speaking

Quebec. Marler himself probably found it a confusing experience and he soon resigned from the government.

Lévesque had met Kierans for the first time only in 1962 but the collaboration between the two men began as soon as Kierans entered the cabinet.

Lévesque enlisted Kierans' help in his preliminary approach to private enterprise about the development of hydro-electric power at Churchill Falls in Labrador. Kierans not only told him that the first cost estimates for the project were too high but suggested to Lévesque that there might be a sound argument for joint public ownership of the development – by the governments of Quebec, as the main customer for the power, and Newfoundland, where the falls are located. His sound argument for such an approach was that "the actual contribution of the private sector was nil except that it had all the equity and got all the profits in perpetuity."

Later, in 1964, Kierans was Lévesque's strongest supporter in the cabinet when Lévesque was developing a plan to tax the production of mineral resources.

Kierans' influence could work in various directions. When Lévesque publicly and prematurely broached the idea of taking over the Bell Telephone system in Quebec, it was Kierans who persuaded him to drop it, not because of any objection in principle but because he felt that the Lesage government's demands on the credit of the province were already as heavy as the market would bear. Lévesque listened to Kierans with a mixture of personal affection and professional respect that he had accorded to none of his cabinet colleagues before 1963.

Kierans and Lévesque were both reformers and individualists. This was the strength and limitation of their political relationship. They came together freely but nothing bound them to one another. There was much that separated them. Despite his radical economic views, Kierans was at heart an English-speaking Quebecer whose loyalties to Lévesque and to his own community came into conflict as Lévesque focused his attention more narrowly on Quebec's political future.

An incident in 1965 revealed the sense of isolation that Lévesque felt in the cabinet even at a time when he was working closely with Kierans on various programs. He was attending a conference in Newfoundland when he read speculation about the candidacies of Pelletier, Marchand and Trudeau in the approaching federal election. Maurice Sauvé, who was also at the conference, telephoned Marchand in Ottawa with Lévesque hovering over his shoulder. Marchand explained that the Pearson Liberals were anxious to recruit himself and Gérard Pelletier but had strong reservations about the "socialist" Pierre Trudeau. After Sauvé had talked with Marchand, Lévesque took the phone to warn Marchand to "avoid the mistake that I had made" and to insist that all three enter federal politics together.

The relationship between Lévesque and Education Minister Paul Gérin-Lajoie was another source of tension within the cabinet.

Gérin-Lajoie had been closely involved in rebuilding the Quebec Liberal party in the Fifties, had contested a riding in the 1956 election against the impressive and sometimes frightening political machine of the Union Nationale, and had opposed Lesage for the party leadership in 1958. There was no doubt that he resented Lévesque's rapid rise to prominence after 1960 and his key role in the 1962 campaign.

"I don't think that Lesage ever regarded Lévesque as a possible successor, or that Lévesque ever wanted to be," recalled another member of the cabinet, "but there could have been a fair amount of jealousy on the part of Gérin-Lajoie."

A Liberal who worked closely with Gérin-Lajoie compared the two men:

> Lévesque was more emotional, closer by nature and instinct to the ordinary man. Gérin-Lajoie was a type of aristocrat, an Oxford liberal.
>
> They often held common views but they seemed to collaborate reluctantly. Lévesque's style really shocked Gérin-Lajoie, while Gérin-Lajoie's style was embarrassing to Lévesque.
>
> Gérin-Lajoie was always a bit threatened by Lévesque's moral ascendancy in the party.

Lévesque's habit of staying up all night talking politics with anyone who would listen to him didn't have anything to do with moral ascendancy but it was a real problem for Gérin-Lajoie and for other ministers of more orthodox habits.

Completely absorbed in the work of his own department, spending his few free evenings with the family that he had moved from Montreal to Quebec, Education Minister Gérin-Lajoie had neither the time nor the inclination to politic informally within the cabinet and party, nor to develop his own sources of information outside the political structure.

Lévesque, with his wife and two children in Montreal during the long legislative sessions in Quebec, was free to go to bed whenever he wanted, for as long as he wanted, and sometimes wherever he wanted. His erratic domestic habits became legendary among his cabinet colleagues and among members of the Press Gallery in Quebec, although that aspect of his activities was almost never reported to the public. There seems to have been an unspoken understanding among Lévesque's former colleagues in the Press Gallery that his nocturnal ramblings would remain as private as their own.

There is at least one cryptic reference to this aspect of Lévesque's life in the official journal of the National Assembly in Quebec. In June, 1967, when the Liberals were in opposition to the Union Nationale government, Lévesque was accused of obstructing the business of the legislature by Maurice Bellemare, a government minister who later became leader of his party. When Lévesque asked sarcastically whether Bellemare had been promoted to the job of "timekeeper" by the government, the minister replied, "No! But I know where you go ... those nocturnal visits that you make to certain places."

Lévesque was so furious that when the President of the Assembly cut short the altercation, he stomped out of the House, without insisting on a reply from Bellemare.

There was another former journalist in the Lesage cabinet, besides Lévesque, Municipal Affairs Minister Pierre Laporte, but Lévesque did not relate well to him in spite of their common background. Laporte also had emerged by 1964 as a leading contender for the party leadership that he eventually failed to win in 1970, only nine months before he was assassinated by Quebec terrorists. A crusading journalist for *Le Devoir* during the Duplessis regime, Laporte developed into a competent and surprisingly traditional type of Quebec politician during the Sixties.

While Gérin-Lajoie regarded the party as a generator of ideas, Laporte treated it as a potential source of personal support. His door was always open to party members who needed help. Lévesque, a newcomer to the party when he was first elected in 1960, never learned to utilize it effectively.

"He had a poor assessment of what the party was," claimed a former senior organizer.

I remember that we had long discussions with the cabinet about the role of the party, in 1960 or 1961. It was either Lévesque or René Hamel – it could have been either – who compared the party members to the *zouaves* – the honorary papal guard that used to be recruited among the men of Quebec parishes.

Lévesque never really understood the party. He thought that most of its members were interested only in patronage. Perhaps five or six per cent were, but 90 per cent of them were in the party because it gave them status in their community, because it gave them something to do, and even because they were interested in the cause.

"Lévesque believed that the party was a necessary organization," said a former member of the policy committee "but he certainly never courted anyone in it. Laporte was a strong practical organizer. He made countless friends by facilitating things for them, trying to help them solve problems in their municipalities and ridings. Lévesque didn't concern himself with that kind of thing."

As the Lesage government settled into office after the 1962 election, the creative optimism of the early years was tempered by financial, administrative and political restraints.

It became clear to Lévesque and the rest of the cabinet that $600,000,000 hydro-electric nationalization schemes were once-in-a-lifetime adventures for a Quebec government. Other major innovations by the Liberals not only generated administrative problems but also encountered mixed reaction from the public. Larger and more modern schools, for instance, seemed to be a good idea in principle until parents began to resent the fact that their children were away from dawn to dark, being bused back and forth to huge schools where it seemed that half of the teachers were bearded atheists and political radicals from the city. Government employees were given the right to strike, an innovation which Lévesque, in particular, had favoured. But no one had seemed to realize that it would mean the closing of hospitals and schools, or that strikers would shut down state-operated liquor stores during the Christmas season.

Tensions within the cabinet began to paralyze its effectiveness. Minor incidents became major confrontations. The 1965 strike at the Quebec Liquor Commission, for instance, triggered a serious dispute between Lévesque and Lesage after the Premier had appealed to the workers over the heads of their union leaders. Lévesque reacted strongly to this display of paternalism and offered his own advice to the strikers: *"Ne lâchez pas* – don't give up!"

When Lévesque's call was published, ministers were summoned to a special cabinet meeting called to order thirty minutes before the regular evening sitting of the Assembly. To at least one of the ministers present, the meeting proceeded "as if it was managed to force Lévesque into the position where he would have to resign."

Toward the end of the meeting, Kierans intervened decisively by saying that Lévesque had not been the only minister who had urged the workers to stick to their guns. He had said the same thing. When Lesage replied that he hadn't read it in the newspapers, Kierans explained that one of the strikers was the husband of the woman who cleaned the Kierans' Quebec apartment twice a week. After Lesage had appealed to the workers to go back to their jobs, the woman had asked Mrs. Kierans for advice. Mrs. Kierans had referred the cleaning lady to her husband and Kierans had given her his personal opinion – that the strikers should obey the orders of their union.

In the silence that followed this story, the members of the cabinet were summoned to the Asembly and the confrontation was over. Lévesque recalled:

I could have kicked myself out then, and probably some of the others would have been very happy – maybe at that point even Lesage himself.

But I felt that it wasn't time to be petulant and there wasn't a bastard among them who could have kicked me out. On what basis? We weren't discussing a matter of policy.

Eventually Lesage chewed himself out of his bad humour, and other problems came up. There were quite a few of them!

"In the two years before the 1966 election," recalled one of the former ministers, "the real initiative and thrust in the cabinet came from Lévesque and one or two others. A lot of this must have been galling to the Premier."

"There was a growing gap between the reformers and the traditionalists in the cabinet," said another. "Lesage was having real difficulty in keeping people together and keeping a unified image of the cabinet before the public."

"Before 1962," remembered a third former minister, "we used to see one another informally but later on, I would find myself eating alone most of the time. Lesage lived in Quebec with his family. Most of the ministers by then had brought their families into the city. The intimacy between us deteriorated and finally everyone was working for himself."

"The government used to function by separate departments," said an experienced observer of the cabinet in those years. "Gérin-Lajoie had his pet projects and Lévesque had his, and it was true even before 1962."

Lesage was the central and perhaps most complex figure. Intelligence, education and experience had endowed him with all the technical abilities of a great administrator and leader. The nationalization issue in 1962 had shown one of Lesage's senior bureaucrats that "Lesage had a very quick mind, a technical mind."

"Once the decision to nationalize was made," he said, "only Lévesque and Lesage really knew what was going on, and they were the only ones who could use the technical arguments coherently."

Lesage also understood government finance and administration. These were two of the weaker aspects of Lévesque's own political equipment.

"It took him a long time to acquire a general concept of the machinery of government," said one of his former associates.

In the various departments that were assigned to him, he was basically concerned at getting to the roots of problems. On the whole, he was a good administrator, but perhaps he didn't have a firm enough grasp of the total government system.

He had a lot of confidence in Lesage and what he regarded as the 'Ottawa system' that Lesage had brought from his days in the federal cabinet. But what we had was a Lesage revision of the Ottawa system, and it didn't in fact provide enough place for discussion of programs in perspective.

Another former associate said that Lévesque "lacked a sense of institutions. He was a marvellous star in the political sky of Quebec," he said, "but he never understood what an institution was, or that at certain times you have to refrain from doing or saying things because of the institutions."

Lesage not only had a better technical understanding of government than Lévesque but he was also an instinctive political animal of at least equal sensitivity. His flaws were personal. The "grand seigneur" manner that often was effective on the political platform could be extremely irritating at close range.

"My own concept of a politician," said one former minister, "is that he keeps his ears wide open and his mouth tight shut. It was the opposite with Lesage."

"The role of a Prime Minister should certainly be to evoke discussion in the cabinet," said another, "possibly to lead the discussion, and certainly to sum it up. But things become impossible if the Prime Minister spends all his time rebutting adverse views. Discussions in the cabinet became disorderly and interminable.

"In the House after 1962, Lesage must really have been unbearable. He wouldn't allow anyone to get a word in. Look up Hansard and you'll see that he's on every page. Johnson and the others in the opposition couldn't make a speech without Lesage interrupting. It was beyond endurance, and it got that way in the cabinet too."

"Lesage was becoming bigger than any possible boots," was the assessment of another former colleague.

He was lording it in a way that was almost Duplessis-like.

But when you start lording it, you also become indecisive because you try to be in charge of too many things at once.

The second thing which became disagreeable for many people in the cabinet was that, after four years or so, certain groups had hardened. Some of the ministers weren't on speaking terms with others. Little cliques sprang up, and some ambitions were beginning to shape up.

In many ways, Lévesque and Lesage complemented one another. They appealed to different generations in Quebec and to different aspects of the Quebec character.

Lesage must have divined this in 1960 when he spent a great deal of time and effort to persuade Lévesque to join the Liberals. The strategy in

1960, according to one of the planners of that campaign, had been to show that "there was an equation between the ideas of the Liberal party and those of René Lévesque which could be equated with the aspirations of Quebecers at the time."

As the years passed, Lévesque remained valuable to the party as a pole of attraction, particularly for young people who were strongly affected by the separatist enthusiasm of the early Sixties. But he rapidly antagonized conservative elements of the population. After 1965, many Liberals felt that he was more dangerous within the party than outside it. Still, despite periodic outbursts against Lévesque, usually when he wasn't present, Lesage kept him in the cabinet. The basic reasons perhaps were simple: he liked him, and he felt confident of his loyalty.

"As far as I'm concerned, Lesage never had any reservations about Lévesque," said a former senior party official who worked closely with both.

> They had their problems but as individuals, they liked one another. Each one had qualities the other didn't have.
>
> Lesage is an extremely intelligent man, not the intelligence of an intellectual but of a man of action. He was a man with a lot of discipline, a hard worker, very punctual. Lévesque had none of these qualities.
>
> In his understanding of a technical problem, Lesage was always ahead of Lévesque, and Lévesque had a great deal of admiration for this.
>
> On the other hand, Lesage knew that Lévesque was loyal, and that he really was a man who would come out and state his opinion. Lévesque was persuasive and intelligent, and often he would carry the day with Lesage even if Lesage had previously said no.

Lesage knew, as did the other cabinet ministers, that Lévesque was no threat to his leadership. As one of Lévesque's senior bureaucrats said, "When you worked for René, you felt that you were working for Quebec and not for his own political future."

This was a characteristic that Lesage valued but it also meant that orthodox political calculations didn't always apply to Lévesque. He had his own goals, and he had already shown an ability to go after them in single-minded, almost reckless fashion, without the politician's usual regard for the immediate consequences on his political career, or on the careers of others.

"The great reservation that I have about him relates to his tactics," as one observer expressed it. "He works for *his* cause, and he cares little about other points of view when he's involved in an important move."

On his part, Lévesque was often uncertain about Lesage's position on many of his projects until the final commitment had been made. Like Lévesque, the Premier maintained his own network of information and influence outside the political world. It was sometimes said that Lesage was, paradoxically, both autocratic and highly impressionable, that he was impressed by money and particularly by "English" money. Rarely could Lévesque be certain that the Premier would back him to the limit on an important issue, especially if business interests were opposed.

"Lesage was always very cautious with him: 'Well, René, what do you think of this? What do you think of that?' He was always trying to take his pulse," said a former minister.

"Lesage often must have felt that he couldn't do anything with Lévesque, and couldn't do without him," another member of the cabinet said. He continued,

> In 1963 or 1964, I don't think that there was any question in Lesage's mind that Lévesque was an asset to the government and to the party. He certainly became of two minds about Lévesque during 1965 because we were pushing too many things all at once. There were many people who wanted to slow down until we had completed a few of the main programs. But Lévesque's mind didn't really work like that. Whenever an opportunity came up, he would absorb himself in whatever it was even if there was no possibility of doing anything with it for two or three years.

"Relations between Lévesque and Lesage started to deteriorate in the fall and winter of 1964-65," recalled another close observer who had worked with both.

> Everything started to deteriorate then. All the major reforms of the party had been started, and now there were so many problems that they couldn't solve. . .so many bottlenecks in education, health services and taxation. Lesage couldn't dominate the strong personalities in his cabinet. He lost intellectual control of cabinet and started to fall into nationalism and to attack the federal government.
>
> At the same time, he began to think that he could become the next leader of the federal Liberal party.

Despite the innovative character of his government in the early years, especially in contrast to the Duplessis regime, Lesage essentially was a conservative politician. He accepted the traditional structures of Canadian politics. As a lawyer, he appreciated the way in which his own profession served as a lubricating medium between the interfaces of commerce and politics. And soon after he retired from politics, he moved smoothly into the boardrooms of some of Canada's largest corporations.

In contrast, Lévesque's first political inclinations had been socialist.

Throughout his career in the cabinet, journalists debated about whether his Quebec nationalism was a medium for his socialism, or *vice versa*.

It was the combination of both in the hydro-electric nationalization of 1962 that had made the scheme irresistible to Lévesque. But the swift achievement of this objective was not to set the pattern for his four remaining years in government.

There were warning signs before 1962 that opposition to Lévesque would be strong on many fronts.

When Lévesque appointed his first senior bureaucrats in 1960, he told them that forest resources as well as hydro-electric and mineral resources eventually would come under his new department of Natural Resources. One of his assistants advised him, at the time, that the pulp and paper companies would never permit this because they would want to continue to exert their influence through a single department devoted mainly to their own industry. Lévesque assured this man that both Lesage and Lapalme had promised that forestry would come under the new department. It never did.

In 1966, following the Liberal defeat, Lévesque suggested the creation of an independent public forestry commission that would be responsible for the administration and management of all state forests. Without sufficient control of their own resources, he said, Quebecers were always in a state of "perpetual panic" when they confronted the four giant companies whose concessions covered 70 per cent of the province's accessible and profitable forest resources. But even after the party had slipped from power, Lévesque failed to carry his colleagues with him on this issue.

Mineral resources did come under Lévesque's control but his principal achievements were relatively modest: the adoption of a new tax on mineral production, the substitution of long-term leases on mineral concessions to replace a system of outright purchase of concessions, and the creation of a state corporation devoted primarily to mineral exploration and research but also involved in production, usually in association with private companies.

It wasn't so much what Lévesque did as what he said that upset the mining companies. One of Lévesque's former associates said:

> They didn't like him very much, particularly after the hydro nationalization of 1962, but after a time, there was a certain grudging respect.
>
> When you look back on it, the corpus of legislation that he left behind wasn't very radical. But there was always a certain psychological fear on the part of the industry. After 1962, his speeches about the need to bring industry into the modern world were interpreted by many people as threats to nationalize them.

Although the former bureaucrat claimed that "Lévesque was very good at playing the rational game and to me, appeared to be a rather cool person in dealing with business groups," there were some memorable flare-ups.

"Sometimes you did get mad," Lévesque has admitted.

> I remember meeting the president of Noranda. He was one son of a bitch – I still don't like them as a corporate entity. We were talking about the location of a new zinc refinery. The company had one idea, we had another. Finally, this guy stops the conversation and says something to this effect, 'Enough of all this irrelevant stuff – I'll tell you what the company has decided.'
>
> When that happened, you felt that something had to change or you might as well give up, because you certainly didn't feel like the government. They were never hesitant about getting subsidies and building roads with the taxpayers' money. But when some bastard comes up and says, 'Well, let's get away from all this irrelevant stuff ... you feel like breaking something.

A close observer recalled:

> He appeared at that time, as a man who had hidden socialist ideas and who had joined the Liberal party as a way to accede to power.
>
> He told me at the time that most of the free enterprise sector was controlled by foreigners who had no genuine interest in the development of our community. But he had no grasp of that aspect of the Quebec reality. His contacts with business leaders were extremely limited. He had come from another sector and had not digested that facet of our democracy.

As time went on, the corporations became increasingly irritated by Lévesque's continual sniping. In the summer of 1965, an illegal eight-day strike by workers at a Noranda subsidiary near Montreal, and the subsequent firing of twelve workers, including three union officials, brought a formal condemnation of the company from the minister's office.

"One can act legally and still behave like a savage," Lévesque reminded the company.

In the same week, Lévesque also accused the huge Domtar corporation of being "heartless" after it laid off fifty workers at a plant near Quebec City. Lévesque didn't claim that the lay-off was unjustified but said that it was "scandalous" for companies in the twentieth century to ignore the social and economic effects of their decisions.

In the autumn of 1966, as Liberal bagmen canvassed these same industries for money to fight the coming election campaign, Lévesque was saying publicly that these electoral funds represented "the most destructive poison" within the parliamentary system. People gained the impression, he said, that large donors to these funds represented a "hidden government." After proclaiming the 1966 election campaign at the outset as "the hypocritical season," Lévesque went on to promise that "the tradition of negro-king governments in Quebec, of governments that slept in the same bed as corporations and where government departments were like branches of mining companies, has been overthrown."

Lévesque's reputation as "René the Red" became so firmly established after the 1962 hydro-electric nationalization that it coloured an otherwise forgettable incident in the cabinet ministers' private dining room in Quebec's parliament building. Lévesque was talking rapidly when one of his dramatic gestures upset a tray filled with glasses of tomato juice that a waiter was holding directly over his head. As Lévesque sat there drenched in juice and covered with red pulp, the conversation around the table came to a dead stop. At least one minister, who recalled the incident years later, was under the impression that everyone had the same thought as they looked at their crimson-stained colleague. An unusual amount of care was taken to smuggle him unobtrusively out of the building.

In many places in North America and Europe, Lévesque's socialism would have been regarded as rather tame. It attracted attention in Quebec because the conservatism of the Duplessis government in the Fifties had maintained an outdated "cold war" mentality about any kind of leftist political thought.

The linguistic as well as economic divisions of Quebec society also gave socialism a highly "national" character in French Canada. The government in Quebec was dominated by the French while the English controlled most of the business activity in the province. In the eyes of many of Quebec's English-speaking business and professional people, any program that enlarged the role of government at the expense of private enterprise was not only socialist but anti-English.

Lévesque's record in government showed that his socialism, no matter how radical it sounded on the platform, was pragmatic when expressed in legislation. No such test existed for his nationalism. As time went on, English-speaking Quebecers and older, more conservative French-Canadians felt that Lévesque was exploring the separatist option more and more deeply.

His fight for the creation of an independent Quebec Liberal Federation in 1964 was taken by some members of the party as a declaration of separatist intent. Lévesque described the Liberal party in Quebec then as a party with "two vocations" that were not always in harmony. One vocation was to "try to group together the ten provinces" while the other was to "work for French-Canadians, to work in relation to the priorities of Quebec." The fact that Lévesque seemed to see these two vocations as being incompatible in a single political party made some people wonder about his faith in the larger national unity of Canada.

As he stimulated questions about the future of Quebec, his journalistic style of speaking encouraged speculation about his own future.

"This is our place," he said in 1963, speaking to a conference of Canadian industrial editors in the Laurentians north of Montreal. "To us, the basic thing is to have a homeland called Quebec. If we are not recognized in this sick Confederation, then we'll move out – and nobody is going to stop us.

"For Canada, it is a matter of life and death," he said. "If we get out, there will be no more Canada."

A few weeks later, answering the questions of an Italian-Canadian audience in Montreal, Lévesque snapped, "The separation of Quebec? It isn't the end of the world."

Audiences of English-speaking Canadians were puzzled and frightened by Lévesque's disjointed speeches and rapid changes of mood. Speaking to a Jewish audience in Montreal early in 1964, Lévesque dazzled them with a typical assortment of contradictions: Quebec nationalism is not an "anti" movement; changes are coming in Canada which "will make old men, whether they are young or old, shake in their trousers"; Quebec will not be satisfied with "constitutional claptrap" or "good grey Canadian compromise"; "a lot of systems are possible inside a federal system"; and the struggle for the survival of French Canada demands "a sort of life-and-death dedication" but it is "a normal development for a people...and I don't feel the need to be aggressive about it."

In an interview with a correspondent of the *New York Times* in February, 1964, Lévesque said that he didn't believe that Quebec would separate but that if it did, "We could get along better without Canada than Canada could get along without us."

Lévesque's most aggressive phrases provided the headlines for English-language newspapers across Canada. By the spring of 1964, the editorial columns of these newspapers were reflecting a widespread feeling of frustration and impatience among their readers.

Treating the whole constitutional debate as a "Quebec-induced controversy," the Toronto *Telegram* complained that trying to discover what French-Canadians want "is like trying to nail jelly to the wall." Even the *Globe and Mail*, the Toronto morning newspaper that gave its readers a more comprehensive picture of events in Quebec than any other English-language newspaper, complained that Lévesque was becoming "something worse than a bore."

"The only surprising thing is that Lévesque should pretend to be surprised by all this," wrote syndicated newspaper columnist Charles Lynch in May, 1964. "Better than most Quebeckers, he knows English-speaking Canada and English-speaking Canadians at first hand. It is inconceivable that he did not know, when he started throwing mud at his old buddies 'les Anglais', that he'd get some of it back, with knobs on."

In Quebec, there were other reactions to Lévesque's words. When he arrived at Montreal's Windsor Hotel in April, 1964, to speak to a nationalist audience, separatists greeted him with placards bearing such slogans as: "King René, when is the republic coming?" and "It will work with René."

The indecision that baffled and frightened many English-speaking Canadians in 1964 reflected Lévesque's own painful exploration of Quebec's role in Canada and his own position in the Quebec government.

"When I'm involved in a project, I try to be as logical as possible," he has said, "but as far as what's going to happen to me personally, I'm no good at figuring out the options."

XVI
Yawn at the Top

By the end of 1965, the main reforms in the Natural Resources Department had been achieved and Lévesque was obviously beginning to lose interest. Eric Kierans was also growing restless in the fall of 1965 when Lesage offered to transfer both men as a team into a new area of activity. Kierans would become the province's Minister of Health while Lévesque would take charge of social assistance.

The new portfolio wasn't totally unfamiliar to Lévesque. In 1963, his assistant deputy minister in the department of Natural Resources, Michel Bélanger, had been a member of an internal task force that had formulated the universal pension scheme that Quebec had proposed to the federal-provincial conference of March, 1964.

The sudden revelation of the Quebec scheme, superior in some respects to the pension plan that Ottawa had proposed, had thrown the conference into confusion and precipitated the first serious conflict between the Pearson and Lesage governments since the federal Liberals had won a minority victory in April, 1963.

Only the swift response of Lévesque and a few other key people behind the scenes had averted a head-on clash. The federal initiative had been undertaken by Maurice Sauvé, a former public relations officer for the Quebec Liberal Federation who had been named Minister of Forestry in the Pearson cabinet in 1964, and Tom Kent, Pearson's policy secretary. Their first and most important contacts in Quebec had been Claude Morin, Deputy Minister of Federal-Provincial affairs and a member of the task force that had drawn up the Quebec scheme, and Lévesque, whom Sauvé had known since 1960.

Lévesque was at Lesage's right hand during the week after the conference when the Quebec Premier met Sauvé and Kent. That had been the beginning of an Ottawa-Quebec negotiation that cleared the way, within a few weeks, for the parallel creation of Canadian and Quebec pension plans. Quebec's success in retaining control of its own plan, and the huge pension fund that would accumulate over the years, had been a striking accomplishment for the Lesage government, made even sweeter by Ottawa's decision to improve its own plan by adopting certain features of the Quebec scheme.

Lévesque had maintained a special interest since then in the Family and Welfare Department while the minister in charge of it, Emilien Lafrance, had gained notoriety as the cabinet's most fervent crusader against alcoholism. When he replaced Lafrance, Lévesque seemed to be anxious to start work in a sector of government activity that had been overshadowed by hydro-electric nationalization and the other dramatic projects of Lesage's "politique de grandeur." For a few months, he responded to the challenge of his new department with some of his old energy and excitement.

The task was herculean. Quebec had been slow to transfer its social services from the Roman Catholic Church to the state. The result was a confused jumble of overlapping systems, and a general standard of assistance that was below the Canadian average. Lévesque threw himself into the work of reform with the zeal of a Charles Dickens emerging from an inspection of a Victorian workhouse.

The time-consuming preliminary work of investigation had already been completed several years earlier by a special government committee on public assistance, and published in the Boucher Report. Six weeks after his appointment, Lévesque made his first public appearance as Welfare Minister "with the Boucher Report in his left hand and, in his right, a pack of cigarettes and five pages of handwritten notes." They contained his philosophic and policy objectives: to replace the stigma of charity by the concept of "investment in social services," to introduce a state scheme of health insurance by the following spring and, within a year, to replace the federal family allowances program by a more flexible and generous scheme administered by Quebec.

"Instead of subsidizing poverty," he said, "we're going to sustain the essential needs of the family."

When a reporter asked how long it would take to implement the seventy-one recommendations of the Boucher Report, Lévesque said "Look at the nationalization of electricity ... that went much faster than I could have imagined."

For a short time, everyone seemed anxious to join Lévesque's new war on poverty. The Montreal *Star*, setting aside its growing doubts about Lévesque's ultimate political objectives, decided that "a fresh and imaginative look is what we hoped to achieve from Mr. Lévesque and that, evidently, we are going to get ... good luck to him." Montreal's *La Presse* described the appointments of Lévesque and Kierans as a "common front" campaign to improve the health and welfare of Quebecers.

Toronto's *Globe and Mail* applauded Lévesque's plan to replace the universal family allowance payments of the federal government with a system of graduated payments that would depend on the number and ages of children in a family.

"It is heartening that the departments are headed by René Lévesque and Eric Kierans, who have proven themselves among the best administrators in the present government," said the Montreal *Star*. "The two men share a concept of 'investing' in people rather than giving them handouts. Both are known for the use they make of research before drafting policies."

The universal applause continued as Lévesque visited old folks' homes and denounced conditions in some of them as a "public scandal." It began to moderate, at least in some business circles, when he opened an attack on finance companies and suggested that they should be gradually eliminated.

"As everyone knows," he told a student audience, "all the finance companies have a bit of the shark in them."

The Canadian Consumer Loan Association, speaking for fifty-four finance companies, challenged him immediately by saying that the companies would have to leave Quebec if the government, as Lévesque had hinted, decided to subsidize consumer loans on a large scale.

That was only a minor skirmish. It soon became apparent that Lévesque's toughest battle would be over his proposal to "recuperate" family allowances. At stake was not only the economic control of $180,000,000 that the federal scheme pumped into Quebec every year but the political impact of the cheques themselves. In the two decades since Ottawa had started mailing these cheques directly to parents, the federal payments had become an accepted part of Canadian family life. Imperceptibly, they reinforced the presence of the federal government in every Quebec household. They were a monthly reminder that the big public cornucopia was in Ottawa.

This highly symbolic issue was the figurehead of the comprehensive social assistance policy that Lévesque prepared for the federal-provincial conference of welfare ministers in January, 1966. Concentrating on practical rather than constitutional arguments, the Quebec memorandum stated that only the Quebec government was in a position to develop an efficient social security system tailored to the special needs of Quebec society.

Lévesque was so closely involved in the preparation of this brief that he personally translated the lengthy document into English for the benefit of politicians and journalists in Ottawa. He also spent a great deal of time discussing the policy with Kierans, who wanted to be assured that transferring control of social security programs to the provinces would not impede Ottawa's control of the national economy.

It soon became clear that Lévesque's forecast of bringing the family allowance program under his control within a year was wildly optimistic. When the Quebec minister told the conference about his "firm and permanent target," Health Minister Allan MacEachen replied for the federal government: "We now occupy the field of family allowances. We have no intention of withdrawing from that field."

"I've known Mr. Lévesque for a long time," Prime Minister Pearson told reporters during the conference. "On our trip to Russia, when Mr. Lévesque was still a journalist, I had the chance to appreciate his sense of humour."

Lévesque made progress with MacEachen on his recommendations for overhauling the family allowance scheme itself but Ottawa was adamant about retaining control. It was one of the first indications that the "cooperative federalism" of Pearson's first years as Prime Minister was coming to an end.

Maurice Sauvé's influence was already on the wane. Pearson was now listening to very different advice from the three men who had been newly-elected from Quebec the previous November – Lévesque's old companions from the evening sessions of 1962 and 1963 – Jean Marchand, Gérard Pelletier and Pierre Trudeau. As their influence grew in Ottawa, it quickly eclipsed any faint hope that might have existed for Lévesque's social security program.

"Jean Marchand, who is quickly becoming a major influence among the Quebec ministers here, is known to feel that Ottawa-Quebec relations have reached the point where certain definitions must be established," wrote the Toronto *Star's* syndicated columnist, Peter C. Newman. "This means not only the drawing up of guidelines for Quebec's 'special status' but also a delineation of the powers that Ottawa needs to remain a viable central administration."

This was a position that Lévesque could understand if not accept. At the end of the conference, he paid tribute to MacEachen's frankness and goodwill, but he was angry and disappointed at the treatment given to the Quebec position by the English-language journalists of the Ottawa Press Gallery. A member of the Quebec delegation to the 1966 conference recalled:

> It was a thoughtful memorandum, but all we could see in the English-language newspapers was: Quebec wants to grab more power. That was the extent of their analysis. No one had tried to figure out if there was any substance to our position.

I don't think that there were five journalists in Ottawa who actually read it. Lévesque had put a lot of work into that paper and he was very bitter about this.

This was evident during a press conference when Lévesque accused the journalists of considering the whole question from an outmoded perspective, and of lacking the imagination to see the new political realities that were emerging in Canada.

"Don't kid yourself," he finally barked at the journalists, "as long as one goddam French-Canadian remains on the soil of Quebec, there isn't a chance of integrating us in the hybrid, bicultural monostrosity that you dream about."

A member of the Gallery asked sarcastically, "Tell us, Mr. Lévesque, what institutions is Quebec ready to leave in Ottawa's hands?"

Lévesque grinned: "The Prime Minister's Office."

Despite his friendly remarks about MacEachen, only a month after the conference Lévesque was attacking Ottawa for taking a "criminally long time" to decide on Quebec's proposals for reforming family allowances. Accusing the Ottawa "establishment" of adopting a "big brother" approach, he said petulantly, "Why don't they ask themselves if it is not the time to meet the problem . . . and accept solutions, even if they come from people who on occasion appear to them to be so incompetent?"

The irritable tone of this speech betrayed the pressure that Lévesque himself was beginning to feel. The switch in portfolios in 1965 had come too late. The task of persuading Lesage to support hydro-electric nationalization now seemed easy compared with the job facing him in Ottawa.

Among the Liberals there, Lévesque had no friends in high places. There would be no miraculous achievements in time for the next Quebec election. And Lévesque was beginning to feel tired. After only a few months, the administrative responsibilities of his new department were weighing heavily on him. It had taken only that long, this time, for the excitement of the new job to evaporate.

Lévesque was also deeply involved at this time in a ministerial committee charged with drawing up a program for the next election. After almost six years in office, this was a much more difficult and less dramatic job than it had been in 1960 and 1962. Now the promises for the future had to take into account the record of the past.

Quebec's traditional opposition to federal authority and its jealous defence of its constitutional rights, for instance, had been seriously affected by the Quebec government's pledge of support in January, 1966, for Ottawa's "Fulton-Favreau" formula to "repatriate" the British North America Act.

As the 1967 centenary of this legislation drew near, there was renewed effort to remove it entirely from British jurisdiction by achieving agreement among the provinces and Ottawa on a formula for amending the constitution in Canada. The Fulton-Favreau formula, named after two Ministers of Justice – E. Davie Fulton of the previous Conservative government and Guy Favreau of the current Liberal one – had seemed to be the long-sought breakthrough, particularly after the Lesage cabinet supported it. But the subsequent reaction in Quebec was so divided that a year later, Lesage was forced to suspend further discussion of the formula indefinitely.

The 1965 decision in favour of the formula placed the provincial Liberal cabinet at the mercy of Quebec nationalists who now claimed that the cabinet had abandoned Quebec interests to please English-speaking Canadians.

This was a particularly painful situation for Lévesque. For the first time, intellectual nationalists attacked him fiercely in public; the first "boos" were heard from his student audiences.

Surveys conducted for the Liberals in 1965 had shown that this negative reaction was spreading through the population, and that the constitutional issue could carry the government to defeat if it were pursued.

The party's electoral organization also was in trouble. Efforts by Lesage and the "old guard" to tame the policy committee of the Quebec Liberal Federation had driven many of its more active members from the party. The spirited "Montreal group" that had dominated the 1960 and 1962 campaigns had largely been replaced by organizers working out of Quebec City in close contact with the Premier.

"They didn't come up with anything very good but Lévesque worked very hard on it," recalled a former party official who worked with the ministerial election committee in 1965 and 1966.

> Lévesque was the most dedicated of the ministers and in the end, it was really Lévesque who drafted the election program. I remember working with him late one night at the Queen Elizabeth Hotel in Montreal. It was about two o'clock in the morning, after the election had been called, and Lévesque was still drafting the final items.
>
> But most of them, perhaps including Lévesque, didn't really know exactly where they were going. They knew that they had excited people in the past six years and now some said – 'We've got to do more!' – and some said – 'No, less!' Lesage was caught in between and he was so tired. He just got mad at everyone.

Lévesque himself had always looked tired, but in the early years of the Lesage government his fatigue had been the result of overwork and excitement. There had been so much to do, and so little time to accomplish it. The grey bags under Lévesque's eyes had been badges of honour for service in the "quiet revolution." In the spring of 1966, Lévesque's tiredness seemed to be part of the atmosphere of disillusion and disunity that clung to the government. For the first time in his career, he began to sound consistently conservative, apologetic and worried.

The man whose political career had started in the midst of a labour dispute at Radio-Canada in late 1958 warned government employees in March, 1966, to look about them carefully as they "composed their impractical gospels."

"We are on the North American continent," he said "We are a mouse, and if our ambitions carry us too far, we'll be squashed by the American elephant and he won't even realize what's happened.

"You have to lose the illusion that everything can be changed by tomorrow morning."

Such explanations were not what the radical left had been accustomed to hear from the "revolutionary" within the cabinet. A new and sarcastic chorus from the far left was added now to the usual right-wing criticism that Lévesque had come to regard almost as essential background music for his political performances. The radical *Parti Socialiste du Québec* accused him of "using social security to win elections in the same way that Duplessis used new roads, bridges and liquor permits."

Pierre Bourgault, the young president of the separatist *Rassemblement pour l'indépendance nationale* (R.I.N.), said that the Liberal regime was more odious than the corrupt Duplessis machine had been because it pretended to be reformist. Bourgault warned:

> Don't forget, that despite all the good that he has done, Lévesque today is the silent accomplice of a party that still practises patronage at a high level, that favours the education of a small and privileged English-speaking minority, that practises punitive justice instead of rehabilitation, that benefits the great centres of business at the expense of underdeveloped regions of the province, that plays up to young people while having no regard for them at all, and that has pushed through an electoral law that stifles the RIN while giving the Liberal party access to millions of dollars in state funds.

Frustrated in their hope of recruiting Lévesque as a separatist leader, Bourgault and his followers were especially bitter about him during the 1966 campaign. However, approving comments from other sources revealed the change in Lévesque's image even more dramatically. *La Presse* of Montreal complimented Lévesque on his "lucidity."

"There have been occasions when his liking for the graphic phrase has led him to something close to injustice," the Montreal *Star* reminded its readers. But this time, the newspaper felt that it had to compliment him "on the kind of clear and needed thinking which makes René Lévesque a most valuable member of the government."

As the campaign progressed, Lévesque told Quebecers that free education throughout university was not yet a realistic proposal. He opposed a strike by engineers at Hydro-Québec as "unjustified." An enthusiastic advocate of centralized economic planning in the 1960 and 1962 campaigns, Lévesque confessed in 1966 that the government had barely cleared the way for the foundations of effective planning.

"We aren't yet ready to really plan," he said. "Planning is always easy on paper. But it isn't merely on paper that one governs.

"But it will come, I promise you that," he insisted. "Quebec will be ready to plan its economic development when it has its hands on the main levers of its own economy."

Quebecers who thought that they had seen every facet of the mercurial Lévesque since 1960 found it hard to recognize this gloomy realist who plodded about the province preaching the virtues of slow and steady. More than any other member of the Liberal cabinet, he showed the effects of riding the whirlwind of the "quiet revolution," and the terrible strains of deceleration as the political momentum of the early Sixties failed to sustain itself.

Even a year and a half later, on the threshold of a new political departure, he still seemed to be gripped by the spirit of 1966 as he recalled the events of that year for an interviewer:

One can't spend seven and a half years in that damn milieu without learning something. One is less willing to improvise in a flamboyant way than six or seven years earlier.

In any event, you can't go back seven years. I think it was Kennedy who said 'The toughest challenge in this business is to maintain an ideal while losing all the attendant illusions.'

I've lost many illusions. There isn't any other business that's better for losing illusions. There isn't a more resistant material than mankind; and people are what politics is all about.

I've always been considered a progressive, a man of the left, but I've seen too many leftists, here and in Europe, to want to be a leftist.

I think that there's one thing that I could never become: a dogmatist. I will never be able to say that there is some way to transpose absolute dogmas into action ...

The limit that restrains every politician is reality, and the changes that you can force the real world to accept. You can underestimate or overestimate this difficulty but you can't ignore it. Those who try to ignore it are either idiots or well-meaning amateurs.

Two days before the 1966 election, Lévesque and other key members of the cabinet addressed the Liberals' final mass rally in Montreal. Instead of giving the traditional pep talk, Lévesque explored the gloomy possibilities of a Liberal defeat.

The path toward progress was extremely narrow, he said. On each side was an abyss. He warned his younger listeners, in particular, against throwing themselves into the abyss of "well-meaning but improvised adventures."

"Bend your impatience and desire for progress to the difficult task of building, with us, a Quebec that truly belongs to us," he said.

On the other side of the straight and narrow, Lévesque saw "the soft quicksand of mediocrity, of a second-rate people."

"When I heard him deliver that speech, I knew we were beaten," recalled one of the planners of the 1966 campaign, "and since I had the same feeling, I said to myself, Christ, that's it!"

XVII
The 1966 Election:
Backward Somersault

For six years, everyone in Quebec had been talking about the "quiet revolution."

"Rarely has a nation indulged in so much talk or devoted itself so rapturously to the cult of the word," wrote Jean-Marc Léger in *Le Devoir* in the fall of 1966.

Every day, as Léger said, Quebec reformulated its own future "in conventions, seminars, round-table discussions and improvised debates that seemed to be going on everywhere, from the antechambers of cabinet ministers to the dining halls of colleges."

"In many respects," he continued, "this has been healthy, but it was less so whenever we took ourselves at our word and gave ourselves the impression that simply by talking, we had achieved the revolution."

What had really been taking place, according to Léger, was "an immense and indispensable job of making up for lost time in a number of key areas." He listed some of the most important: the strengthening of the role of the state in Quebec, the reorganization of the public service, the creation of the first "instruments of economic action" by the state, the foundation of coherent social and cultural policies, educational reform, and the examination of Quebec's constitutional status.

"But we have yet to make our quiet revolution," Léger concluded.

That was one way of looking at it but, as many Quebec politicians were fond of saying, all the voters weren't on the editorial staff of *Le Devoir*. They were on farms, in villages and in the factories and offices of Montreal and Quebec City, and it was clear that many of them thought that the "quiet revolution" had gone far enough by 1966.

"There was a feeling in the province that everything was really going haywire with all these reforms," said one of the strategists of the Liberals' 1966 campaign.

In the city, we didn't feel these things. But after the election, when I met businessmen outside the cities, I realized how serious this had been. They had wanted the government to act with more reflection. They saw Lévesque as the man who wanted things to go faster. I had the impression that a great number of people were growing a bit afraid of him, although they still liked him.

At the beginning of the election year of 1966, most Quebecers assumed that the Liberals couldn't possibly lose. The government itself was supremely, dangerously confident.

One party official spent three weeks trying to reach Lesage for approval of the kind of motivational survey that had been invaluable to the party in the two previous campaigns. Lesage finally agreed to the survey but stipulated that the results would have to be ready within sixty days, not the usual ninety. The survey was completed on schedule, two days before a spring get-together of cabinet ministers in Florida. Despite the generally optimistic reports of public opinion experts, some of the findings were worrisome. The number of "undecided" respondents was unusually high. Education appeared to be a matter of primary concern to the public, as in 1960 and 1962; but this time, the issue seemed to be working against the government.

The survey also underestimated, by about half, the proportion of voters who ultimately cast their ballots for the separatist parties that would make their first appearance in this election, the *Rassemblement pour l'indépendance nationale* and the *Ralliement Nationale*.

By allocating the votes of undecided respondents in the same proportions as those who had expressed a party preference, the survey predicted that the Liberals would win up to 85 of the Assembly's 108 seats. This was the figure that warmed the hearts of the Liberal ministers as they gathered under the Florida sun. Some of them even became seriously concerned at this meeting about the stability of the parliamentary system in Quebec, should the opposition suffer such a devastating defeat.

The survey encouraged Lesage to schedule an election for June 5 and to stake his own political reputation firmly on the result.

His image needed a boost. The previous fall, the Premier had spent three weeks in the western provinces trying to interpret the "quiet revolution" to English-speaking Canadians. The trip was a disaster. The autocratic Lesage style had antagonized the informal westerners. After it was over, Lesage's own conclusions about the visit were pessimistic, with respect to the future of Canada and his own future in federal politics.

"I pleaded with him not to go," said a former associate. "I warned him that it would boomerang. But Lesage was determined.

"He attacked the federal government and adopted the theme that Quebec was getting a raw deal. Everywhere he went, he created resentment."

Lesage was still on tour in the west when the opening phase of the 1965 federal election campaign made English Canada aware that new voices were being heard in Quebec, and that the new voices were opposed to the kind of special status for Quebec that Lesage insisted was essential.

With English-speaking Canadians becoming more suspicious and skeptical about the aims of the "quiet revolutionaries" in the Lesage government, with Marchand, Trudeau and Pelletier undercutting the foundations of his political position, with his cabinet ministers pouring venomous stories about one another into the ears of journalists, Lesage desperately needed a triumph of some sort to restore his authority as a spokesman for Quebec in the rest of the country, and to enable him to become master of his own cabinet once again.

If the surveys were right, the 1966 election seemed made to order for this.

Dumping the "Montreal group" that had directed his earlier campaigns, Lesage worked with a few people in Quebec City on plans for a campaign that would put most of the work and glory on his own shoulders.

Other ministers would take part in the campaign, particularly Lévesque who was used extensively on television, but this time Lesage would be the star. One of his senior cabinet ministers recalled sitting for a full week in his office in Quebec City at the height of the campaign without a single public appearance on his calendar. A party official in Montreal who had played a major role in the two earlier campaigns and whose job on paper was the same in 1966, was able to meet Lesage only once during the campaign.

"Lesage was a very tired man," said a member of his 1966 entourage. "He was a preoccupied man, on the phone every night with government business, who did not believe that it was possible for him to lose."

"The party publicity this time featured Lesage," recalled one of its advertising consultants. "They actually wanted to put billboards in the rural areas showing Lesage talking to a farmer – with Lesage wearing a homburg!"

"My attitude was," said a former minister, "that if Lesage wanted to do it by himself, let him go ahead and do it."

"We should never have been defeated," said another former minister. "Reforms in education had turned some people against us, but a party that wants to implement reforms of that scope has to compensate politically. Our organization was bad.

"One of the ministers was so nonchalant that he didn't even use all the campaign expense money that was allocated to him from public funds under the new legislation."

"Jean Lesage was the artisan of his own defeat," in the opinion of another former minister. "On election night, when it was very clear that we were beaten, Lesage was still repeating that he would form a government the next morning. It seems to me that this gives a picture of the man at that time."

The Liberals won a majority of the popular vote: 47.2 per cent of the total against only 40.9 per cent for the Union Nationale led by Daniel Johnson, a former junior minister of the Duplessis government of the late Fifties. But the Union Nationale's traditional strength in sparsely populated rural ridings gave it fifty-five seats to fifty-one for the Liberals. The new separatist parties won 8.8 per cent of the 1966 vote but failed to win any seats. The remaining two seats were won by Independents.

If Johnson's victory took the Liberals by surprise, it stunned the rest of the country, and particularly the journalists and politicians who had made a specialty of interpreting Quebec during the early Sixties. How had a former minister in the corrupt Duplessis government been able to sell himself and his old party to the new, sophisticated generation of Quebec voters? Had they elected him because he promised a financially conservative administration or because he had written a nationalist book in 1965 entitled, "Equality or Independence?"

Clear answers to these questions never emerged, but Johnson's own popularity continued to increase up to the time of his death in September, 1968. He gave Quebec a quieter style of domestic politics, although it was enlivened by such spectacular visiting attractions as the Quebec tour of French President Charles de Gaulle in 1967.

The Liberal defeat of 1966 still presents many interesting speculative questions. If Lesage had won, would he have been able to press his arguments for "special status" more effectively on the rest of Canada? Would he have opposed Pierre Trudeau for the federal Liberal leadership in 1968? Would Lévesque have remained then in the Liberal cabinet? Would he have succeeded Lesage as Premier?

In the short term, the 1966 defeat seemed to have little apparent effect on Lévesque's political thinking. His immediate reaction was to blame it on Quebecers' inability to absorb progress rather than on any shortcomings in the government. He told a television interviewer that Quebec apparently had to progress by "somersaults" and wasn't able to maintain a "consistent rhythm of progress."

XVIII
Lévesque Chooses

Within the party, Lévesque's response to the 1966 election defeat was immediate and practical. He telephoned a few friends to suggest that "a little group" should meet to consider some organizational changes in the party.

This was, as it turned out, the first concrete step taken by Lévesque toward the creation of a new party, but at the time, it was a spontaneous move that might have led anywhere.

It brought Lévesque, a few days after the election, to a country home in the Eastern Townships near Lake Memphremagog, about eighty miles southeast of Montreal, for an informal get-together with a small group that included François Aquin, a young lawyer and past president of the Quebec Liberal Federation who had just been elected in the Montreal riding of Dorion and who would bolt the Liberals in 1967 to become the first separatist member of the Quebec Assembly; and Marc Brière, another lawyer who had been active in the party since 1955, a long-time member of its policy committee and an associate of Gérin-Lajoie's. Brière would become one of the founding members of Lévesque's new party; Aquin would become one of its most troublesome.

Within a few weeks, Lévesque's "little group" had grown into a loose collection of perhaps a hundred Liberals who met regularly during the summer and fall of 1966. The meetings of these survivors of the 1966 defeat were held in the comfortable surroundings of the private St. Denis Club on Sherbrooke Street, Montreal's most fashionable boulevard, in a salon dominated by a painting of a nude on a stormy beach entitled "*Le Salon d'Epave* – The Shipwreck Room."

The dominant members of the group at the outset were Lévesque, Kierans and Gérin-Lajoie – the leaders of the reform wing of the cabinet before the election. Pierre Laporte came to one or two of the meetings but "wandered away because he knew that it was upsetting Lesage." Some of the members assumed that Laporte was there in order to keep Lesage informed.

Leaving people out was "a curious and ruthless process," according to one member of the group. Not invited were the former ministers who had formed the "old guard" around Lesage and a few of the newer members such as Claude Wagner, the crime-busting judge whom Lesage had appointed as Justice Minister shortly before the election.

The rank-and-file of the St. Denis group was made up of people like Brière, Aquin and Yves Michaud, another newly elected Liberal member of the Assembly who had been active on the party's policy committee during the Sixties and who had resented Lesage's efforts to tame the committee during his last years as Premier.

The policy committee had always been dominated by Montrealers who were treated as radicals by the more conservative party group in Quebec City. Before 1960, the Montrealers had been the creative element in the party, close to the former leader, Lapalme, who continued to live in Montreal during his years in the Quebec legislature. The program of the 1960 election had emerged within the Montreal group. Nationalization in 1962 had been a Montreal issue in the sense that Lévesque and Hydro-Québec symbolized the political assertiveness and technical capability of the city's growing French-Canadian middle class while the head offices of Shawinigan and the other privately-owned utilities symbolized the financial dominance of the city's English-speaking population.

The importance of the nationalization issue had always been hard to appreciate in Quebec City where all the executives of the privately-owned utility were French-Canadians, as were virtually all the other residents of the city.

In 1964, Montreal Liberals on the party's policy committee had led the battle to establish an independent Quebec Liberal Federation against the opposition of most Quebec City Liberals led by Henri Dutil, a Quebec advertising executive who eventually became secretary-general of the Federation. The idea of an independent federation had been reluctantly accepted by Lesage, who lived in Quebec City, but from then on, the Montreal influence in the party had waned. Lesage's campaign in 1966 had been plotted by his own staff and in Dutil's office in Quebec City.

After 1964, the policy committee had been reorganized and brought to heel by Lesage but its original spirit had continued to make itself felt in the party. In the early Sixties, members of the committee had often adjourned after their meetings to the Auberge St. Tropez on Montreal's Drummond Street, a Provençal-style bar and restaurant. Lévesque would often join them there, along with some of the younger Liberals such as Aquin and Michaud and Robert Bourassa, a Montreal economist who had married into the wealthy Simard family and who was becoming one of Lesage's most trusted advisors.

After the Liberals were defeated in 1966, the suppressed spirit of St. Tropez exploded in the St. Denis Club.

"The split in the party became evident after the election," recalled a leading member of the St. Denis group.

> Lesage and the old guard of the party felt that we had lost the election because of intellectual ideas that had led the party astray and created a popular backlash.
>
> We felt that the party had gone astray between 1964 and 1966 because it had betrayed the quiet revolution. We had lost because we had not been successful in explaining clearly enough how we were going to carry on the program of the quiet revolution. So we had been left with only the backlash of the revolution – and the Lesage charm.

"The St. Denis group certainly undermined Lesage's position and alienated all those who weren't invited to join it," said another of its members, "but it never was directed against Lesage. Quite frankly, Lesage after the election wasn't making much of a contribution to anything."

"The attitude of Lesage and others in Quebec City was negative," said another. "If you want a meeting of elected members, they said, we have a caucus. If you want a meeting of party members, there's the Federation. So what are you doing in the St. Denis Club?"

Two objectives took shape during the discussions in the Shipwreck Room. The most immediate was the control of the Federation itself through the election of Kierans and two other members of the St. Denis group to the top executive posts of the Federation at the annual convention in November, 1966. The second was a new program for the party.

A new program meant yet another difficult expedition into the issue of constitutional reform, this time in the context of the pragmatic and highly political Quebec nationalism of Premier Daniel Johnson. If the Liberal Party was going to find a distinctive constitutional position, it was going to have to return to a strong federalist position or try to beat Johnson at his own game by defining a more nationalist option. The first alternative hardly seemed worth discussing, at least in the opinion of most members of the St. Denis group. Lévesque and his friends began to explore the second.

It wasn't long before rumours of dissension in the party began to appear in print.

One of Lévesque's favourite targets for criticism, since the election, had been the privately-owned radio and television stations in the province. He blamed the government's defeat, in part, on a "lack of objectivity" among journalists who wanted to "take the government down a peg or two." This had developed during the summer into persistent criticism of the "degrading" and "scandalous" programming on the privately-owned stations.

Eventually Lévesque proposed that media monopolies in Quebec should be disbanded, that stations should be required by law to invest some of their profits in original programming, and that the privately-owned stations should be required to offer free time to political parties during election campaigns, as did the state-owned networks.

Lévesque's attack on the owners of radio and television stations seriously alarmed some people in his own party, and it soon became a symbolic issue between the Montreal and Quebec factions. Lévesque's stand was publicly criticized by Dutil while Kierans and his two running mates at the November convention sided with Lévesque.

By the end of October, disagreement over the composition and role of the party executive, and the control of the party's election funds, had become so severe that three members of the St. Denis group – Lévesque, Gérin-Lajoie and Bourassa – were designated to negotiate a compromise with other elements in the party before the November convention. Bourassa's role as mediator was to increase in importance during the coming year.

Lévesque was now beginning to be identified publicly by some Liberals as the real source of division. An article in the Quebec City daily *l'Action*, written by Auguste Choquette, one of the province's Liberal backbenchers at Ottawa, suggested that Lévesque's resignation would be the solution to all the party's problems. In a subsequent letter to his constituents, Choquette accused Lévesque of "crypto-separatism." Lévesque replied by accusing the federal Liberals of trying to interfere in the provincial party's affairs.

When the convention opened, compromises had been negotiated on most of the differences between the various factions. The reformers elected Kierans to the presidency; their opponents defeated his two running mates. But the "abscess" within the party, as one journalist described it, was punctured when the Federation's outgoing president, Dr. Irénée Lapierre, told a radio interviewer that Lévesque no longer belonged in the Liberal party and, in fact, would be a liability for any party.

"If he doesn't leave us now," he predicted, "he'll go tomorrow."

Dr. Lapierre also described Kierans as "Lévesque's puppet" and hinted that Lévesque's real objective was to replace Lesage at the head of the party.

On the final day of the convention, all of Lesage's diplomatic skill was required to avert a split. When he tried to protect Dr. Lapierre by blaming the format of the interview, Lesage was booed and shouted down by a majority of the 1,000 delegates. It took only a few seconds for him to bring the meeting to order again but the unprecedented outburst shook him. Newspapers the next day headlined it as a "blow to the prestige" of the former Premier.

"The contest ended in a tie," wrote Claude Ryan in *le Devoir* after the convention. "There were neither winners nor losers. The real confrontations will take place in the months to come. We won't know until then if the conflicts will bring new unity to the party or spectacular and irreparable divisions."

The election of Kierans as president of the Federation was an important victory for the reform element of the party but it did nothing to advance the constitutional debate. Kierans made his own position clear at the convention: "As an economist, I think that the time isn't ripe for Quebec to go it alone without suffering a serious drop in its standard of living.

"And when the time comes," he added, "I hope that Quebec won't make that choice. The solution lies in a Canada in which the rights of the French-Canadians, as equal partners in Confederation as far as language and culture are concerned, are everywhere recognized and respected."

As a confirmed federalist, Kierans had no interest in furthering the constitutional debate within the party. But for others, particularly Lévesque, this had been the main thrust of the St. Denis Club discussions. He continued to develop the issue after the 1966 convention with other members of the original St. Denis group. It was the start of a process that was to transform Kierans from Lévesque's closest ally in 1966 to his political executioner only a year later.

Separatism had loomed as a possible option for Lévesque since the early Sixties. Lévesque himself has given 1965 as the decisive year. One of his close associates recalled coming away from a conversation with him about that time with the feeling that the attraction of separatism was becoming irresistible to Lévesque.

"As a member of the government," recalled the same man, "he discovered how decisive was the control of Quebec affairs that was left in the hands of outsiders, particularly in the economic field, and how profoundly the collective life of French-Canadians was affected by the political decisions made in Ottawa.

"These were the two cardinal discoveries that he made, and they literally grew inside him. You could sense that."

It was a time of discovery for many people in Quebec. Lévesque's journey toward a final political decision was taken in the company of hundreds of thousands, including some of the most important figures in the Quebec Liberal party. A few, among them Robert Bourassa, who would later become Premier, followed him almost to the end of his journey.

"I didn't realize that it was beginning to be an all-or-nothing effort with him," said a former member of the Liberal caucus, recalling the winter and spring of 1967.

It was still a question of thinking: well, he's been talking like this for three or four years: how far he goes when the crunch comes is a different question.

I certainly didn't feel that the party as a whole would go for something like that. Five members of the caucus at the most were flirting with it. You had to pay attention to it because Lévesque was there but you still felt that in the last analysis, he would back down from an outright declaration.

It was just a feeling that if he couldn't get a majority in the party, he would drop it as something that wasn't feasible. He's very pragmatic and realistic; he always was.

"You know how René proceeds; he has intuitions, feelings," said a member of the St. Denis group. "He puts all kinds of things together and gives you a direction. We were following that but we didn't know exactly where it was leading."

At the beginning of April, 1967, about fiteeen or twenty Liberals held a constitutional seminar in a Laurentian resort hotel at Mont-Tremblant north of Montreal. It was essentially the St. Denis group; it was also, as one of the participants recalled, the end of the St. Denis group:

It was an important moment for Lévesque and I'm sure that he had prepared for it for a long time. He told us that it was time to be more precise about the party's program, and then he spoke for about half an hour.

It was already there – his whole thesis of sovereignty-association. It was the best speech that I ever heard him give. It was so logical, so well done, that many people didn't see the full importance of what he was doing. It was really explosive, a bomb, but it didn't give that impression.

As reports of the Mont-Tremblant meeting began to reach the press, commentators couldn't seem to decide whether it signified even greater divisions in the party or a move toward unity.

"It was less a defiance of party authority," decided Pierre-C. O'Neil of *La Presse*, "than an attempt of the Liberal left to reach agreement on minimum constitutional objectives."

After Mont-Tremblant, the group continued to meet about once a month, often in the basement of Bourassa's home in the prosperous English-speaking Montreal suburb of the Town of Mount Royal. One by one, the federalists withdrew as Lévesque's leadership and the direction of the group became more apparent. The significant departure of Gérin-Lajoie, the party's constitutional authority and an advocate of special status for Quebec within Confederation, came early in the summer of 1967. He told the group that its discussions were leading nowhere.

Lévesque himself seemed to pause at this point. Lesage had ordered a truce in the constitutional debate and it was generally respected except for a brief outburst by Aquin in a speech at the end of June. There was speculation that Aquin might be expelled from the party but the matter was dropped by the caucus after both Lévesque and Bourassa defended Aquin's right to express his own views.

For a few weeks, as Canada celebrated the centenary of Confederation and as Montreal's Expo '67 attracted visitors and dignitaries from all over the world, there was a lull in the interminable debates within the party. Then, as if the quiet period had really been a contrived dramatic pause, President de Gaulle spoke from the balcony of Montreal's City Hall on July 24.

"*Vive le Canada!*" he intoned. "*Vive le Québec!*"

As the crowd held its breath in anticipation, de Gaulle thundered, "*Vive le Québec libre!*"

There was an immediate, explosive reaction from the people jammed into the plaza below the balcony. Separatist and federalist alike could hardly believe their ears. Neither could Prime Minister Pearson, who delivered such a severe rebuke on national television that night that de Gaulle cut short his visit and returned to France the next day.

The exact proportion of spontaneity in de Gaulle's gesture will always be difficult to calculate. Certainly it came as a surprise to the President's entourage in Canada and to the Quebec government. That same evening, the French ambassador to Ottawa was so confused that he left behind his briefcase in the limousine of one of the Quebec ministers.

About an hour after de Gaulle took off from Montreal, he sent a formal telegram of thanks to Premier Daniel Johnson who received it in his Montreal office, which was at the headquarters of Hydro-Québec.

"Well, de Gaulle is now up in the air," quipped Johnson, "and so are we."

A few months later, a member of Johnson's cabinet spent almost an hour with de Gaulle in Paris. The Montreal speech was never mentioned but the conversation was mainly about Quebec affairs.

"I can't say that de Gaulle was in favour of the separation of Quebec," related the former minister.

He never made a remark that would enable me to say that. But he was in favour of the Johnson position on renewal of the constitution. Before his trip he had read all the documentation that Johnson had sent to him, including the Quebec submissions to the federal government. His position was this: France will do all that it can, but only what you want it to do.

Through contacts between Quebec ministers and de Gaulle's entourage, the story circulated in Quebec that de Gaulle, on his arrival in Canada from Paris, had said privately that he felt compelled to make a decisive gesture in Quebec.

Even if this story is authentic, the occasion for his "*Vive le Québec Libre!*" appears to have been accidental. On the following day, Mayor Jean Drapeau was at pains to explain to a visitor from Ottawa that no speech by de Gaulle had been planned, that he had ordered the microphone to be removed from the balcony earlier in the day, and that it had remained there only at the insistence of a television technician. He also claimed that de Gaulle had turned to Premier Johnson after his speech and had inquired about the deafening ovation that had greeted his final words, saying, "What did I say?" or something to that effect. Johnson is supposed to have replied, "You have just used the slogan of a party that I defeated last year."

De Gaulle's speech created another crisis within the Quebec Liberal party. A few days after the event, at a caucus in Quebec, the conservative wing took the initiative.

"The first part of the meeting was dominated by those who were critical of de Gaulle," recalled one participant. "They seemed to be more emotional and aggressive about it than about anything that had ever come out of Ottawa or Toronto. The great anxiety of the Liberal party since 1964 had been separatism, and they resented de Gaulle's intrusion.

"I think Lévesque realized at that time that his position had no chance in the Liberal party."

It was François Aquin who brought the issue to a head by threatening to resign unless the Liberal caucus issued a statement in support of de Gaulle's action. And it was Lévesque, along with Michaud and Bourassa, who tried unsuccessfully to talk him out of it during lunch before the afternoon session of the caucus.

When Aquin resigned to become the first separatist member of the Quebec Assembly, Lévesque stated publicly that his reasons were "insufficient." Aquin felt at the time that Lévesque already had a new party in mind but didn't want to relate its creation to a single incident, particularly to an incident imported from France in the person of a politician whose autocratic character had been criticized by Lévesque in the past.

Unlike many members of Quebec's political elite, including Aquin, Lévesque was no Francophile. His wartime experiences had left him with greater admiration for the British than the French, and his journalism had given him more familiarity with American than European politics. During his ministerial visits to France, the rigid divisions of French society had grated against his own "American" informality. While the traffic of politicians, journalists, writers and entertainers between France and Quebec grew heavier year by year during the Sixties, Lévesque continued to feel more at home in New York than in Paris, and on the beaches of Cape Cod than at Cannes.

In the summer of 1967, Lévesque vacationed as usual in the United States. Before he left, he promised the survivors of the St. Denis group who were still with him that he would return with a written statement of his constitutional position.

"There were about ten or twelve of us left," recalled one, "and we decided that Lévesque had to let us know where we were going. When he came back from his holidays, he had a few notes. It was the skeleton of his first statement on sovereignty-association."

During the next few weeks, Lévesque continued to work on his statement, but the members of the group already had a clearer idea of his ultimate destination. At the end of the summer, there was a final meeting in the basement of Bourassa's home when the economist, who had worked closely with Lévesque up to this point, told Lévesque that he could no longer support his position.

Bourassa's reasons were technical, arising from the monetary aspects of Lévesque's sovereignty-association proposal. On a personal level, the two men remained on close terms; and it was known in Lévesque's group that Bourassa's decision to leave went against the personal sentiments if not the political instincts of his wife.

On September 18, 1967, Lévesque issued his "Option for Quebec."

In about 6,000 words, Lévesque outlined his vision of a new political order for Canada. It was disjointed and emotional, the work of a propagandist rather than a political philosopher, but it was specific enough to serve as a line of division in the years to come as individual Quebecers made up their own minds about the future of their homeland. Lévesque's credo began:

We are Québécois. What that means first and foremost – and if need be, all that it means – is that we are attached to this one corner of the earth where we can be completely ourselves: this Quebec, the only place where we have the unmistakable feeling that 'here we can be really at home.'

Being ourselves is essentially a matter of keeping and developing a personality that has survived for three and a half centuries.

At the core of this personality is the fact that we speak French.

Lévesque's option was justified and amplified in stages in his proposal:

– He addressed Quebecers as members of a community that was something more than a nation, almost a family. The struggle for survival had made Quebecers "heirs to the group obstinacy which has kept alive that portion of French America we call Quebec." Their common recollections of the past are "things that made us what we are ... enable us to recognize each other wherever we may be ... tune in each other loud and clear, with no one else listening."

– "In this little corner of ours," Quebecers who grew up in the old, inward-looking and defensive society are enduring a "sudden acceleration of history" in common with the rest of mankind. The unprecedented development of science, technology and economic activity contains "potential promises and dangers immeasurably greater than any the world has ever known."

– Quebec society has "grave, dangerous, and deep-rooted illnesses which it is absolutely essential to cure if we want to survive." The cure consists of making this "trying and thoughtless age ... accept us as we are."

– Some progress had been made. During the "quiet revolution," Quebec had reformed its social welfare system, strengthened administrative structures of the state, cleaned up electoral practices and "taken the first step toward collective control of certain essential services such as *la Société Générale de Financement* (General Investment Corporation, the state-sponsored investment and management company); *la Société d'Exploration Minière* (the state-owned Quebec Mining Exploration Company); and the *Caisse de dépôts* to invest the savings accumulated by the Quebec Pension Plan." But these achievements are merely the beginning for a nation "condemned to progress" that "must guard against the loss of impetus, against the periodic desire to slow down."

– The Canadian political framework of "two nations in a single country ... has had its day." To develop normally, the Quebec nation must have jurisdiction over certain essential services: Citizenship, immigration and employment; certain aspects of international relations; and social security and welfare. There would have to be greater Quebec control over industrial and commercial corporations, fiduciary and savings institutions, internal agencies of development and industrialization "as well as the power to exercise a reasonable control over the movement and investment of our own capital." Other questions which would have to be settled would include certain disputed territorial claims between Quebec and Canada, along the Labrador boundary, and the jurisdiction of the Supreme Court.

– This "bare minimum" demanded by Quebec will be regarded as a "frightening maximum" by the rest of the country.

– "But there are moments – and this is one of them – when courage and calm daring become the only proper form of prudence ... Quebec must become sovereign as soon as possible."

– This sovereignty should be open to association with others. Areas of collaboration with Quebecers' former compatriots might include the monetary system, tarrifs, the postal system, the national debt, treatment of minorities, and defence and foreign policies.

– This "new adaptation of the current 'common market' formula" might be called the Canadian Union – *l'Union canadienne*.

"Well, that's it!" was the first sentence the next day in the *La Presse* report of Lévesque's announcement.

"René Lévesque has at last put an end to the rumours which have surrounded him for months," said the Montreal *Star* in an editorial. "He wants sovereignty for Quebec because only through it can Quebecers achieve the 'security of our collective existence.' In other words, Mr. Lévesque has opted for separatism."

Having stated this clearly enough, the editorialist of the Montreal *Star* proceeded to muddy his own assessment. He seemed to be confused by Lévesque's "most practical of arrangements, a union constantly seeking *ad hoc* solutions through permanent consultative committees which sounds in a curious way like the federal parliament under another name.

"There would be all the trappings of statehood but there would be very little increase in the responsibilities of sovereignty" in the *Star's* opinion. This revealed to the *Star* that Lévesque's option was "based on emotion" rather than the practical needs of the province.

"It is here that Confederation has failed, for Mr. Lévesque and for many others like him," the *Star* concluded. "It is this failure which produces the great solitude of French Canada and sparked the extraordinary reception given General de Gaulle ...

"But if Confederation fails to provide the emotional nourishment which French Canada needs, equally economic logic is also on the side of the federal state."

In its first editorial reaction to Lévesque's statement, the *Gazette* of Montreal sent another French-Canadian against the new convert to separatism. It quoted from a recent speech by Jean Ostiguy, a Montreal stockbroker and outgoing president of *la Chambre de Commerce du district de Montréal*, to assert that "the constitution has not served us so badly." The *Gazette* stated that Ostiguy represented a majority of French-speaking Canadians when he had said, "We must beware of breaking windows, of abruptly exchanging the progress and economic growth we are now experiencing for a political freedom which could not be counted on to produce economic freedom."

In *La Presse* the same day, editorialist Renaude Lapointe rejected Lévesque's depressing analysis of Quebec's future in Confederation "at a time when the Quebec personality is confidently affirmed, better educated, more dynamic and more influential than ever before." She accused Lévesque of failing to admit that "90 per cent of our weaknesses and shortcomings are our own fault."

"How can anyone imagine," asked *Le Soleil* of Quebec City, "that the withdrawal of Quebec, which would throw the rest of the country into the arms of the United States in short order, would be permitted with any good grace?"

The editor of *Le Devoir*, Claude Ryan, on the day after Lévesque's statement, emphasized the positive results of this "very important event." He congratulated Lévesque on breaking free of the "intellectual iron collar" that had given him so much discomfort in the past few years. Ryan perceived that this gesture would help to bring an end to the "era of ambiguity" that had existed in Quebec.

"The truly strong men of the era that is about to begin," he predicted, "will be those who have the courage to take definite positions and who have the intellectual vigour to defend them."

Commenting directly on the separatist option, Ryan's editorial of September 23 gave continued but qualified support to federalism.

"For the time being," he wrote, "it seems to us to be the better path toward freedom and co-operation."

The reactions of Quebec Liberals, at first, seemed less decisive. While Kierans predicted immediately that the Lévesque option would be rejected by the party, Lesage merely affirmed Lévesque's right to publish his position and bring it before the Liberal convention in October. Pierre Laporte suggested that Lévesque's minimum requirements might be contained within some sort of "special status" formula for Quebec without the need to create "associate states."

The week after Lévesque's statement, Sylvio St. Amant of the the editorial staff of *Le Nouvelliste* in Trois-Rivières, a small city midway between Montreal and Quebec, was still predicting that "a compromise will be reached at the coming convention." But by the beginning of October, the party line had started to harden.

A significant defeat for Lévesque was the sixty-seven to forty-five vote against his position at the annual convention of the Quebec Young Liberal Association. Lévesque's style had always given him a large following among younger members of the party. This time, he was guilty either of carelessness or bad tactics. After making a good impression on the convention on the first day, he abandoned the field to Lesage on the second day when the vote on his position was taken.

Lesage's success in robbing Lévesque of this bloc of support at the Liberal Federation's convention led one newspaper to predict, accurately, that "the final victory may go to the one who has the best organization on the floor of the convention."

The opposing forces were beginning to take shape. Lesage now stated publicly that he would "never lead a party that preached separatism." Kierans promised that "if the Liberal party accepts René's resolution for separatism, for a sovereign Quebec, I could not remain in the Liberal party."

The survivors of the St. Denis group continued to dwindle as the pressure increased. There were no more meetings in Bourassa's basement in the Town of Mount Royal. Now the young economist, who had worked with Lévesque on developing his option, was placing as much distance as he could between himself and Lévesque in a series of speeches and press conferences. He insisted that Lévesque's monetary policy left a basic question unanswered: How could a central bank deal with two equal and sovereign states? Bourassa also claimed, along with Kierans, that independence would mean serious economic problems for Quebec, and hardship for ordinary wage earners.

Among the last to leave Lévesque was Yves Michaud, the new member for the Montreal riding of Dorion, a former journalist and close friend of both Lévesque and Bourassa. Michaud identified himself in October as a supporter of the "associate states" format, claiming that Lévesque's scheme for association between Quebec and Canada was politically fragile. Michaud preferred to see Quebec voters continue to elect representatives to the federal parliament.

At the last meeting of Lévesque's group before the convention, at an east end Montreal restaurant owned by former Canadien hockey star "Butch" Bouchard, Michaud told Lévesque that "the Rocky Mountains are part of our heritage ... Marquette and Joliette ... we were there first."

"You are going to deprive us of a heritage that is ours," he said.

"Well, if you still want your Rocky Mountains," replied Lévesque, "keep them!"

Michaud didn't abandon his mountains until six years later, when he left a comfortable post in the Quebec civil service to run as a separatist candidate in the election of October, 1973. Later he became the founding editor of *Le Jour*, the separatist movement's first daily newspaper.

Often it seemed, as in Michaud's case, that the technical differences between constitutional positions had little to do with the political decisions that were being made. When old political and personal loyalties broke down over minor differences in the proposed constitutions of projected federations, it was obvious that other factors were at work. Personal ambition, friendship and temperament could be decisive. The final decisions often appeared to rest on grounds that were psychological rather than political.

133

"Lévesque was thinking about it perhaps six or seven months earlier," said one of the St. Denis group. "He was looking for a way out.

"And I said, 'What if you created another party?' 'Well,' he said 'we might not win, but we'd make a hell of a lot of noise.'

"Why didn't I go with him? Because I was a federalist, maybe because of opportunism, I wouldn't know."

"What began to coalesce around Lévesque," said another member of the group, "was a nucleus of people who shared his thoughts. He could stay up with them in bull sessions all night long and at the end, be convinced that they reflected the innermost feelings of the province.

"If he had tried to give speeches in Sept-Îles and in Lac St. Jean, he would have found out that independence was not the number one concern of the majority."

"I almost left him during that meeting at 'Butch' Bouchard's," confessed another member of the group who ultimately stayed with Lévesque. "Michaud wasn't ready to accept independence, even with the kind of association envisaged by Lévesque, and I had the same feeling. I was very reluctant to be known as a separatist. It was a hard move to make, from something accepted to something that was labelled erratic."

Throughout September and October, efforts had been made to reach a compromise. Bourassa went back and forth between Lesage and Lévesque so often that some members of Lesage's staff referred to him as "the missionary." Bourassa kept open the contact with Lévesque for so long that he almost compromised his own position. Even now, some of those who were close to events claim that Bourassa had given Lévesque a commitment to leave the party with him.

"I think that Bourassa was too prudent a man to have committed himself to René," said a close observer. "He had made up his mind long before that he would try for the leadership of the party."

Neither Kierans nor Lévesque had many illusions about the outcome when they met in Montreal for an hour-long television debate that was organized by the CBC and broadcast on September 26. As soon as Lévesque entered the studio, he went to Kierans, extended his hand and said, "I'm sorry."

"I'm sorry, too," replied Kierans.

Kierans then said to Lévesque that one or the other was going to be out of the party by the end of the October convention. It was clear, he said, that whoever was identified as the man who had led the drive to oust Lévesque would himself have little future in the party and perhaps in Quebec politics, regardless of the outcome. Six months later, Kierans was to run against Pierre Trudeau for the leadership of the federal Liberal party.

"René and I are two predictable people," said Kierans on the air that night. "I knew he was heading to this. He knew I would fight him."

"Basically, I am a Quebecer first," commented Lévesque, "and Eric is a Canadian first."

Those who were involved in the Liberal convention of October 14, 1967, are still divided about who did what to whom. Was the procedure of the convention rigged to force Lévesque out of the party, or did Lévesque force the party to expel him?

Lévesque has said, about his decision to join the Liberals in 1960, "I used the party and the party used me." The same comment could apply to the events of 1967 as the Quebec Liberal party struggled toward a more federalist position and Lévesque attempted to control the scenario of his own departure.

"Lévesque was not expelled by anyone," said a close observer. "The initiative came from Lévesque and his group. They faced the party with a take-it-or-leave-it proposition.

"It was tactics – let's not be under any illusion – just bad tactics in my opinion, as I told him at the time. But he was resolved to make his option."

"I remember meeting him in 1967 and discovering that he was toying with the idea of launching a new party," said an old friend of Lévesque's.

I remember telling him – René, if you go that way, you'll either be the von Papen of a rightist revolution or the Kerensky of a leftist revolution but you won't be Hitler or Lenin. He laughed and said – well, you might be right.

We also discussed his own role and Gérin-Lajoie's in the legislature, and I told him that they had been very poor in opposition. I wasn't too surprised about Gérin-Lajoie but I had thought that Lévesque would have been very dangerous for the Johnson government. I remember half-realizing then that he was already out of the game as it was set up then. He was looking for something beyond that.

Later, on reflection, it seemed to me that he didn't see the scenario as it took place, that he was probably taken by surprise.

"The night before the convention," recalled one of the St. Denis group, "there was a meeting of Lévesque's people in the Clarendon Hotel in Quebec City, and I heard Lévesque saying – if we have 25 per cent, then I'm staying. At that point, he still believed there was a possibility of remaining in the party.

"And he did have the support of 25 to 30 per cent of the members of the party. But with the coalition against him – Laporte, Kierans and Lesage – it dropped down to something like seven per cent at the convention.

But he was still confident the night before – perhaps in his own charisma – that he could deliver."

Lévesque himself recalled a final session with Laporte on the Friday that the convention opened at Quebec's Château Frontenac Hotel. His manifesto had been approved by his constituency association in Montreal and embodied in a resolution submitted to the convention. Lévesque had asked for a secret vote on his resolution. Laporte, who had been in Florida during the preceding few weeks and who had stayed aloof from the preliminaries of battle, was functioning as a mediator between the Lévesque group and Kierans.

"We had three or four specific requests and the answers were no, no and no – and that was it," said Lévesque. "At that moment, on Friday, we knew that the convention was over. So then the question started to be discussed in our group: What do we do afterward?

"I didn't have any idea."

"Right up to the convention, we felt that there might be a miracle," a former member of Lévesque's group said. "After what had happened at the 1966 convention, we knew what was coming – that Lévesque would have to leave or we would be thrown out. But we were very reluctant to leave."

Negotiations continued up to the last moment. Maurice Sauvé, no longer powerful in Ottawa but still with many contacts in Quebec, appeared at the door of Laporte's suite before the crucial Saturday afternoon session of the convention, saying that he had talked with Lévesque and that something might still be worked out. Kierans, Laporte and a few others saw him for five minutes and rejected the suggestion that a *modus vivendi* could be achieved at that stage.

An hour before the afternoon session began at 2.00 p.m., a small number of key Liberals met in Lesage's suite to make final plans. Their main concern was that Gérin-Lajoie might try, after Lévesque had made his move, to bring about a vote on the "special status" report that he had completed as head of the Liberal Federation's committee on constitutional affairs. Kierans told Gérin-Lajoie that if he presented a resolution on special status to the convention that afternoon, he would go out with Lévesque that night.

"I'll get up myself and move that it be defeated," he threatened, "and I'll be seconded by Gérard Lévesque."

"Is that right?" Gérin-Lajoie asked Lévesque, another former cabinet minister.

"That's right," confirmed Lévesque.

Kierans and Lesage knew then that when René Lévesque walked out of the party that afternoon, no other major figure would go with him.

In fact, it was Pierre Laporte later that day who moved that the Gérin-Lajoie report be studied further by the party's political commission. This was embodied in a resolution which also included a general statement of opposition to "separatism in any form." It was adopted late Saturday evening by a show of hands, reported by the newspapers as 1,500 votes against seven. The Lévesque resolution received the support of only four delegates but by then, Lévesque and most of his followers had left the convention and the party.

For most of the delegates, the issue had never been in doubt. Arriving at the Château Frontenac the previous day, a group of delegates from northwestern Quebec had told reporters, "We haven't come to discuss Lévesque's thesis. We're after his head." When the rules of procedure were being adopted on Friday, the Lévesque group's demand for a secret ballot on the separatist resolution was hooted down by the other delegates.

About 6.00 p.m. on Saturday, at the end of a long afternoon of debate in the ballroom of the Château Frontenac, Lévesque was given the right to speak again for five minutes as the proposer of one of the two resolutions before the delegates. "On the verge of tears," according to one of the journalists covering the meeting, Lévesque quietly thanked the convention for permitting him to present his resolution. Those who had spoken against it, he said, had tried only to create fears about the unknown. Instead of giving serious attention to the option that he had announced in September, they had tried to create the impression that Quebec independence would lead to anarchy.

Finally, he repeated a warning that he had given to Lesage in a letter the previous August: that "the party is in danger of dying if it returns to being a private club."

Cheered by a small band of supporters at the front of the hall, Lévesque then left the stage and walked the length of the ballroom to the exit, followed by every eye in the audience. After the months of public debate and secret negotiation, the actual moment of departure had a predestined, almost programmed character. Lévesque's final speech as a Liberal was far from being a call to revolution. It was a fatalistic acceptance of the inevitable.

A few minutes before Lévesque had approached the platform, Bourassa had stopped him and urged him to think of the example of Aneurin Bevan, who had stayed with the British Labour Party despite his unwavering opposition to nuclear weapons. Lévesque had simply shrugged his shoulders and mumbled that it was too late. The only thing that remained, at that stage, was to go through the final act with as much dignity as possible.

The bitterness erupted later that evening. An hour before midnight, as the delegates closed their convention by singing "O Canada" beneath the

Canadian flags that had been hurriedly unfurled that morning beside the original display of Quebec flags, Lévesque held a press conference surrounded by about 200 supporters in the smaller Clarendon Hotel a few blocks away. He accused Kierans of having employed "economic terrorism" against his thesis.

"It isn't the man in the street who is sowing the seeds of panic," he said, "but the newspapers and the dominant English-speaking element in our province – three or four dozen people of the same race that managed to put up very well with Duplessis as they finagled behind the scenes with the economy of Quebec."

Kierans replied that the Liberal party had refused to permit "an elitist minority to drag the Quebec population into a separatist adventure."

Behind the propaganda, the dominant emotion among those who had been closest to Lévesque's development over the years was sadness. Only the members of the party's "old guard" were jubilant, men like the former Minister of Lands and Forests, Bona Arsenault, who quipped, "Suicide is always a sad thing." Bourassa told reporters that Lévesque's departure was "a great loss for the party – it will be difficult to replace him." Months later, Bourassa was still speculating in public that Lévesque might have stayed in the party if the issue had been negotiated more carefully.

There were similar opinions within the Lévesque group.

"We felt rather sad," said one of Lévesque's supporters, recalling the events of that day. "we were leaving but we didn't know exactly where we were going."

"I'm sure that if Kierans, Gérin-Lajoie and Lévesque had stayed together, things would have been different," said another. "I'm sure that they could have persuaded Lévesque toward a more flexible conclusion of his views. But I don't know whether that would have been better in the long run. It probably would just have delayed the issue."

"I had ambiguous feelings that afternoon at the Château," Lévesque remembered.

All I wanted to say was that we knew we were beaten, and to tell them that was the end of our living together. And to walk out.

Gérin-Lajoie was about the only one who had the decency to say goodbye and to shake my hand. All the others were looking kind of scared.

It was a mixed feeling. On the one hand, after more than six years, and working hard with people ... agreeing, disagreeing, having fights ... even if you're not friends in the real sense of the word ... you get close enough ...

On the other hand, there was the feeling that ... oh my god ... at last we can get out from under all that stuff that's been building up for the last three years ... a sort of small-scale continuous night of the long knives.

That evening, we had a meeting with perhaps fifty of the most dedicated people at the Clarendon. A decision in principle was made that we had to have further political action, that we were starting, not finishing.

Once the decision had been made, most Quebec newspapers looked back almost wistfully on Lévesque's era in the Quebec Liberal party. Even the English-language press indulged in a few second thoughts. The *Gazette's* political correspondent in Quebec, Gordon Pape, reported that "the party emerged from the convention as a much different type of political movement from the one which swept to power in 1960 and 1962.

"Lévesque's original thinking and reforming zeal have stirred and excited Liberal party members for more than seven years," he wrote. "When he left, he took with him not only a fair number of youthful supporters but most of the party's crusading spirit as well."

The Montreal *Star* editorialist agreed: "Now those who feel as he did – not about separatism but about social reform – are left without their strongest ally. A new responsibility falls on them. Somehow, without Mr. Lévesque, they have to maintain the forward movement of the party."

French-language journalists were more interested in the effects of the split on Quebec's growing separatist movement. Claude Beauchamp, the political correspondent for *La Presse* in Quebec, called the convention "the first step in a realignment of political forces" in the province. Commenting on the "expressions of relief" on the faces of delegates to the convention after Lévesque's departure, Claude Ryan of *Le Devoir* warned that "the truth is that a major surgical operation has been performed, and no one can yet predict what the long-term effects will be."

Ryan foresaw that Lévesque would be called upon within a short time to lead separatist forces in Quebec. The federalist-separatist confrontation at the Liberal convention, he wrote, was simply the first of many, leading up to "a final and decisive rendez-vous when the participants won't be merely the members of a single party but the people of Quebec themselves."

In a 1971 interview, Lévesque said that he had moved toward separatism "bit by bit, without even noticing." It seemed to him, in retrospect, to have been a "normal" development.

He saw his 1967 decision as the inevitable outcome of his personal and political experiences. The past explained his decision, his decision explained the past. It made sense out of his life, and it made Quebec history make sense to him, particularly the history of the Quebec nationalists who had struggled generation after generation for the religious, linguistic and political rights of French-Canadians.

Once Lévesque had made his decision, he believed that only the ultimate goal of independence made this historic national effort, as well as his own career, seem logical and productive. Without independence as a goal, the struggle was a sad tale told by a minority on the road to oblivion. Only the achievement of independence could transform it forever into the saga of an extraordinary struggle for national survival.

French Canada's struggle began long before the British conquest of 1759. Despite the centralizing policy of the French monarchy and the absolutism of French state institutions imposed on New France, a distinctive *Canadien* nation emerged over the years. Visitors from the mother country in the early part of the eighteenth century soon discovered that the colony was not simply an overseas extension of France.

A Jesuit who twice visited Canada at that time commented not only on the Canadians' "frivolity, aversion to assiduous and regular labour" but on the "spirit of independence" that made many of the men prefer the adventurous life of the fur trade to the settled routine of farms and towns.

When Britain conquered the French colony, its first policies were directed toward assimilation. This was done as a matter of course by the

British and probably accepted as automatically, at least at first, by the remaining French. Gradually both sides acquired an appreciation of the political leverage that French-Canadians could exert in their own interest, but it was more than seventy years after the conquest before the idea of an independent French-speaking state in North America emerged as a clear and influential political objective.

In 1837, as a radical element in Quebec moved toward armed revolt, a meeting of 1,200 people sponsored by the rebellious "*Patriotes*" at Saint-Ours, a small town southeast of Montreal, passed twelve resolutions corresponding to the first American Congress's declaration of rights and grievances and to the French declaration of the rights of man in 1789.

"Regarding ourselves as no longer bound except by force to the British government," the "*Patriotes*" decided that "sad experience forces us to recognize that our true friends and natural allies were on the other side of the 45th parallel."

The rebellion was a failure but the idea of independence had been sown. The idea was there thirty years after the rebellion when Quebec opponents of Confederation said that the new federal constitution would mean "the political suicide of the French race in Canada." It served as the fiery inspiration in the Saint-Jean-Baptiste Day speech that the Premier of Quebec, Honoré Mercier, delivered in 1889: "Our enemies are united in the hatred of the French homeland ... in the name and for the prosperity of this province of Quebec that we love so well, let us clasp hands like brothers ..."

In Henri Bourassa, at the turn of the century, the spirit of independence was shaped by his resistance to British imperialism. The scale and intensity of Bourassa's fight for Canadian independence showed the interdependence of French and English-speaking Canadians. The issue came to a head during the First World War in the crisis over conscription. After the war, and during the economic recession that began in 1920, Quebec nationalism returned again to the ideas that had inspired the "*Patriotes*" of 1837. Speaking to a conference of Quebec intellectuals in 1923, a Quebec priest said that "at last we are beginning to realize the need to sever our destiny from that of our neighbours."

"Will this separation extend as far as political independence?" the priest asked. "Our staunchest and best-informed leaders predict it, wish it, and even suggest that all efforts be devoted to this ideal."

The separatist wave peaked in the Thirties, then lost momentum as the Canadian economy improved; but it revived during the conscription crisis of the Second World War. This time, nationalist opposition to compulsory military service in Quebec created a new political instrument, the *Bloc Populaire* party, that won 15 per cent of the vote and four seats in the 1944 Quebec election.

When the conscription issue ended with the war, many of the most outspoken leaders of the *Bloc Populaire* moved slowly toward the mainstream of Canadian political activity. The classic example – André Laurendeau – who went from the leadership of the group of young doctrinaire nationalists in the *Bloc* to the co-chairmanship of Canada's Royal Commission on Bilingualism and Biculturalism two decades later.

In the late Fifties, rising unemployment again stimulated nationalist activity in Quebec in what had become a predictable response to adverse economic conditions. Little attention was paid in 1957 to the creation of *l'Alliance Laurentienne* and to the election of a young naturopath, Raymond Barbeau, as its president. The few political observers who noticed the event saw the Alliance as a rather quaint reproduction of an antique Quebec political model. No one realized that it was the first of a new generation of separatist parties.

Separatists were still so rare in 1961 that Barbeau's first book was called *I Chose Independence*, as if it were a personal and exotic adventure story.

In September, 1960, the most important and enduring of this new breed of separatist movements came into being: *Le Rassemblement pour l'indépendance nationale*. However, even two years after that, one of Quebec's most respected sociologists could still write about the separatist phase that had begun in 1957 as if it belonged to a movement in decline.

"Once more the separatist movement rallied only a minority, and a very chequered one at that," wrote Fernand Ouellet in an essay published in 1962. "Despite widespread propaganda, it never gained a firm foothold among workers, farmers and capitalists. Support for the movement came mostly from young people, with a few intellectuals thrown in.

"Haven't we often before witnessed this familiar phenomenon?"

If the spirit of separatism was familiar to Quebec observers, this time the setting was different.

In 1960, when the *Rassemblement pour l'indépendance nationale* was formed, Quebec politics had undergone a year of dramatic upheaval, following the sudden death of Premier Maurice Duplessis. His successor, Paul Sauvé, had sensed the pressure of suppressed demands for change in the province and had begun to reform not only Duplessis' old party but the nationalist stance that had been an essential part of his defences against alien forces within the province and English-speaking Canada. Federal assistance to universities and a national program of highway construction, rejected by Duplessis, were acceptable to Sauvé under certain conditions. So too was federal involvement in a proposed program of universal state hospital insurance, although Sauvé did not live to accomplish the reforms.

He died suddenly at the age of fifty-two, less than four months after he had succeeded Duplessis. This time there was no obvious successor. The Union Nationale caucus elected an ineffective replacement who was defeated by Jean Lesage and the Liberals in the election of June, 1960.

"It's more than a change of government," proclaimed the new Premier after a few days in office, "It's a new lease on life."

The Lesage government exploded into action with all the intellectual energy that had been pent up during the Duplessis' years. After their first month in office, the correspondent for Le Devoir in Quebec compiled an astonishing list of decisions: the appointment of Paul Gérin-Lajoie as, in effect, the province's first Minister of Education; the reorganization of the corrupt Quebec Provincial Police; the opening of discussions on hospital insurance with the federal government; creation of a Treasury Board as the first part of a sweeping reform of government administrative practices and the bureaucracy; announcement of the first public tenders for road building; and the first of many Quebec demands during the Sixties for greater access to tax revenues controlled by the federal government in order to finance the enhanced national obligations of the Quebec government.

The government encouraged the idea that a revolution was in progress. When Premier Lesage proclaimed an end to "economic colonialism" in Quebec, he often sounded more like a guerrilla leader down from the hills than a sleek corporation lawyer.

Part of the sloganeering was just that – an effective propaganda campaign to persuade Quebecers that they were involved in a revolutionary crusade. Without this fervour, many changes might have been resisted more stubbornly. But part of it arose from the sincere belief of some members of the government, the most active and influential, that Quebec was undergoing fundamental changes that would produce a quite different type of French-speaking community requiring a new relationship with the rest of North America.

Quebec also began to see itself during the Sixties, for the first time in its history, as part of a global political development.

The world that television brought into Quebec farmhouses and tenements during the Fifties was shaken by the disintegration of old colonial empires and the birth struggles of new nations. French-Canadian journalists, Lévesque among them, were particularly intrigued by the independence movements among the French colonies in North Africa. In 1960, the first year of Quebec's "quiet revolution," independence was achieved by no less than seventeen African nations.

In the late Fifties, Lévesque and other Quebec journalists had reported extensively from Algeria. By the year of Algerian independence, 1962, young French-Canadians were influenced by the struggle there just as an earlier generation of North Americans had been inspired by the Spanish

Civil War. In the month following his dramatic "liberation" tour of Quebec, President de Gaulle promised independence to the last French colonial territory in Africa, French Somaliland.

Young French-Canadians identified themselves during the Sixties with oppressed national groups around the world. Their own national struggle gained stature, as well as an exciting new vocabulary, when it was seen as part of a global revolution.

"The French-Canadians of 1963," wrote Raymond Barbeau of *l'Alliance Laurentienne*, "are colonized economically to a greater extent than any other civilized people."

In the past, there had always seemed to be overwhelming practical reasons against the idea of Quebec independence. Now French-Canadians saw underdeveloped African states, one after another, realize the dream that had lurked for more than a century in the dark recesses of the French-Canadian soul. Now Africa bloomed with nations that were smaller than Quebec, in some cases; even less populous, in a few instances; and in almost every case, less adequately equipped with the commercial, technical and educational instruments essential for a prosperous existence in this century. In every practical way, Quebec appeared to be far better prepared for independent nationhood than most of the new nations that were coming into being in the Sixties.

Perhaps the preparation already had lasted too long. The political and economic power that French-Canadians had achieved, without independence, were not going to be given up lightly for an untested hypothesis. The lowest economic level of French-Canadian society was still far above the poorest populations of many of the newer nations.

Many Africans had almost nothing to lose in a political upheaval. The French-Canadian worker in the east end of Montreal had plenty – a car, radio, television set, travel, a chalet in the country, and a state social security system that protected him against the extreme hardships of sickness, unemployment and old age.

There had been a price to pay for all this. Unlike most other North Americans, apart from the blacks and native groups, French-Canadians had accepted their material well-being from the hands of another group. English-speaking Canadians and non-Canadian interests traditionally controlled most of the major financial and commerical enterprises in Quebec and influenced the political development of the province.

In the Sixties, it seemed to many Quebecers that the time had come to reckon up the profits and losses of this arrangement. Everyone else seemed to be doing it.

Closer than Africa, black activists in the United States drew the attention of French-Canadians, for the first time, to another immigrant and alien North American minority. *White Niggers of America* was the title of an influential book written in the Sixties by Pierre Vallières, a young journalist and separatist leader who had once been a protégé of Gérard Pelletier's at *La Presse* and *Cité Libre*.

Quebec consciously began to reach out to the world. In 1891, the nationalist Premier Honoré Mercier had made an unprecedented and triumphant tour of France, Belgium and Italy. Seventy years later, Jean Lesage followed Mercier's almost obliterated trail to Paris to inaugurate Quebec's first overseas *délégation générale* while the new *Rassemblement pour l'indépendance nationale* held a joyous, simultaneous celebration in Montreal on the sidewalk in front of the French consulate. In the following decade, Quebec offices and commercial missions were established in New York and four other U.S. cities, as well as in London, Milan, Dusseldorf and Brussels.

Lesage visited Paris again in 1963 and 1964, being received at the Elysée Palace by President de Gaulle and treated more as a head of state than a provincial leader.

Quebec and Ottawa clashed frequently over the province's right to conclude international agreements in areas of provincial jurisdiction such as education. The defeat of the Lesage government in 1966 did nothing to soften the clashes. Premier Johnson spent five days in Paris in the spring of 1967, concluding agreements for cultural and technical exchanges and preparing the way for de Gaulle's return visit to Quebec two months later when the General, in the words of a statement issued subsequently by the French government, "unmistakably told the French-speaking Canadians and their government that France intended to help them to realize the aims of freedom that they have set themselves."

The limits of Quebec's diplomatic independence were reached, however, in 1968 when Ottawa suspended relations with the Republic of Gabon after the French-speaking African state invited Quebec rather than the federal government to an international conference of French-speaking ministers of education. Ivan Head, the professor of international law at the University of Alberta who was about to become the Prime Minister's foreign policy advisor in Ottawa, wrote at the time that Gabon's invitation and Quebec's acceptance "could have opened the way for Quebec to attain sovereign status by the same gradual process adopted by Canada in gaining independence from the United Kingdom."

French-Canadians rapidly absorbed the concept of an independent Quebec during the Sixties. The "state of Quebec" became an everyday phrase in speeches of Quebec politicians. In 1966, when the appointed members of the Legislative Council were paid off and sent home, the Legislative Assembly was re-christened the National Assembly. Also in 1966, with the blessing of the Quebec government, the "Estates General" gathered together 1,750 representative French-Canadians to discuss and prepare, over a period of several years, the type of constitution that would express Quebec's new sense of statehood.

Statistical measurements of separatist feeling among Quebecers were, at first, as dramatic as they were unreliable. In March, 1961, the Montreal daily *La Presse* published a questionnaire that was mailed back by 11,000 people, with 45 per cent favouring separatism. A few months later, *Le Devoir* ended a series of fifteen articles on independence with a similar questionnaire. Three-quarters of the respondents this time agreed that a separate Quebec state was desirable.

A telephone survey of 300 French-speaking Quebecers by *Le Magazine Maclean* at the end of 1961 showed that 26.2 per cent of the respondents supported independence while 34.5 per cent were opposed. A more elaborate survey of more than 1,000 Quebecers published in the same magazine in 1963 indicated that 16 per cent of the French-speaking residents of Montreal favoured independence. Elsewhere in the province, the separatist proportion was 11 per cent.

These percentages have tended to remain fairly constant over the years. Maurice Pinard, a McGill University sociologist who helped to design many of the surveys in the Sixties, has stated that "the many polls taken over the past ten years indicate that the proportion of people favouring independence has scarcely increased at all during this period."

The results of public opinion polls couldn't be translated directly into votes, as the separatist parties soon discovered. In the 1966 Quebec election, the scattered efforts of the two new separatist parties, the *Rassemblement pour l'indépendance nationale* and the *Ralliement Nationale*, gave them only 8.8 per cent of the vote.

Another new element was added to the traditional English-French confrontation in Canada when the first acts of political terrorism were conducted in 1963 by the *Front de Libération du Québec*. Global fashions in nationalist tactics were clearly evident here. In the Sixties, Canadian newspapers and television programs carried many reports about the training of Quebec guerrillas in Cuba, Algeria and various Arab countries of the Middle East. Two of the earliest terrorist groups were directed by immigrants – a Belgian who had fought in the Resistance against the Nazis, and a Hungarian who had served in the French Foreign Legion.

The first wave of mailbox bombings by the F.L.Q., in the spring of 1963, was mainly the work of a small number of French-Canadians who were still in their teens. There was one death – a night watchman who opened a garbage container at the wrong moment – and a military bomb disposal expert was seriously injured. The police investigation eventually produced sixteen guilty pleas in court and sentences ranging up to twelve years.

Terrorist activity continued in Quebec throughout the Sixties. The F.L.Q. of 1963 was followed within a few months by *l'Armée de Libération du Québec*, half-a-dozen young French-Canadians who robbed banks and stole military equipment from armouries until they were arrested in April, 1964. That summer, another *Armée Révolutionnaire du Québec* invaded a gun shop in Montreal and two people were killed as the terrorists were surprised by the police.

The international connections of Quebec terrorists, never of central importance, were illustrated by a bizarre event in February, 1965. A thirty-eight-year-old Montreal woman was arrested in New York after she had driven from Montreal with a load of dynamite for a group of black activists. Michelle Duclos, who had visited Algeria soon after it had obtained independence, had met the leaders of the New York group in Montreal and had agreed to assist them in blowing up the Statue of Liberty. One of the French-Canadians accused of stealing the dynamite committed suicide in prison.

The hold-ups, bombings and deaths by miscalculation continued throughout the decade. Most of the victims were ordinary French-Canadians: a sixty-four-year-old woman employed in the office of a shoe company that received a bomb during a labour dispute; and another woman who worked for the Department of National Defence in Ottawa who died simply because she happened to be near a terrorist bomb when it exploded. In the summer of 1966, a sixteen-year-old youth became the first and only member of the F.L.Q. to be killed "in action" when a bomb that he was trying to place outside a textile plant exploded prematurely.

As the police broke up F.L.Q. cells, the terrorist movement's underground newspaper *La Cognée* (The Hatchet) encouraged new recruits. For a short period in 1966, it appeared twice a month and published special editions for workers, university students and high school students.

"The F.L.Q., the bombs, the fireworks, that was a wonderful time!" stated a 1966 article in *La Cognée*.

> Things were happening in Quebec, it gave us the urge to get into the boat! We thought that something was going to happen at last.
>
> But today the F.L.Q. is nothing but a little paper appearing every two weeks! You hear these defeatist remarks at times. Others are on the point of saying it: no more bombs, no more F.L.Q. But their impressions are unjustified. They are due to the silence that the newspapers have wrapped around our actions for several months now.

In the spring of 1970, as police inspected an F.L.Q. cache of arms, money and dynamite in a summer home thirty-five miles north of Montreal, they came across evidence of a plan to kidnap the U.S. Consul General in Montreal.

"The disgusting representative of the U.S.A. in Quebec is in the hands of the F.L.Q.," proclaimed the *communiqué* that had been printed in advance. It also listed conditions for the release of the Consul General, including the liberation of "political prisoners" held in Quebec jails, settlement of labour disputes and payment of a "voluntary tax" of $500,000 in gold ingots.

The plan could have served as a blueprint for the political kidnappings and assassination of the following October, the final and most spectacular action of the F.L.Q. of the Sixties.

Terrorist activity was an integral part of the political upheaval in Quebec during the Sixties. As political independence movements appeared and disappeared during the first half of the decade, they attracted radical extremists as well as those who believed in conventional forms of political activity. The movements at first tended to welcome everyone. Convicted F.L.Q. terrorists were frequently identified in the newspapers as card-carrying members of the *Rassemblement pour l'indépendance nationale* and other political organizations.

After the 1964 gunshop raid when two men were killed, R.I.N. president Pierre Bourgault threatened the Montreal *Star* with a libel suit for suggesting that there might have been a link between the raid and the R.I.N. It was then more than a year since the movement had turned itself into a political party and announced that it would field candidates in the next Quebec election.

Like many of the smaller and more radical movements, the R.I.N. wrote much of its early history on the streets of Montreal and Quebec City. Demonstrations of solidarity with striking French-Canadian workers were a routine part of its activities. But its relatively moderate leftist policies and the quality of its leadership gave it a broader base of support than any of the other early movements. By 1964, the *Rassemblement pour l'indépendance nationale* had established its primacy among a clutter of separatist groups.

André d'Allemagne, its first president, a former journalist and translator who had once worked for the federal government in Ottawa, was a youthful, attractive and articulate spokesman. When he visited Paris in the fall of 1963, the influential newspaper *Le Monde* noted the occasion by publishing an article on Quebec independence under his byline. Several days later, d'Allemagne was listened to carefully by French journalists at a press conference sponsored by the International Committee for the Independence of Quebec, one of a number of pro-separatist groups that appeared in France during the Sixties and that were used as channels of communication and funds between Paris and Quebec.

D'Allemagne was succeeded in 1962 by Guy Pouliot, a Quebec City lawyer. Two years later, the leadership had been won by Pierre Bourgault, a young actor and journalist, a protégé of Gérard Pelletier's at *La Presse*, who became the principle spokesman for the separatist movement until Lévesque's arrival in 1967.

Despite its 1963 decision to engage in conventional political activity aimed at the 1966 Quebec election, the R.I.N. always remained to some extent a party of street demonstrators and radical extremists. Officially, the party opposed violence but it also provided a congenial milieu for young French-Canadians who were impatient with the tempo of the "quiet revolution."

In moments of crisis, Bourgault always kept the R.I.N. from going over the barricades. When Queen Elizabeth visited Quebec in October, 1964, it was Bourgault's responsibility alone, at one point, to decide between a conventional protest meeting and a clash with police that probably would have turned into a bloody riot. He chose the conventional protest.

The previous February, the president of the foundering *Parti Républicain du Québec*, Dr. Marcel Chaput, had told a Toronto interviewer that "some separatists had resolved to let her (the Queen) know brutally that she is not welcome in Quebec." When the journalist had asked if Quebec City could become another Dallas, Chaput had muttered darkly, "It could."

Eight months later, the atmosphere in Quebec City on the eve of the Queen's visit was explosive. After a noisy meeting and street demonstration in a working class district, Bourgault sent his followers home rather than ordering them to march into the city. The next day, sparse crowds along the Royal route were an eloquent expression of the Queen's uncertain welcome. Foreign journalists compared the thin lines of spectators and massed ranks of riot-equipped police with the usual welcome given to the Queen in Canada and concluded that another bit of Empire was on the brink of independence.

After the Quebec police stupidly and brutally clubbed the few demonstrators who did venture into the streets, Bourgault opened a speaking tour of the province that helped to make "The Saturday of the Truncheons" a day to remember in the annals of separatism.

In 1964, one of Bourgault's problems was to keep his followers in the streets but away from violence. The young separatist movement already presented a discouraging history of false starts and misguided leadership. The career of Dr. Marcel Chaput was a warning to Bourgault. Fired from his federal job with the Defence Research Board for making separatist speeches, the McGill-educated chemist had founded and lost control of his *Parti Républicain du Québec* by the end of 1963. Remnants of the party regrouped in 1964 as the more militant *Front Républicain pour l'Indépendance*, an organization that kept its membership and activities secret.

At the peaceful end of the separatist spectrum, the movement overlapped the concerns of some elected politicians. At the end of 1964, Bourgault led a five-man delegation before a special committee of the Quebec legislature that had been created a year earlier to study a revision of the Canadian federal system. The Montreal *Star*, noting that the R.I.N. presentation "won the grudging admiration of observers and committee members alike for its clarity, logical force and moderation," also drew attention to Lévesque's sympathetic interest in the separatist delegation.

A week after the R.I.N. appearance before the constitutional committee, Lévesque was quoted as saying, during a speech in Plattsburgh, New York, that "I'm not a separatist but I could become one."

In the eyes of at least some Canadians, his response to the terrorists in Quebec was also ambivalent.

Lévesque repeatedly denounced the young members of the F.L.Q. as "stupid, oafish fools," as he did in Toronto in 1963 a few weeks after the wave of mailbox bombings in Westmount. But the condemnation was usually accompanied by an attempt to explain the pressures that impelled some young Quebecers toward violence.

"Believe it nor not, I am a forty-year-old moderate," Lévesque told the Toronto audience, "and there are others, younger people, behind me who frighten me."

Many English-speaking Canadians took this kind of explanation as a warning, perhaps even as a threat. In May, 1964, when Lévesque spoke to a student audience at Montreal's Collège Sainte-Marie, a single phrase was enough to create a furore among apprehensive English-speaking Quebecers. Lévesque told the students that negotiations with Canada's Anglophone majority should be carried on "if possible without bombs or dynamite."

Earlier in the speech, he had said that "to succumb to the temptation of violence, to kill someone without reason, is a criminal act no matter how noble a principle is involved ... it is useless to try to create in Quebec, artificially, the climate of Cuba or Algeria." But little attention was paid by the English-language media to the context of Lévesque's remark. The Montreal *Star* accused Lévesque of saying, in effect, "not dynamite necessarily but dynamite if necessary."

Reaction to his speech was so violent that Lévesque defined his position more closely a few weeks later by reading a prepared statement over one of Montreal's English-language radio stations:

Quebec is, and must remain a democratic society ...

In this context, violence, that is physical violence and the method of terrorism, are both criminal and stupid. Their use also reveals a lack of courage along with a lack of sense ...

What it does require is a rather degrading absence of human dignity and contempt for human life, and the weakness of minds who have so little confidence in their own ideas that they're afraid to fight for them democratically.

Lévesque described the Quebec terrorists as "aliens – they've read about terrorism elsewhere, without any real knowledge of situations that brought it about, and which have absolutely nothing in common with our own.

"So they are isolated, and really reach no one," he said. "If what they do weren't so dangerous, they'd be more to be pitied than anything else."

But Lévesque also warned his English-speaking audience to guard against being "easily led into hysterical denunciation and even personal abuse against anyone whose ideas they dislike."

"Such people obviously do not understand the real strength of the desire for rapid and fundamental change in French Quebec," he said. "Quite obviously, also, they would far prefer a return to the old status quo of the quiet and conservative French Canada. They are tempted to use the terrorist fringe as a pretext for calling for a stop, and a return to some sort of 'quaint old Quebec.'"

It was symptomatic of the atmosphere in Quebec at that time that the Montreal *Star* rejected Lévesque's explanation.

"Admirable as it was," said the *Star*, "it does not wipe out the incitement to violence he indulged in two weeks before."

The *Star* continued to regard the Collège Saint-Marie speech as having opened the door "to the use of violence by a group of adolescents whose age and training alike lead them easily into extreme courses."

Having condemned nearly an entire generation of French-Canadians, and accused their parents and teachers of educating them for extremism, the newspaper hinted that Premier Lesage should seriously consider asking for Lévesque's resignation from the cabinet.

"We have had enough of demagogues blowing off steam as it suits them," the *Star* decided.

The next day, Gérard Pelletier signed an editorial in *La Presse* accusing the *Star* of "flagrant bad faith which disgraces the profession of journalism."

"To reject facts, to quote someone erroneously, to manipulate words to suit your own prejudices, have been the shameful practices of those who pretend to serve truth," he wrote.

Less than two weeks earlier, the *Star* had commented favourably on a

Pelletier editorial about the dangerous power of words in Quebec's volatile political atomosphere. The *Star* editorial of May 22 began: "Writing with his usual modesty and grace, Mr. Gérard Pelletier . . ." On June 3, the *Star* opened its editorial by saying: "The considerable powers of invective enjoyed by Mr. Gérard Pelletier . . . were employed against this newspaper yesterday."

The *Star* insisted on its right "to criticize or condemn the Minister of Natural Resources whenever his remarks seem to us to open the door to the kind of extremism which has marred Quebec's record now for more than a year."

The editors of the *Star*, illustrating their isolation from the French-Canadian community, confessed that they were unable to understand why their reaction to Lévesque's speech should have been so different from the reaction of their French-speaking neighbours.

"It set off a shock wave in English-Canada," wrote the *Star* editors. "It should have set off a shock wave in French-Canada.

"The trouble is," the *Star* continued, "that the decent moderates who write the best editorials in the French press today, who are its responsible spokesmen, are all old friends of René Lévesque.

"When they try to examine him objectively, old loyalties break in to cloud their vision."

If the *Star* had broadened the scope of "old loyalties" to include almost the whole French-Canadian community, it might better have understood the divisions between the two linguistic communities in Canada that Lévesque's speech had illuminated.

René Lévesque was among the leading protagonists of a communal adventure that affected every French-Canadian during the Sixties. So were the terrorists. French-Canadian readers of *La Presse* might quarrel with Lévesque's tactics, as they might abhor terrorism, but they knew instinctively that all the main actors of the "quiet revolution" were expressing, in total, all the varied and conflicting tendencies of the whole group. As far as the terrorists were concerned, most French-Canadians neither condemned them outright nor made heroes of them. They were "all in the family."

When Lévesque said that changes should occur "if possible without guns or dynamite," French-Canadians knew that he was expressing their own desire for peaceful and orderly evolution, as well as their own impatience. And they held that opinion as instinctively as Quebec's English-speaking community sensed a general threat to its own security in the changes that were altering the old political and commercial alliances of the province.

The Montreal *Star's* worried reaction to a single phrase in Lévesque's speech was a measure of the insecurity felt within its own community.

The French-speaking group's acceptance of Lévesque's words indicated its confidence in its own unity and stability.

In the first half of the Sixties, this stability was always beneath the surface as Quebec was caught up in the revolutionary game, and Canada with it, to a lesser extent. It was a time when even the most conservative politicians dabbled in innovation and radicalism.

When Lévesque was calling for an "associate state" relationship between Quebec and the rest of Canada in 1964, Premier Lesage was preparing to tour the western provinces to promote "particular status" – another catch-phrase that was used at the time to describe Quebec's political objectives in Confederation.

In the general election campaign of 1965, even the strongly federalist New Democratic Party supported the "two-nation theory" – another fashionable term that illustrated both the benevolence and vagueness of English-Canada's response to Quebec's new sense of special destiny. Like most of the other slogan-definitions of a new federalism, the "two-nation theory" appeared to recognize Quebec as the national homeland of French-Canadians without venturing very far into the practical implications of this position.

Attempts to define the terms of Quebec's "special status" in Confederation obsessed the Quebec Liberals after their defeat in 1966. They felt that it was imperative to locate a distinctive constitutional position for the party in response to the traditional, pragmatic Quebec nationalism of the new Premier, Daniel Johnson, and the tough federalism that Pierre Trudeau, Jean Marchand and Gérard Pelletier had brought to the Pearson government after their election in 1965.

It was in the framework of the Quebec Liberals' search for a satisfactory definition of "special status" that Lévesque made his initial definition of Quebec independence. He called it, confusingly enough, "sovereignty-association." But there was little confusion now about his ultimate political destination. It was the beginning of a new era both for Lévesque and the separatist movement.

XX
The Virgin Birth of the Parti Québécois

"Aie!" exclaimed a startled René Lévesque, according to a report in his own weekly column in *Dimanche-Matin*, when he opened his mail a few days after his departure from the Quebec Liberals in October, 1967. Out of an envelope postmarked Ottawa and bearing the crest of the Secretary of State tumbled one of the Centennial Medals awarded that year "for service to Canada" to about 20,000 Canadians, including all members of Parliament and the provincial legislatures.

History might yet show that Lévesque's award was one of the more appropriate. Even at the time, despite apprehension about Lévesque's personal impact on the scattered forces of separatism in Quebec, there was a widespread sense of relief that the great debate of the Sixties was crystallizing – that the question of separatism was moving into conventional political channels for a decision.

The editors of many Canadian newspapers, particularly those in western Canada, seemed to feel that Lévesque had performed, perhaps inadvertently, a service to his country. *The News* of Medicine Hat, Alberta, stated:

> Because we have confidence in the future of Canada, we cannot but rejoice in the decision of the Quebec Liberal Federation to reject separatism and to expel René Lévesque from its ranks ...
>
> The decision of the Liberals may signify that opinions about separatism are starting to crystallize among the population. This is a welcome development. Canadians are particularly anxious to know the attitudes of all parties toward Confederation.

"Since I quit the party about fifteen days ago, I feel much more relaxed," Lévesque told a newspaper reporter. "I feel that I'm ready to start afresh with something that I'll be able to carry forward."

The immediate beneficiaries of Lévesque's departure were his former colleagues among the Quebec Liberals. As soon as their 1967 convention ended, the constitutional question that had absorbed so much energy since 1960 began to fade into the background.

Although some commentators predicted that the failure of the 1967 convention to deal with Gérin-Lajoie's report on "special status" would mean trouble in the future, by the following spring the issue had all but disappeared. Even Gérin-Lajoie seemed to be relieved by the fact that constitutional issues "were remaining somewhat on the sidelines," as he said in April, 1968, leaving him a clearer field for his run at the Quebec Liberal leadership.

In the spring of 1968, Gérin-Lajoie and some of the other members of the St. Denis Club group were still having to deny rumours that they might ultimately join Lévesque's new movement. Their denials sometimes were vague enough to maintain the speculation.

But by the autumn, a year after the 1967 convention, positions had hardened considerably.

"Lévesque's option and mine are as different as night and day," Gérin-Lajoie had decided by this time. "Lévesque wants an independent Quebec within an association where Quebec will have the right of veto. That is real independence. My option is clearly federalist with a federal parliament responsible for almost all the matters that come under it within the present constitution."

The young economist Robert Bourassa, whom Lévesque had told friends in 1966 to keep an eye on as a prospective party leader, also disentangled himself slowly, in 1967 and 1968, from his recent history as a close collaborator in the preparation of Lévesque's option. So gradual was his retreat that four months after the October, 1967, convention, he was still wondering in public "whether Lévesque would have quit the party if it had not been for the Kierans' ultimatum on the constitutional question."

Bourassa continued for some time to insist that differences between himself and Lévesque related to methods rather than objectives, and to technical arguments about the monetary system of an independent Quebec. Even after Lévesque started to accuse Bourassa of "demagogy," the young economist-politician persisted in stressing the similarities rather than the differences between his "neo-federalism" and Lévesque's separatism.

Even less clear immediately after the Liberals' 1967 convention was the position of Jacques Parizeau, an important economic advisor to both Liberal and Union Nationale governments who admitted to having had "conversations" with Lévesque during the preparation of his separatist option. When Eric Kierans, speaking as an economist and also as president of the Quebec Liberal Federation, claimed that independence would cost Quebec $2,300,000,000 in the first five years, Parizeau had helped Lévesque to assemble statistics showing that an independent Quebec with a minor defence role would save $500,000,000 a year by leaving Confederation.

When journalists badgered Parizeau for his own opinion of Lévesque's option, the economist snapped, "I don't know yet. When I know exactly if I agree with it or not, I will say so."

After Lévesque made his decision in October, 1967, it became more and more difficult for Parizeau and thousands of other French-Canadians to remain uncommitted. The political confusion of the early Sixties was settling rapidly into three principal options: the old-fashioned, practical, conservative type of Quebec nationalism that the Union Nationale represented, based more on attitudes than constant constitutional objectives, the renewed federalism of the Quebec Liberals, and the left wing nationalism of Lévesque's movement. Particularly among the intellectual and economic elites of Quebec, Lévesque's decision posed a question that could not for long be ignored.

The architect of Lévesque's exit from the Quebec Liberal party, Eric Kierans, took his own leave soon after to make an unsuccessful attempt, against Pierre Trudeau, for the leadership of the federal Liberal party in April, 1968. By that time, Gérin-Lajoie, Bourassa, Pierre Laporte and other potential leaders among the Quebec Liberals were preparing for the retirement of Jean Lesage and their own campaigns to succeed him in 1970. Lévesque's departure made it almost certain that they would not have to run the Quebec Liberal leadership race over the constitutional hurdles that had preoccupied everyone before 1967.

While the Liberals benefited politically from Lévesque's departure, many separatists looked on his arrival on their side as a mixed blessing.

The separatists had viewed Lévesque as a possible leader since the early Sixties.

Pierre Bourgault, who had joined the *Rassemblement pour l'indépendance Nationale* in 1960, three weeks after it started, and who became its president in 1964, first met Lévesque in 1962 at a Liberal campaign meeting. The R.I.N. at that time had fewer than 500 members, and nearly all of them voted Liberal in the 1962 election because of Lévesque's presence in the cabinet.

After 1963, Bourgault saw Lévesque informally at least several times a year. By 1965, Lévesque was giving Bourgault and other separatists the impression that he was increasingly restless in the Liberal party. "He always said," recalled one, "that he would be quitting the Liberals soon, in three months, in six months ... this went on for years."

By 1966, with the R.I.N. and the more conservative *Ralliement Nationale* planning to contest their first election, some separatists were beginning to regard Lévesque as a more dangerous opponent than the confirmed federalists in the Lesage cabinet.

"He took our momentum away from us," explained one. "He was nationalist enough to seduce a lot of people. So we decided that Lévesque was nothing but a Liberal who was playing the nationalist chord to get votes."

"The honeymoon between René Lévesque and at least a part of the Quebec left is over," reported *La Presse* during the 1966 campaign.

A convention of Quebec leftist groups at that time denounced Lévesque for permitting the Liberals to exploit his reputation as a progressive, saying that this was merely the "paternalism of Duplessis" in a new guise. Bourgault accused Lévesque of condoning an electoral system that favoured the large parties and "muzzled" his own.

After the 1966 election, many separatists became extremely bitter about Lévesque. In a newspaper interview in the summer of 1967, Bourgault scornfully dismissed Lévesque as a vapid nationalist of no importance to the independence movement. Unfortunately for Bourgault, publication of the interview was delayed until a few days after Lévesque's split with the Liberals.

At the end of that year, when he was interviewed during a European tour, Bourgault predicted that all separatists would soon group together under Lévesque. However, he returned home to discover that Lévesque wanted little to do with him or his party.

"It was our 'bum' image that he really didn't like," recalled a former member of the R.I.N. executive. "We were always out in the streets demonstrating and Lévesque was completely against this."

It was soon clear that Lévesque intended to ignore the political structures that had evolved within the independence movement since 1960. He wanted to give his own party a fresh start.

A new party wasn't a new idea for Lévesque. Many of his conversations in 1962 and 1963 with Marchand, Pelletier, Laurendeau and Trudeau had concerned the need for an effective Quebec party of the left. The group had analyzed the failure of the socialist C.C.F. party to establish a base in Quebec after its foundation in English-speaking Canada in the Thirties.

In 1956, Trudeau had written that "the renewal of democracy in our province ought to originate outside the existing parties."

In the 1963 federal election, Trudeau had supported the New Democratic Party, the successor of the C.C.F., and had published denunciations of the Pearson Liberals' decision to accept nuclear arms from the United States; but the adherence of intellectuals such as Trudeau, and a few union officials, was all the C.C.F. or the N.D.P. had ever achieved in Quebec, except among the province's English-speaking minority.

The conclusion of Lévesque, Trudeau and the others in 1962 and 1963 was that an effective Quebec party of the left would have to originate in authentic Quebec aspirations. Lévesque has stated as much:

But there was nothing definite about ideas like that before the 1967 break with the Liberals. It was something in the back of one's mind. It was post-midnight political philosophy.

My attitude in 1967 was – let's go as far as we can with the Liberals and see what happens. But you could see that the whole party was being organized against the idea. So some thing had to be brewing in the back of your mind. We were becoming more and more convinced that our position was not only an option but the way we saw the future politically.

After the break with the Liberals in October, 1967, Lévesque moved swiftly and deliberately toward the founding of his own movement. The first step came two weeks later when fifty-four members of his old constituency association in the Montreal riding of Laurier, including the entire executive council, resigned from the Liberals to create *l'Association Laurier-Lévesque*. A similar organization, *l'Association Lévesque-Nouveau-Québec*, was formed by dissident Liberals several weeks later at Sept-Îles on the north shore of the St. Lawrence River.

On November 18-19, little more than a month after his departure from the Liberals, Lévesque presided over the birth of the *Mouvement Souveraineté-association* (M.S.A.) by 380 supporters during a weekend meeting at a Dominican monastery in Montreal.

While Lévesque moved quickly to gather his followers into a para-political organization, he was cautious in public about his ultimate objective. In a three-hour speech to a group of Montreal businessmen a few days before the M.S.A. was created, he talked only in general terms about the formation of a new party or "common front ... able to marry efficiently Quebec's urgent need for political freedom to its economic and social progress."

Lévesque placed more emphasis at this stage on the "association" part of his option than the "sovereignty" aspect. This had already caused trouble during a preliminary meeting with Bourgault to discuss the future of the established party and the new, nebulous movement that Lévesque had organized.

The break with the Liberals seemed to leave Lévesque, at first, in a contemplative, moderate frame of mind, as if the schism had temporarily satisfied his appetite for radical action. He repeatedly warned his supporters against "improvised and artificial" political organizations.

In a long interview with Pierre Olivier of *La Presse*, published at the beginning of November, 1967, Lévesque was able to consider his new position with cool detachment.

Olivier treated Lévesque as part of the "generation of the Fifties" that had prepared itself during the Duplessis years for the "explosion of 1960."

"There is perhaps less distance between Trudeau and Lévesque," stated Olivier, "than between Lévesque and some of the twenty-year-olds who belong today to various separatist organizations."

Lévesque told Olivier that he still regarded Trudeau, Pelletier and

Marchand as friends, and said that it was time to stop the old habit of Quebecers in Ottawa and Quebec calling one another traitors.

He talked also about the complexity and difficulty of modern government: "Notice how quickly men of thirty-five and forty years of age go grey in that harness ... it's no sinecure."

Pragmatism dominated his view of the future. Repeating Olivier's question, he said:

The type of society that we should have? It should be a society obsessed by the idea of efficiency. That's the only objective for a small people who want to have a chance of success in the world today.

On paper, it's easy to agree that what we need is a revolution to change the basis of society. But all that seems terribly theoretical to someone who is trying to grapple with reality. His job is to improve the quality of the instruments available to society and to keep his objectives as precise as possible.

Having made the radical jump to separatism, Lévesque seemed determined to emphasize his conservatism. This made it almost impossible to discuss common strategy with Bourgault and his followers. In fact, Lévesque had to be dragged to the negotiating table to deal with the R.I.N. and once there, he was content to let the delegations from each side embroil themselves in endless ideological arguments.

"Lévesque wanted to get most of the R.I.N. members but he didn't want the image or the history of the R.I.N.," recalled one of the men who negotiated for Lévesque with the R.I.N.

"It was very clear from the start that Lévesque hated our guts," said one of the R.I.N. participants.

We kept proposing things and he always found a way to get out of them.

But Lévesque didn't want to be known publicly as the one who broke off negotiations. And believe me, he's a very patient man when he wants something, and even more patient when he doesn't want something. And he's a formidable man at the discussion table, like a snake, brilliant.

"He hated the way we behaved," said another R.I.N. executive member. "Lévesque wanted to reassure people and he thought that we frightened them."

Lévesque had sound tactical reasons for dealing carefully with the R.I.N. It suited his purpose to have most of the extreme separatists bottled up there, making the job of controlling the M.S.A. easier and clearly defining the conservatism of Lévesque's own policies.

"At times, Lévesque expressed the idea that it wasn't a bad thing to have an extreme movement on our left," recalled one of his former asso-

160

ciates in the M.S.A. "It enabled him to say, 'Well, you see, there are people who are worse than we are.' "

Negotiations with the R.I.N. dragged on until June 24, 1968, when they were terminated by Pierre Trudeau who, less than three months earlier, had been chosen leader of the federal Liberal party and had assumed the office of Prime Minister. At the end of a successful election campaign that had resembled a Beatles tour at times of extreme "Trudeaumania," the Prime Minister decided to go ahead with plans to attend Montreal's evening parade on the feast of Saint Jean Baptiste, the patron saint of French Canada.

Lévesque called the decision "phenomenally stupid." It was certainly as open to question on moral grounds, as an incitement to violence, as it was undeniably right as a political tactic. On the night of the parade, the reviewing stand in front of the Municipal Library on Sherbrooke Street was a source of hypnotic attraction for Bourgault and his followers. They gathered in the darkness of Lafontaine Park on the opposite side of Sherbrooke Street, encouraging one another and making tentative rushes at the line of police guarding the reviewing stand.

And which side actually started the riot was as uncertain as it usually is. Suddenly the reviewing stand was bombarded by a hail of empty pop bottles as the police started to round up the demonstrators and drag them toward paddy wagons.

While the state-owned television network resolutely kept its on-air cameras trained on the parade, film cameramen recorded the brutal suppression of the demonstrators by police. Eventually the television audience did catch a few glimpses of the street action as well as the extraordinary scene on the reviewing stand: while the Mayor of Montreal and other dignitaries scrambled for shelter, Prime Minister Trudeau angrily shook himself free from the mass retreat and stood alone at the front of the stand, watching the demonstrators subside beneath the truncheons of the police.

The picture of a resolute French-Canadian federalist literally standing up to the separatists was the scene that reached television viewers across Canada on the late news that night and that flickered in their minds the next day as they gave Trudeau the first majority victory in a federal election since the Diefenbaker landslide of 1958. It was an irresistible picture to most English-speaking Canadians, as well as many French-Canadians, in that decade of uncertainty.

Two days after the election, Lévesque emerged from a long session with leaders of his movement to repudiate the actions of Bourgault and the R.I.N.

"Too many people are playing sorcerer's apprentice with violence," he said, "including many who ought to be among the most responsible of our leaders."

Charging that Bourgault had engaged in "unequivocal incitement to violence as a means of political action" in the days before the parade, Lévesque accused the R.I.N. of promoting "adventures in anarchy that disgrace everyone." He also blamed the organizers of the parade for inviting the Prime Minister. The only protagonist who escaped Lévesque's censure was Trudeau. Once the invitation had been made, said Lévesque, the Prime Minister had no alternative but to accept.

Lévesque also pointedly told reporters that his new separatist colleague in the Assembly, François Aquin, had not taken part in the M.S.A. meetings that had voted to censure Bourgault.

There had already been a major public confrontation with Aquin, two months earlier, and it had almost destroyed the new movement at its first general meeting. The point at issue had been the continued existence of English-language schools in an independent Quebec – a policy favoured by Lévesque.

Sentiment among the 1,200 M.S.A. delegates meeting in April at the Maurice Richard Arena in east end Montreal had run strongly against the "Lévesque" line adopted by the M.S.A. up to that time. When a cultural affairs workshop at the convention proposed to permit the existence of English-language schools in an independent Quebec only during a transition period, Lévesque had had to place his own leadership on the line to bring the delegates closer to his own position.

At the end of the meeting, both Lévesque and Aquin had set conditions on their continued membership in the movement. Aquin had said that he would continue to work in the M.S.A. until the founding convention of the separatists' new political party later that year, in an effort to influence the policies of the new party. Lévesque had been reported in the newspapers as threatening to quit his own movement if the radicals prevailed.

The dispute over language and education tended to obscure the convention's impressive advance toward the social, political and economic elements of the new party's platform. The main planks were a "negotiated and peaceful" achievement of independence and a "flexible" treaty of association with the rest of Canada; development of the state's role in Quebec's economy; and a list of such progressive social measures as a higher minimum wage, equal pay for women, and universal and total medical coverage under a government health insurance program.

Some of the younger, more radical delegates had referred to Lévesque that weekend as a "crypto-federalist," sounding curiously like the older members of the Liberal party who had accused Lévesque of "crypto-separatism" only a year before.

"We'll go with Lévesque as long as it's true that he's the only one who can lead us to power," a twenty-three-year-old delegate had said. "But later on, we'll know what to do ..."

An older observer, Claude Ryan of *Le Devoir*, had been more interested in comparing the M.S.A. with nationalist movements of a quarter-century earlier such as *la Ligue pour la Défense du Canada* and the *Bloc-Populaire*. He noted "the same nationalist fervour, the same loyalty to French Canada ... the same support drawn preponderantly from the middle classes."

In one respect, Ryan observed, this gave strength and authenticity to Lévesque's movement. It was rooted "deeply in the conscience and the political tradition of French Canada." But it also indicated that the M.S.A. could be hindered by the same limited appeal that had prevented the earlier movements from developing into enduring political institutions. Lévesque, like his nationalist predecessors, seemed to be attracting a large following among intellectuals, civil servants, the professional class and radicals without creating an appreciable base of support among the workers and rural population of Quebec.

Divisions within the M.S.A. on the language question reflected this weakness. For students, teachers and other intellectuals, the status of the French language in Quebec was a matter of personal and passionate concern. It was an issue that loomed large in Montreal, where the two language groups were in direct and constant competition. But even in the metropolis, most ordinary French-Canadians had little contact with the English language and no social contact at all with English-speaking people. In smaller urban centres and in rural areas, the language issue was extremely remote from the practical concerns of French-Canadians.

The same division in another guise made itself felt at the very beginning within the structures of the new movement. By early 1968, the M.S.A. had established itself in modest quarters on a residential section of St. Denis Street in the eastern central part of Montreal. After the main office had been opened on one side of the street, several apartments were rented in a building across the street to accommodate the party's research and records centre.

"Right away, we had two groups," recalled a former M.S.A. official. "The people in the research centre were saying that those in the main office were just old-style political hacks, while the ones in the main office talked derisively about the 'poets' across the street."

Creating a viable political organization was Lévesque's first objective. He had no intention of founding another nationalist debating society and he was supported in this by most members of his provisional executive, including many political veterans who had worked with Lévesque in the Liberal party or his own constituency organization. Personal loyalty and affection for Lévesque had been important elements in their own decisions for separatism. They saw no contradictions in organizing the new movement around what their opponents in the M.S.A. began to call "the religion of René."

In the spring of 1968, Lévesque seemed to be everywhere in Quebec. Contacts in almost every constituency were selected from lists of labour union leaders, activist teachers and students – all those who had been at the founding M.S.A. meeting in Montreal in 1967 and a special list that Lévesque and his old associates had drawn up of Liberals who had belonged to his "fan club" when he had been in the Liberal party. Provisional executives were appointed in most constituencies, membership cards were issued, and policy discussions were devoted to the timetable that would lead up to the founding convention of the new party in October, 1968.

Outside of Montreal and Quebec, the most promising territories for the new organization were Chicoutimi in the Lac St. Jean region north of Quebec, and Rouyn-Noranda in northwestern Quebec, both industrial and mining communities with strong unions; Sherbrooke in the Eastern Townships and Trois-Rivières between Quebec and Montreal, industrial cities with university and college communities; industrial and semi-rural areas near Montreal such as Sorel-Tracy and Joliette; and the south shore suburbs of Montreal where the bungalows of the growing French-Canadian middle class were spreading over farmland and orchards.

As the party organization grew, the "poets" watched uneasily from their quarters across the street from Lévesque's office, dismayed at the way he free-wheeled through the province, speaking his own mind on any subject, as always, and consulting anyone who cared to stop and talk with him. The theorists of the party soon discovered what Premier Lesage and his cabinet colleagues had had to contend with only a few years earlier.

This was as true in practical affairs as in political principles. Lévesque continued to be late for party meetings, to make himself unavailable in the morning until he had decided that it was time to start work, and to jealously guard his private affairs from the intrusions of the political schedule. Various systems were designed by his separatist colleagues to keep track of his extra-party activities and to organize his time more efficiently but none of them was particularly successful.

"I always thought it was a mistake to try to treat Lévesque as simply a salesman for the party," said a former executive member of the M.S.A. who had little sympathy for the theorists.

I remember hearing Lévesque several times, in preambles to speeches in those days, say that he hoped that he wasn't going to stray too far from the party line. I always thought that this was wrong.

Lévesque had to be able to give his own opinion. He was a member of the party, too, as well as its leader. The theorists all talked about 'participation of the base' but wasn't Lévesque also a part of that base?

164

The theorists, on their side, were honestly concerned that Lévesque's popularity made it difficult for the party to undertake the grassroots organization and ideological formation that they wanted. After the M.S.A. meeting of April, 1968, when the language issue almost wrecked the movement, a young Montreal delegate, in a letter to *Le Devoir*, had expressed his concern that the Lévesque phenomenon in the M.S.A. was simply another expression of the French-Canadian instinct to "unconsciously look for a fascist government ... and to put the whole weight of our impotence on the shoulders of a single individual while refusing to take our collective responsibilities in our own hands."

Lévesque's disregard for ideology was illustrated shortly after the Saint Jean Baptiste riot in June, 1968 when the *Ralliement National* was absorbed into the M.S.A. without any of the prolonged negotiation that had marked the futile dealings with Bourgault and the R.I.N.

In its political philosophy, the conservative *Ralliement National* was at the opposite end of the spectrum from both the R.I.N. and the M.S.A. It was led by a former member of the Social Credit Party, Gilles Grégoire, who had served as Créditiste leader Réal Caouette's lieutenant in the federal parliament after his election in 1962. The sleek, adroit Grégoire had nothing in common with Lévesque in 1968 except a consistent history as a Quebec nationalist and an appreciation of political realities, but that was enough to bring them together. The assimilation of Grégoire's party was negotiated by the two leaders on a July weekend.

Grégoire's arrival on the scene was greeted with suspicion by the "poets" of Lévesque's movement. *Le Devoir* had reported "irritation and uneasiness" among many separatists about this alliance between Lévesque, "the democrat of the quiet revolution," and Grégoire "who has never repudiated his Social Credit principles and who, regardless of whether it is true or not, is viewed everywhere as an opportunistic demagogue."

There also had been skepticism about the real value of Grégoire's assistance. At the time of the merger, the M.S.A. had claimed to have about 13,000 members. This total had been achieved from an initial membership list of about 500 at the end of 1967, and represented by far the largest separatist movement in existence anywhere except in the mind of Gilles Grégoire. Grégoire boasted of having 25,000 members in his *Ralliement National*, and claimed that most of them were in rural areas where the M.S.A. was weak.

Unlike the M.S.A., the R.N. lacked proper membership records. By September, Grégoire's opponents in the M.S.A. were letting the press know that the effective membership of the R.N. was less than 5,000. Even this was an exaggeration. One former official of the M.S.A. claimed finally that his own estimate of R.N. membership, at the time, was about 500.

In terms of numbers, as the 1966 election had indicated, the R.I.N. would be a more valuable acquisition for Lévesque than the R.N. Total membership of the R.I.N. was usually estimated in 1968 at about 8,000, but this figure included everyone who had ever been a member of the party at any time since 1960. The true membership figure was less than half of this, and many of these active R.I.N. members already had joined Lévesque's group by the summer of 1968.

Grégoire had been accepted by Lévesque because he had promised to deliver votes in rural Quebec, and because his conservative image was an asset for the kind of party that Lévesque had in mind. The R.I.N., by contrast, was strong in Lévesque's own urban territory, and a merger or alliance with the R.I.N. would strengthen the radical character of the M.S.A. at a time when Lévesque was convinced that this would be electorally disastrous.

As the date for the founding convention of the new party approached, a language dispute in the Montreal suburb of St. Léonard emphasized one of the basic distinctions between Lévesque and the R.I.N., and between Lévesque and many members of his own party.

St. Léonard was a working class suburb where the French-speaking majority co-existed uneasily with a substantial Italian-Canadian community whose children attended English-language schools along with more than 90 per cent of the children of all immigrants in Quebec. In St. Léonard, a proposal to reassign school facilities between the two language groups brought all the underlying conflicts to the surface. *Le Mouvement pour l'Intégration Scolaire* (M.I.S.) sprang into existence to demand that the children of immigrants be forced to attend French-language schools.

The M.I.S. was also inspired by some relatively new population statistics. Calculating the effects of a declining birth rate in Quebec and the assimilation of immigrants to the English-speaking community, some demographers at the University of Montreal had predicted that the city, by the year 2000, might once again be dominated by its English-speaking population as it had been in the nineteenth century.

The arguments in St. Léonard of Montreal's English-speaking community in favour of parental freedom of choice in education carried little weight with French-Canadians who were frightened by the prospect of losing political control of a city where the English already controlled the economy. In the centre of this dispute in 1967 was the Italian community of St. Léonard whose choice of school was dictated by obvious practical reasons, and who had little understanding of the centuries-old conflict that raged around them.

It would have been easy and popular for Lévesque to support the M.I.S. Instead, he tried to distinguish between the general objectives of the M.I.S., which he supported, and its tactics in St. Léonard, which he deplored. He thought that St. Léonard was useful as a means of alerting and educating French-Canadians but he also believed that English-speaking Quebecers should not be forced to send their children to French-language schools. Lévesque enraged the M.I.S. leaders by saying that outsiders were manipulating the French-language students of St. Léonard for their own political purposes.

"I could understand what they were up against in St. Léonard," Lévesque later recalled.

It was a cancerous case from their point of view. But they didn't offer a political attitude that we could take hold of. It led nowhere.

Eventually we aim to assimilate as many English-speaking Canadians as possible into the French-language mainstream. But you don't do that by beating them over the head and saying you've got to speak French. You do that by having a prosperous society, jobs. If things work out well in Quebec, there's no reason why they won't assimilate.

Lévesque stayed away from St. Léonard while his closest associates in the M.S.A. joined the demonstrators on the streets of the suburb, and while many local M.S.A. associations passed resolutions of support. When he finally visited the school occupied during the protest by French-speaking students, it was one of the few times during his political career that he was booed and jeered by French-Canadians. Leaders of the M.I.S. publicly burned their M.S.A. membership cards.

"It was a dramatic and difficult time for Lévesque," said one of his former associates in the M.S.A. "He was torn apart by the effort to find a position somewhere between Bourgault and the Liberal government.

"When he saw what was going on in St. Léonard, he asked himself: Is this the kind of intolerance that we want in Quebec?

"And the bad reception by the students made him feel that he was getting old. A few weeks after that, he started to talk again about getting out of politics."

In September, 1968, the R.I.N. announced that it was no longer interested in a merger with the M.S.A., mainly because of Lévesque's stand on minority language rights. At a September meeting to celebrate the eighth anniversary of the R.I.N., François Aquin announced that he was retiring from politics, and hailed the R.I.N. as "the only true independence party in Quebec."

Celebrating the anniversary with Pierre Bourgault were Marcel Chaput, the original "martyr" of the cause; André d'Allemagne, the first president of the R.I.N. in 1960; and Pierre Renaud, secretary-general of the R.I.N. and one of the brightest young men of the movement. Save for Lévesque, the R.I.N. contained the true succession and orthodoxy of the independence movement; but without Lévesque, it had no future. Its anniversary celebration was a piece of nostalgic bravado.

With Aquin in retirement and most of the leftist radicals still engaged in the R.I.N., the founding convention of Lévesque's new party in October, 1968, was relatively serene. It was, as Lévesque said in his opening speech, a "rendez-vous of adult and responsible citizens." He promised that the new party would be neither an "academic club" nor a place where "the passion of a great cause degenerates into improvised agitation."

Even the language question was resolved without drama or bitterness by the 800 delegates as they recognized the right of Quebec's English-speaking minority to have schools in its own language in a nation where French would be the only official language. A resolution to reduce progressively state funds to English-language schools was easily defeated.

"We'll treat the English people the way that they have treated us for 200 years," said one delegate. "We're going to permit them to educate themselves in English, but then they're going to have to work in French."

The convention went a step farther than the M.S.A. meeting the previous April when it stated that an electoral victory for the party would be, in effect, a declaration of sovereignty by Quebec. Only the "modalities of applying this acquired sovereignty" would be negotiated with Canada by the government of an independent Quebec. The M.S.A.'s original position, and one that Lévesque's party eventually would return to, had been that an electoral victory would provide only a mandate for a separatist government to negotiate Quebec's "accession to independence" over a period of time.

Delegates spent most of the weekend describing the utopian features of an independent Quebec under a social democratic government – everything from salaries for doctors to nationalization of urban real estate for housing. Then they voted on a name for the new party, Lévesque had let it be known that *Parti Souverainiste* was his own choice but the convention gave 285 votes to *Parti Québécois*, 131 votes to Lévesque's choice and 84 votes to *Parti Souveraineté-Association*.

While journalists covering the convention were impressed by the seriousness of the delegates, they criticized the academic tone of their debates.

"There was very little discussion about the policies of the government now in power," wrote Michel Roy of *Le Devoir*, "and even less about measures to combat it."

He quoted an organizer of the Union Nationale party as saying, "At one time, we were worried that the televised proceedings of the convention might upset the average voter. But for the time being, we feel reassured. The majority of Quebecers won't go for that. It was much too intellectual, thank God!"

"The party is full of teachers," wrote David Dent, the Montreal *Gazette's* Quebec City correspondent, "and they seem intent on running Quebec a bit like they run their classrooms.

"They say the people should make the decisions but they spent Saturday debating the most picayune aspects of policy, before they even got within sight of the historical point where they may be able to consult the people."

Only 12 per cent of the membership of the M.S.A., before the convention, had been identified as coming from the working class.

"On the day after its birth," reflected Claude Beauchamp of *La Presse*, "the Parti Québécois seems clearly to be the political movement of a single class in our society, the white collar workers, the intellectuals and the professions."

The creation of the *Parti Québécois* (P.Q.) had an immediate and totally unexpected effect on the R.I.N. Watching the P.Q. convention on television, Bourgault telephoned the secretary-general of his party, Pierre Renaud, to ask, "Are you thinking the same thing as I am?" Renaud said, "Yes." Several days later, at a meeting of his executive, Bourgault asked them, "Do we go into an election like this, or do we do something?"

Prodded by Bourgault, the executive agreed to try to kill their own party at its annual convention in less than two weeks.

Despite opposition from his own radical wing, Bourgault's resolution to disband the party was carried by a vote of 227 to 50.

"For the last time in my life, I shout: *Vive le R.I.N.!*" cried Bourgault. "For the first time in my life, I shout *Vive le Parti Québécois!*"

The practical reason for Bourgault's enthusiasm was that half to two-thirds of the R.I.N. members already were members of the P.Q.

The sudden, formal disappearance of the R.I.N. came as an unpleasant surprise to Lévesque. For once, he was at a loss for words, at least in public. In private, a close friend of Lévesque's told Bourgault two weeks after the convention that "he had never seen Lévesque so enraged."

At an oyster party in his own riding a few weeks later, Lévesque refused to be photographed with Bourgault. At subsequent conventions of his party, he made every effort to prevent Bourgault from being elected to the P.Q. executive. It was only after Bourgault conducted a futile but respectable election campaign in 1970 against the Quebec Premier, Robert Bourassa, that Lévesque began to relent and eventually agreed to work with him on the Parti Québécois executive.

A few months before the 1970 election, Bourgault impulsively insisted on a face-to-face confrontation in Lévesque's office. It lasted about forty-five minutes and Bourgault later told a friend that "no man in the world had ever humiliated me to that extent."

Lévesque told Bourgault that he didn't represent 300 people in Quebec, that his hands were bloody from the violence of the Sixties, and that he would never appear with him on a public platform. Finally, Lévesque told him to "go home, like Aquin, get out of the party."

There were sound political reasons for Lévesque's dislike of Bourgault. The R.I.N. leader had singled out Lévesque as a special menace to Quebec independence during his last years in the Liberal cabinet. As a member of the P.Q., Bourgault would keep alive the identification with F.L.Q. terrorism that had damaged his own party in the 1966 election. Lévesque complained to his own colleagues in the M.S.A. after 1968 that Bourgault's statements continued to feed "that kind of distortion."

But some of the reasons for Lévesque's aversion were more personal. Bourgault's dramatic platform style and his genius as a coiner of slogans were detested by Lévesque who shared, with Pierre Trudeau, Gérard Pelletier and other members of his own generation, a hateful memory of the old-time soapbox oratory of the Quebec politicians of the Fifties.

During the negotiations with the R.I.N., Lévesque had been angered by the R.I.N.'s theoretical certainty "that independence had to be a virginal kind of thing, pure and total," and by the insinuation that Lévesque had prostituted the idea of independence by trying to sell it to the rest of Canada.

The sudden suicide of the R.I.N. looked to Lévesque as if Bourgault was trying to have the last laugh. By dissolving the R.I.N., Bourgault had simply ignored Lévesque's objections to the merger. Now the Parti Québécois would have to cope with the radical remnants of the R.I.N. as well as extremists in future who would hang around the fringes of the P.Q. because there was no place else to go.

"I would still like them to start a party on the left," Lévesque said years later. "It would be damn useful but you can't force people to cut their own throats. The radicals are still playing the game in a typically traditional way, talking very loud and doing very little."

None of these circumstances fully explain the virulence of Lévesque's rejection of Bourgault in 1968. Perhaps it had something to do with Bourgault's tendency to treat the forty-six-year-old Lévesque, at that time, as an elder statesman of the separatist movement or, worse still, as an old star introduced into a new act to help attract the public.

When Lévesque broke with the Liberals in 1967, Bourgault had told journalists that he would gladly make way for Lévesque at the head of an independence movement because the former Liberal minister was older than he was and, consequently, more pressed for time.

Those who knew Lévesque well suspected that he found this elaborate courtesy on the part of Bourgault more unforgivable than anything in the younger man's political record.

XXI
The 1970 Election:
The "Rhodesian" Campaign

René Lévesque's commitment to separatism in 1967 substantially altered the character and electoral prospects of the movement.

Up to that time, separatist organizations had ranged from dangerous and disreputable to barely respectable. Their leaders had been unknowns who owed their political reputations to their separatist activities. The only exception to this rule, before Lévesque, had been Gilles Grégoire, and his previous career as a leading figure in the right-wing Social Credit movement in Quebec had made him unacceptable to most young separatists.

Lévesque came to separatism with an unassailable record of achievement as a Quebec cabinet minister. He was widely regarded as a politician of rare integrity. In a province noted for political corruption and public cynicism, among both the English and French of Quebec, Lévesque was in a class by himself, a saint to his friends and the devil incarnate to his enemies.

The reputation and personal following that Lévesque brought to the independence movement was a mixed blessing. He was the first separatist leader who appeared to be indispensable. Under his leadership, it became increasingly difficult to estimate accurately the growth of support for independence. After 1967, the future of the movement was always assessed, to some extent, in relation to Lévesque's own political future.

Opponents of independence immediately recognized the authority and respectability that Lévesque gave to the option of separatism. Several months after his break with the Liberals, when Quebec labour leaders paid him a formal visit, the Montreal *Star* warned that

> while the idea of sovereignty plus economic union might not have any great appeal to people intimately concerned with bread and butter is-

sues of work and unemployment, René Lévesque, one of the few cabinet ministers, past or present, with any real feeling for them and their problems, has a very distinct appeal.

The two must not be allowed to become confused.

In September, 1969, a public opinion poll commissioned by the Montreal *Star* in Montreal, Quebec City and Trois-Rivières, showed that Lévesque was the second choice of respondents who were asked to select, from a list of six, the politician best suited to be Premier. The first choice was Claude Wagner, a former Justice Minister in the Lesage cabinet who would come within a few votes of winning the federal Conservative leadership in 1976. Among Montreal respondents, Lévesque was the first choice.

In the following month, a Gallup poll in Quebec gave him a 35 per cent "favourable" rating against 41 per cent who were listed as "unfavourable" to him and 24 per cent who were undecided.

Polls showed that Lévesque's personal following was consistently larger than the number of avowed separatists in the population, which remained fairly constant throughout the Sixties, at about 15 per cent.

In the 1966 election, hindered by poor organization, a shortage of campaign funds, and a leadership of limited appeal, the R.I.N. and R.N. parties had captured only about half the separatist support shown by the public opinion polls. Lévesque gave the movement the prospect of holding this committed support while attracting new votes from people who were suspicious or afraid of the idea of independence.

In July, 1969, a survey in Quebec by journalists of *Le Devoir* and the Toronto *Telegram* led the Montreal newspaper to conclude that "the Parti Québécois isn't really considered to be a separatist party by French-Canadians." Much of its strength, said *Le Devoir,* was in Lévesque's reputation as "the embodiment of new hope" and in the fact that many Quebecers regarded him as a true leader.

Lévesque's own commitment to independence was qualified. In 1968, his emphasis on the "association" aspect of his sovereignty proposal persuaded many people that he was merely an exotic type of federalist. As the years passed, the debate about whether Lévesque was more nationalist than socialist, or *vice versa*, was as popular as it was inconclusive.

It remained a question that his own party felt compelled to try to answer at every annual convention, but Lévesque never hesitated to show his impatience with those of his followers who "waste the credibility that we have on amateurish excitements."

"We have to look like a new and professional party," he reminded them at the start of the 1969 convention.

Not all the internal battles in the party ended in victory for the leader.

The effort to keep the party from running to ideological extremes produced many casualties, particularly among men of Lévesque's generation who had joined him when he left the Liberals and who had helped to lay the foundations of a viable party. Lévesque's personal intervention was not enough, at the 1969 convention, to save the party's policy committee from abolition by younger members who regarded it as undemocratic. The committee had been headed by Marc Brière, a lawyer and a veteran of the Quebec Liberal policy committees of the Fifties and Sixties who had left the Liberals in 1967 largely because of his personal regard for Lévesque.

"The evolution of the party demoralized many good men," recalled one of its central figures in those early years.

It was easy for a young teacher to waste one or two years arguing about ideology but it was a different matter for a lawyer or businessman who was giving up time, money and a great deal of family life for the sake of the party.

I remember a restaurant owner in Rouyn-Noranda who gave a large part of his time and income to the party for two years but who was treated with contempt because he wasn't able to spend hours discussing policy resolutions. They lost many people because of that kind of thing.

On a personal level, this became a serious problem for Lévesque. There were fewer and fewer people in the party of his own age and with the same political memories.

"He was always asking about the health of Brière and the others," recalled the same former colleague. "Some of us went through personal depressions as a result of our experiences in the party."

An important addition to the party in 1969 was Jacques Parizeau, a professor of political economy at the University of Montreal and a former economic advisor to successive Quebec governments. Parizeau had also continued to work as a consultant for the federal government up to the time of his commitment to separatism, and perhaps past it. His influence in the party grew during the Seventies until he was widely regarded as one of the likeliest successors to Lévesque. Parizeau was later joined by Claude Morin, chief advisor on federal-provincial relations to four Quebec premiers. Parizeau and Morin enabled the party to produce an informed and professional economic and constitutional critique of federalism that bore little resemblance to the wild ideological assaults of the separatists of the early Sixties.

As Parizeau joined forces with Lévesque, another economist, former associate and former advisor to Lévesque began his successful drive for the leadership of the Quebec Liberal party. From an initial disagreement with Lévesque in 1967 about the monetary system of Lévesque's "Canadian Union," Robert Bourassa had developed the position that independence would be less profitable for Quebec than continuing the economic and political union with the other provinces. As his own leadership convention drew near, at the end of 1969, Bourassa made opposition to separatism his main theme, promising to work for the destruction of the Parti Québécois.

The political debate between Bourassa and Lévesque, although bitter at times, took place against a faded background of personal friendship. There was no such moderating influence when events brought Lévesque into confrontation with Pierre Trudeau, his old antagonist of Jean Marchand's Friday night "club" of the early Sixties. Having described Trudeau as an inconsequential "hippy" when he was chosen federal Liberal leader in 1968, Lévesque dismissed his majority victory in the national election that year as being of little interest to Quebec. Perhaps it would delay independence "for a few months," he said.

In the early Sixties, Trudeau and Lévesque had steadily disagreed about the origins and effects of Quebec nationalism. In the later Sixties, the unfinished debate was resumed before a national audience, with no noticeable increase in sympathy or understanding on either side.

Trudeau saw the separatist movement as an expression of "the profound insecurity and ancient fears" of the French-Canadian people, and as an anachronistic attempt to "shut the doors and block the frontiers" against the outside world. For Lévesque, the movement was exactly the opposite: an escape from the stifling restrictions of Confederation to the freedom and responsibility of adult nationhood.

Both men looked at the history of French Canada since the conquest, saw the same story of "shame and humiliation," and reached opposite conclusions. Each saw freedom in his own option, and saw the other as a prisoner of Quebec's past.

Perhaps a more fundamental difference between the two men was rooted in racial heritage. In contrast to Lévesque's French-Canadian ancestry, Trudeau carried in his bloodstream, in his speech, and in his mannerisms the legacy of his Scottish-Canadian mother. He personified the dual nature of Quebec society. And it was this duality, the existence of this large and relatively wealthy English-speaking minority in Quebec that was, from the outset, an almost insuperable barrier to any party that aimed at Quebec independence through an electoral victory.

Calculating and accommodating the political strength of the English-speaking minority had become an instinctive art for successful Quebec politicians. A typical assessment of political reality was given to Lévesque before he left the Liberals by Lucien Saulnier, a haberdasher who had become the tough chairman of Montreal's executive committee at the right hand of Mayor Jean Drapeau. Saulnier remembers telling Lévesque, in the 1964-66 period when they met to discuss federal-provincial problems, that it was easier to change existing political structures in Quebec than to create new ones.

"Always remember," he said, "that almost 25 per cent of the voters in this province are English-speaking. A separatist party could never win 1 per cent of this 25 per cent. So you're left with the prospect of having to get about 75 per cent of the remaining vote in order to have a bare majority, and that's impossible."

In the early Seventies, the French-English "numbers' game" became even more topical than usual. The declining birth rate of French-Canadians, and the ability of the English-speaking community to attract nine out of ten immigrants to the Quebec province, began to cast doubt on the ability of French-Canadians to hold their own in Montreal. Demographers at the University of Montreal forecast that even under the most favourable conditions, assuming a minimum flow of immigrants into the city, the French-speaking element in Montreal would decrease from 66.2 per cent in 1966 to 60 per cent by the year 2000. Assuming larger flows of immigration, the demographers warned that the French-speaking proportion could drop as low as 52.7 per cent by the end of the century. This would return the city almost to the point it had reached in the middle of the nineteenth century, when English-speaking people accounted for more than half its population.

"When you are just over half, you're finished, especially if you're economically weak," Lévesque had warned as early as 1968. "We are on the road to becoming a second Louisiana."

After a new English-language radio station was established in Montreal in the Sixties by a Newfoundland broadcaster, Lévesque drew attention to the fact that there were now more English than French radio stations in "our so-called second largest French-language city in the world–city of happy imbeciles that we are.

"Good God! We've been colonized by Newfoundland!" he cried. "At least being colonized by the United States is semi-respectable."

In an attempt to cope with vociferous demands from French-Canadian radicals who wanted to legislate English out of official existence in Quebec, the Union Nationale government of Premier Jean-Jacques Bertrand introduced Bill 63 in the National Assembly in October, 1969. Bertrand himself had grown up in the Eastern Townships between Montreal and the U.S. border, the last stronghold of the English in rural Quebec, and Bill 63 reflected his own acceptance of Quebec's bilingual character as well as the conservative nature of his government. It provided for measures to improve the teaching of French in Quebec and to encourage the use of French in business and industry, but it also respected the traditional right of Quebec parents to send their children to English or French schools, depending on their own preference.

The bitter debate over Bill 63 saw the government lose one of its members, Jérôme Proulx, to the Parti Québécois, giving Lévesque a seconder for his motions in the Assembly.

As the controversy in St. Léonard had shown, Lévesque's opposition to the unilingual movement was unshakable. He defended the historical right of Quebec's English-speaking population to a publicly-financed English-language school system. But he also believed that it was suicidal for French-Canadians to leave this English-language system wide open to children from their own group and to immigrant children. French-Canadians and immigrants, declared Lévesque, should be required to send their children to French-language schools.

Unrestricted freedom to choose the language of education was described by Lévesque as "fundamentally vicious" in its effects on the French-speaking majority.

The language legislation polarized opinion in Quebec, sending a spurt of new members into the Parti Québécois. Lévesque claimed that membership applications during the debate on Bill 63 increased from 700 to 2,000 a week.

By its second convention in October, 1969, the Parti Québécois bore little resemblance to the groups of "little bearded intellectuals" that had preceded it. According to Claude Beauchamp of *La Presse*, it was now a party "capable of thinking in electoral terms."

"If the Parti Québécois were not proposing independence," said the Montreal *Star* in an editorial, "it's stand would make sense."

Despite internal difficulties with radicals from the old R.I.N. and opposition between "organizers" and "poets," the Parti Québécois entered the election year of 1970 with a relatively moderate program and public image, a total membership approaching 40,000 and a broad base of financial support that enabled it to budget for administrative expenses of $100,000 in 1970, an equal amount to purchase television time, and $1,000,000 for the expected election campaign. The party was able to stand on its own feet financially, and they were clean.

In 1967, in order to start his organization, Lévesque had accepted $10,000 from an old nationalist sympathizer in St. Hyacinthe, a small industrial city near Montreal, who had made a fortune by selling his propane gas distribution system to U.S. interests. There were also loans from time to time from wealthy members of the party such as Guy Joron (a successful P.Q. candidate in the Montreal riding of Gouin, in 1970). But as a general rule, contributions were limited to less than $1,000 and the party drew up its own "black list" of contractors, architects and others who had contributed heavily to the Liberal and Union Nationale parties.

A backhanded compliment to Lévesque's personal honesty was paid in September, 1969, by Pierre Laporte, former minister of Municipal Affairs in the Lesage cabinet and a contender against Bourassa for the leadership of the Liberal party. Laporte claimed that a P.Q. organizer, in accepting a cheque for $1,000 from a consulting engineer without following the party's rules by consulting a senior party official, had told the donor, "All these rules are just to keep Lévesque quiet. When we need money, we take it."

At this time there was also an offer of financial support from France, through channels that had existed between the *Ralliement Nationale* and certain groups in France.

"The offer came from a movement that was very close to de Gaulle," recalled one of the party's officials, "and it was a good offer–more than we needed–a question of hundreds of thousands of dollars, paid in instalments."

The offer was quietly investigated by a member of the party's executive who went to France in 1969, and found to be serious. But it was rejected by Lévesque, who felt that the proposal was politically dangerous and who, in any case, had never had a strong attachment to France.

After more than two years of recruiting members, raising funds, organizing the party at the local level and creating a moderate left-of-centre platform, Lévesque and his followers were prepared for their first campaign when Premier Bertrand announced that the election would be held on April 29, 1970. In fact, as far as Lévesque was concerned, the campaign had really started soon after Robert Bourassa's election as Liberal leader on January 17 of that year. Perhaps because of their earlier close association, or Bourassa's avowed objective of destroying the Parti Québécois, Lévesque attacked the new leader with an intensity that Claude Ryan of *Le Devoir* described as "almost hysterical."

Calling Bourassa a "mini-Trudeau," Lévesque said that he had been the weakest of the three candidates for the Liberal leadership, that he was a tool of the party establishment and that he was simply unable to cope with Quebec's complex problems. When Ryan accused him of being too vitriolic, Lévesque retorted that he was not going to treat Bourassa with the "traditional hypocrisy."

Early in March, the two leaders confronted one another in a Montreal radio studio for "the debate of the year." Calling the results a tie match, Claude Ryan decided that Lévesque had made a tactical mistake by agreeing to debate economics with an economist while Bourassa had made a mistake by agreeing to any kind of debate at all with Lévesque.

"Bourassa didn't beat Lévesque," wrote Ryan in *Le Devoir*, "but the fact that Lévesque didn't gain any points against him was, for Bourassa, a moral victory."

This debate perhaps made Lévesque take a more careful look at Bourassa. During the campaign, he treated Bourassa as a serious opponent. He had already, during a speaking tour of western Canada, predicted that Bourassa would be the next Premier of Quebec, perhaps as leader of a minority government. After the first week of the campaign, Lévesque made what turned out to be, for a politician on the hustings, a fairly realistic prediction of his own party's strength in the election: from 20 to 35 per cent of the French-speaking vote and ten to twelve seats in the Assembly. This would be, he said, a "decisive first stage" in the development of the party.

Lévesque's campaign expressed the interplay of fear and hope within the French-Canadian spirit. He spoke frankly and movingly to his audiences about their "fear of independence, fear of the flight of capital, fear of the attitude of the English-speaking Canadians and Americans"; but he also held out the hope that "if we want it to be, this can be the beginning of the normal history of Quebec."

"Do you believe that it can be?" he asked the 12,000 people who crowded into his opening election rally at the Maurice Richard Arena in east end Montreal.

"Oui!" roared the audience, in a response that sounded "like a clap of thunder" to one of the journalists at the meeting.

Lévesque presented various forms of this verbal catechism to many audiences during the campaign. When more than 1,000 people came to hear him speak in Hull, across the Ottawa River from the national capital, Lévesque reminded them that "many people on the other side are watching you."

"Does that make you afraid?" he asked.

"Non!" shouted his audience.

More than mass professions of faith were needed to overcome the traditional insecurity and conservatism of French-Canadians. The "Brinks' affair" showed this as it quickly became one of the symbolic and memorable episodes of the campaign.

A few nights before the election, in an efficient and well-publicized operation, a convoy of eight armoured trucks was loaded with securities at the main office of the Royal Trust in Montreal, and dispatched to points outside Quebec. Lévesque claimed that the incident was "dramatized for electoral purposes," that the transfer of securities was a normal procedure and that it had no significance for the province's economy. Once the stories and photographs had been published, officials of the trust company also played down the importance of the transfer, but no one really underestimated the effect of the "Brinks' affair" on the vote a few days later.

"That doesn't work any more," Lévesque bravely insisted in public.

"They can try all they want—the long hesitations and divisions of Quebecers are going to disappear."

And again:

The winter of Quebec's impotence is over. Even if the Parti Québécois doesn't take power, our essential objective has been achieved—to shatter, once and for all, the old ice of our fears and complexes.

We've had enough of standing at the end of the line. We are the first citizens of a normal nation, as good as any other.

He was single-handedly trying to work a psychological miracle on French-Canadians under the pressure of an election campaign, knowing in his heart that it was impossible. Frequently the defiant screen of optimism would give way to reveal a brooding, dangerous expectation of failure.

"If we miss our chance in 1970," he said, "there will be a temptation to upset the whole applecart. The thousands of students and workers who took to the streets to protest Bill 63...

"If we don't pay attention, there will be anarchy, and it will cost us dearly.

"If we don't take an option that will enable two generations to look at one another without being ashamed," he said at an election rally in March, "things can go from disgust to open revolt, and it can happen faster than we think."

Eight years of sporadic terrorism had left many English-speaking Montrealers allergic to this "or else" approach. Lévesque regarded it as simply a description of the actual situation in Quebec; they took it as blackmail. It seemed to many of the English that, under pressure, Lévesque too often succumbed to the temptation to point enigmatically at the young terrorists on the extreme fringes of the independence movement. The English never knew whether it was a genuine warning or a veiled threat.

The uncertainty and exasperation of English-speaking Quebecers rarely found its way into the published record during the Sixties. Only the hot-line radio shows gave some insight into the apprehension and hostility that had built up in the working class districts of English-speaking Montreal and among Montrealers of European origin who felt helpless and claustrophobic as they were squeezed between the two main language groups. In the 1970 campaign, these feelings burst into print in a weekly newspaper published in Côte St. Luc, a Jewish suburb of Montreal sometimes called "the golden ghetto."

The last issue of *The Suburban* before the election carried the headline "O Canada" above a large picture of the Canadian flag and an unsigned editorial that most readers in the west end of the city identified immediately with the founder and director of the newspaper, Sophie Wollock.

"YES–a thousand times YES–O CANADA–we stand on guard for thee," the editorial began.

"We defy you, René Lévesque, and your bands of arrogant, thoughtless and grasping separatists. We defy you to take away the rightful heritage that belongs to all Quebec people. We defy you to threaten us with nationalism and a police state. We defy you–period."

The editorial concluded with a "post-election warning to all Canadians. . .lest one think that come April 30th, all will be calm and quiet."

"Is it civil war you want?" asked *The Suburban.* "You will get it–with dividends. No longer are the people of Quebec going to sit quietly back come May 1st, and let their country be divided and hyphenated.

"If the separatists want a fight on their hands, then the citizens will give it to them."

Less blatant but even more revealing was an editorial, published in the Montreal *Star* the previous week, that depicted Lévesque as the Kerensky of a separatist revolution who would soon be replaced by the Lenins and Stalins of Quebec. The editorial alluded to "the propensity of Quebec leaders, throughout history, toward authoritarianism and dictatorship" and said that the federal authority was the province's "fundamental guarantee" of protection against extremism of the right or left.

The editorial brought an immediate formal protest from twenty-five of the *Star's* own journalists, including a number of prominent French-Canadian reporters who had recently been hired by the *Star* to strengthen its ability to interpret Quebec developments for English-speaking readers.

In an open letter to their own newspaper, the journalists accused it of publishing an editorial with "racist connotations."

The editorial goaded Lévesque into making one of the most intemperate speeches of his career. He described the editorial, the day after, as the "first, lovely, total confirmation" of the English-speaking community's judgement that "we, basically, are not civilized enough as a society for self-government." Speaking in English for television, Lévesque fumed:

> That's an insult, a collective insult to a civilized people which in fact has no God-damned lesson to get from the Montreal *Star*, or from any of the exploiters of both the English and French groups in Quebec–and they're among the worst.
>
> And I'd like to say we've got no lesson on that score to take. . .from

anyone that has been dominating Quebec like a bunch of Rhodesians–the white group. If we had colours here, you'd feel it.

Rejecting the "paternalistic WASP arrogance of the ones that have been leading our governments, and to the slush funds that they contribute to, leading both of our hack parties by the nose for too long," Lévesque urged English-speaking voters to look seriously at his party's program on minority rights. He described it as "more civilized, I think, than any nationalist movement anywhere that I know of has ever been able to put on its program."

Lévesque and his party made a serious attempt during the campaign to persuade English-speaking voters that "the best guarantee of your own future is the normal and healthy attainment of self-government by the French-speaking majority." Literature was distributed in English. In the west end riding of D'Arcy McGee, the party nominated its most striking English-speaking candidate, Paul Unterberg, a thirty-five year-old lawyer whose father was executive treasurer of the Canadian Jewish Congress.

Lévesque's own riding, Laurier, in central Montreal reflected the widespread importance of the English-speaking vote, particularly in urban areas. Almost one-third of his constituents were English-speaking or immigrant voters. As a Liberal in 1966, Lévesque won two-thirds of this ethnic vote, a higher proportion than his over all 56.6 per cent. But there had been resentment among many of these people, a year later, when Lévesque switched parties but continued to sit in the Assembly on the strength of their votes.

In the final weeks of the campaign, it was clear that the Parti Québécois organization and Lévesque's message were reaching a significant number of people. Large crowds were turning out for his meetings, and Lévesque handled them carefully. During four days in the middle of April, according to one of the journalists accompanying him, the word "independence" was mentioned only four times. There was less emphasis than usual on the past failures and shortcomings of French-Canadians. Lévesque talked about the decision for independence as a common-sense choice that would be respected by other Canadians.

Lévesque travelled an estimated 10,000 miles during the campaign. He delivered thirty-five speeches. About 30,000 people, according to one newspaper estimate, heard him in person. Some were persuaded but a majority remained, along with editor Claude Ryan, "among those who prefer to look before they leap." There were still too many unanswered questions.

The election result that was supposed to provide a guide to the future of the independence movement left itself open to a number of conflicting interpretations. By winning 23.1 per cent of the vote, almost triple the separatist vote of the previous election, the Parti Québécois established itself as a force to be reckoned with in Quebec. The party's showing looked even more impressive if the votes of English-speaking Quebecers were put aside. This gave the P.Q. 28.7 per cent of the francophone vote compared with 32.6 per cent for the victorious Liberals. It was estimated that one out of every two French-speaking Montrealers had voted for Lévesque's party.

On election night, Lévesque asked a cheering, weeping crowd at Montreal's Paul Sauvé Arena, "Don't you find that this defeat has the smell of victory?"

The vote statistics lent substance to Lévesque's claim that the P.Q. was the opposition party in fact if not in title. But it wasn't possible, no matter how the statistics were arranged, to make the English-speaking vote disappear, or to ignore the urban-rural distribution of ridings that had enabled the Union Nationale to capture nineteen seats with only 19.7 per cent of the vote, and Social Credit to win twelve seats with only 11.2 per cent.

Both these factors had limited the Parti Québécois to seven seats in the Assembly despite its impressive total of votes.

Lévesque himself lost the Montreal riding that he had held since 1960 as his old supporters among the ethnic voters continued to vote Liberal.

Opponents of independence saw Bourassa's majority as a clear victory for federalism. One of the *Gazette's* Ottawa correspondents reported that "the question being asked by many observers here today is: Has separatism really peaked?"

"Mr. Lévesque forced the French-Canadian to make his choice and everybody discovered what some of us have been saying for years–the French-Canadian chooses to be Canadian," said Industry, Trade and Commerce Minister Jean-Luc Pepin in Ottawa. "If I were he, I would go away and hide."

Despite his brave words on election night, Lévesque was bitter. In particular, he blamed the English-speaking population of Quebec for voting en bloc, blindly, for the Liberals.

"If they don't want us to make Quebec independent with them, we'll do it in spite of them," he said. "We're not going to waste any more time or energy on them."

He blamed all newspapers for the outcome, and promised a report that would show the people of Quebec "how they were tricked by their newspapers."

A few personal friends found Lévesque moody and depressed after the election. He talked seriously of resigning from the leadership of the party and retiring from politics. The strains of the election campaign, the disappointment over the result and, at least for the time being, the end of his career in the National Assembly seemed to leave him deflated and restless.

His party also needed time to absorb the result and regroup its forces. One of the questions that came to the surface immediately was whether the Parti Québécois should continue to emphasize social and economic issues rather than independence, as it had during the campaign, or perhaps even drop the independence issue entirely.

Writing in *Le Devoir* two weeks after the election, Louis-Marie Bouchard, a professor at the Chicoutimi campus of the University of Quebec, urged the Parti Québécois to regroup as a party of the moderate left rather than risk becoming a sterile nationalist group. The undeniable fact of the election, he said, was that three-quarters of the Quebec population had rejected independence. This expression of public opinion could not be ignored by a party that considered itself to be democratic.

The Parti Québécois, wrote Professor Bouchard, could not continue indefinitely to force a political idea on people who had clearly rejected it.

XXII
The October Crisis:
The Elusive Coup

Speaking before a convention of Quebec Liberals in October, 1969, Prime Minister Trudeau had described "the climate of terror, the climate of violence" in Quebec as "the real outcome of separatism in the last ten years." The same conclusion was drawn by many people outside Quebec because of the prominence given to the terrorists by the news media.

But the *Front de Libération du Québec* and the other terrorist groups did more than merely publicize the separatist movement, particularly during such international events as the Royal visit of 1964 and the de Gaulle tour of 1967. They achieved some success in identifying the campaign for Quebec independence with the liberation struggles of other national groups in different parts of the world.

They forced others to see French-Canadians, to some extent, as some of them saw themselves, and as the F.L.Q. theorist, Pierre Vallières, described them in his book *White Niggers of America.*

In terms of numbers, the half-dozen deaths caused by the Quebec terrorists were insignificant compared with the casualties of racial conflict and of opposition to the Viet Nam War in the United States, or the heavy price paid by independence movements in Africa and Asia. But Quebec terrorists were noticed in other countries because they clashed so blatantly with the familiar stereotype of Canada as a prosperous and orderly country.

Europeans were puzzled by the phenomenon of urban guerrillas in a nation that some of them still regarded as an unspoiled wilderness. In less developed countries, the sympathy of nationalist patriots for the "colonized" people of Quebec was mixed with envy of their industrial development and standard of living. Hardened revolutionaries in other countries sometimes treated the linguistic and cultural concerns of

French-Canadians as the neurotic amusements of a prosperous and bored minority.

In Quebec, neither French nor English saw anything humorous or artificial in the bomb explosions, the deaths or the constant procession of young people who appeared before the courts shouting slogans and demanding treatment as political prisoners.

Organized terrorism started little more than a year after the R.I.N. began its political activity for an independent Quebec in 1960. It gained respectability from the existence of the political movement, and it gave the movement its own sense of commitment.

The most spectacular achievement of the terrorist wave of the Sixties was the "October Crisis" of 1970. Two small bands of terrorists kidnapped a British diplomat and, subsequently, a Quebec cabinet minister, killed the Quebec minister and created a situation where the federal government felt that it had to enact wartime emergency legislation suspending some civil liberties.

The "October Crisis" was a landmark event in the history of Quebec. Years later, interpretation of the event remains as partisan and confused as it was at the time.

For the terrorists, it was the culmination and the conclusion of almost a decade of activity–the death of Labour Minister Pierre Laporte put an end to the F.L.Q.

At least in the short run, the crisis benefited Prime Minister Trudeau and the federal Liberals. It also helped Premier Robert Bourassa, although this took longer to become apparent. And surprisingly enough, it helped Lévesque, although he might easily have been destroyed by it.

The cops-and-kidnappers part of the story was a classic of the Sixties. On the morning of October 5, 1970, two armed men kidnapped the senior British trade commissioner in Montreal, James Richard Cross, from his home in Westmount. They soon identified themselves, through *communiqués* delivered to radio stations, as members of an F.L.Q. cell. Their conditions for the release of Cross included publicity for their political manifesto, a "voluntary tax" of $500,000 to be paid by the Quebec government, the liberation of F.L.Q. members from Quebec jails as "political prisoners" and an aircraft to take the kidnappers to Algeria or Cuba.

Five days later, a second cell of the F.L.Q. kidnapped Pierre Laporte, the forty-nine-year-old Minister of Labour and Immigration in the Quebec cabinet and a contender for the leadership of the party the previous spring.

On October 16, acting on requests from the Quebec and Montreal governments, the federal government brought the War Measures Act into force. Among other things, this outlawed the F.L.Q., empowered the po-

186

lice to search without warrant, and provided for arrest and detention without bail.

Pierre Laporte was murdered the following day.

James Cross was freed on December 3 when police located and surrounded the suburban Montreal duplex where he was being held. His abductors were flown to Cuba in exchange for his release.

On December 27, police located and arrested three men hiding in a farmhouse twenty miles southwest of Montreal and charged them with the kidnapping and murder of Laporte.

The "October Crisis" was an experience of unprecedented intensity for all Canadians and particularly for those near the centre of events. Some of the many questions that remain unanswered are similar to those that the assassination of President Kennedy still generates, questions about alleged political conspiracies and the actual roles of those who were arrested and charged. Other questions relate to the social and political impact of the kidnapping and murder. The question that has been asked most persistently and unsuccessfully is: Was there a likelihood of serious civil disorder and a political coup during the "October Crisis"?

The question was first raised during the crisis by some of the main political actors.

Three days before the War Measures Act was brought into effect, in an impromptu interview outside the House of Commons, Prime Minister Trudeau talked in general terms about "the emergence of a parallel power...which is challenging the elected representatives of the people."

The evening before the Act was proclaimed, Claude Ryan wrote an editorial for the following day's edition of *Le Devoir* that concluded: "We must at all cost avoid the downfall of Quebec into civil war and its subjugation to martial law. But this will only be possible if the legitimate government of Quebec manages to assert its moral authority more firmly and to broaden its basic support among the people over the next four weeks."

In retrospect, particularly in view of similar kidnappings elsewhere before and after the Canadian episode, the discussion of "parallel power" and "civil war" seems exaggerated. Despite the suspension of civil liberties and the presence of soldiers in Quebec to guard federal buildings, diplomatic missions, and some politicians, everyone appeared to be behaving at the height of the crisis in a fairly predictable fashion.

Despite reports of internal dissension and indecision, the Bourassa cabinet remained united behind its new leader. Nationalists like Claude Ryan urged a more flexible attitude toward negotiations with the kidnappers. Quebec's union leaders went further in their criticism of government handling of the crisis, while the radical left attempted to close the universities and arrange public demonstrations to support the objectives of the F.L.Q.

All this activity was the least that could have been expected under the circumstances. But at some point in the week following Laporte's disappearance, the situation seemed to pass the point of predictability in the minds of those who were attempting to control it. A feeling of apprehension developed rapidly within the centres of authority in Ottawa and Montreal, supposedly in response to situations hidden from the public.

Campaigning for re-election at the height of the crisis, Montreal's Mayor Drapeau was asked during a radio interview about the reasons for proclaiming the War Measures Act.

"It is because the revolution is in preparation that we asked for help from a higher government; we didn't refer to any specific acts," he said.

"The revolution was started–this is what people don't believe. I don't know what evidence is needed. It was not only apprehended; it was started."

On the night of his election, October 25, after winning 92 per cent of the votes, Mayor Drapeau declared that "the vote expressed approval of the measures taken during the tragic moments of the last weeks...

"The tragic circumstances of the last three weeks could have modified the course of history," he continued in a speech televised from a heavily guarded City Hall. "There was a provisional committee that was going to take power by way of revolution."

The Mayor referred to "not only the known attacks made by revolutionaries but also the attempts to set up a provisional government charged with carrying out the transfer of constitutional powers to the revolutionary regime."

The following day, the Toronto *Star* quoted "top-level sources" in Ottawa as saying that

the Trudeau administration believed that a group of influential Quebecers had set out to see whether they might supplant the legitimately elected provincial government with what they conceived of as an interim administration having enough moral authority to restore public order.

Dominique Clift gave another version in the Montreal *Star* on November 2:

Premier Robert Bourassa himself was at the very centre of consultations which could have led to the formation of a government of national unity in Quebec, a move which was later misrepresented by Mayor Jean Drapeau and anonymous federal sources as an attempt to create a provisional government sympathetic to the cause of revolution.

Two unrelated developments during the week of Laporte's kidnapping contributed to the "parallel government" scare.

The first was a series of meetings and consultations, directed by Claude Ryan of *Le Devoir*, where the idea of a government of national unity was discussed as one of a number of hypothetical responses to the F.L.Q. challenge.

The most important of these meetings between Ryan and his editorial staff took place on the Sunday following Laporte's disappearance. At its conclusion, Ryan undertook to test the conclusions of the *Le Devoir* group with Lévesque and Lucien Saulnier, the chairman of Montreal's executive committee. He was unable to contact Lévesque but drove to Saulnier's home later that afternoon.

Saulnier apparently took the *Le Devoir* hypothesis more literally than Ryan could have imagined. Later that night, one of the *Le Devoir* journalists who had participated in the morning discussion at his newspaper was interviewed by Premier Bourassa, who said that Saulnier had warned him in very dark terms about the conspiracy being hatched by Ryan at *Le Devoir*.

The journalist's explanation apparently satisfied Bourassa. None of the Premier's statements subsequently lent any support to the conspiracy theory, and he was later to deny specifically that this "illusory hypothesis" had played any role at all in his decision to ask for the War Measures Act.

The second development that was related to the "parallel government" scare began a few days later, on the afternoon of October 14, when Ryan received a call from Lévesque suggesting that a group of representative Quebecers should issue a statement urging Bourassa to seek a negotiated solution with the F.L.Q. At a downtown Holiday Inn in Montreal that evening, Ryan and Lévesque made a final copy of the draft statement that Lévesque had brought to the meeting before releasing it to journalists in the company of the thirteen other signatories—union leaders, academics, members of the Parti Québécois and the president of a Quebec-based cooperative insurance company.

There was a tentative agreement among members of the group to meet again the following Saturday to suggest a plan of emergency action for the Quebec government. But by then, the federal government had proclaimed the War Measures Act and Lévesque had released his own plan in the name of the Parti Québécois. The Holiday Inn group never met again.

Perhaps the meetings at *Le Devoir* and the Holiday Inn were enough to start and sustain the idea of a "provisional government" conspiracy. The truth remains elusive. One of the few men who knows the full story still maintains, "I don't think I'll comment on it as long as I live."

Individual responses to the 1970 situation have remained contradictory. One of the chief protagonists told me years later, "I had to agree that there was a very great danger there." But a moment later, he said; "On the other hand, it was so immature that there was really no danger."

During the week between Laporte's abduction and the proclamation of the War Measures Act, Lévesque's public statements reflected the intense pressure felt by all Quebec leaders. His most extreme statement was delivered on Friday, October 16, in response to the War Measures Act: "Quebec no longer has a government."

Speaking at a press conference, Lévesque said, "The bit of country over which we had any control has been swept away by the first hard blow. The Bourassa cabinet has stepped down and is no more than a puppet in the hands of the federal leaders."

Lévesque's statement concluded with a careful but nonetheless dangerously vague response to the power vacuum that he perceived in Quebec:

> In view of the extremes which have for all practical purposes caused the destruction of our government, Quebec's democrats must overcome their differences of opinion immediately and find the means or the organizations for building the moral power necessary to defend our basic liberties and, at the same time, all our hopes for the future.

If Lévesque had been merely a journalist writing his daily column in *Le Journal de Montréal,* the commentary would have been provocative. However, from the leader of a political party that regarded itself as the alternative to the Bourassa government, the comment was dangerous. It could have been interpreted as an invitation to replace the elected government with some other form of authority.

Lévesque's position was supported the following day by the leaders of Quebec's two labour federations and the president of the Quebec teachers' union, all of whom had been members of the Lévesque-Ryan group at the Holiday Inn earlier in the week.

"Faced with the urgency of the situation," he said in a statement released after their meeting, "the executives of the three parent unions have decided to call an extraordinary plenary session, the supreme authority of their organizations between conventions, in order to decide the methods of action to be taken to save democracy in Quebec."

Early the following morning, Pierre Laporte's body was found in the trunk of an automobile in suburban Montreal. The murder almost obliterated the weak forces of opposition to the War Measures Act in Quebec and the other provinces.

"This is not the time to split hairs," wrote the editor of *La Presse*, Jean-Paul Desbiens. "As of today, the people of Quebec must declare their support of the government in every way possible..."

At *Le Devoir*, Ryan no longer appeared to doubt that extraordinary measures were necessary, although he still found the War Measures Act excessive and urged the government to apply its provisions "with a maximum of discretion."

Laporte's murder ended opposition to the federal and Quebec governments' handling of the crisis for all but a small minority of Canadians. Public opinion polls showed that the ratio of support for the governments' action was from 70 to 90 per cent. From then on, the governments moved confidently through the final phase of the crisis. There was no further significant public discussion of alternative governments or other radical methods of "saving" democracy.

In all this, Lévesque's position remained somewhat ambiguous.

Speaking at a regional party conference the following November 8, he accused Trudeau of "fascist manipulation" and "calculated errors . . . when he mentioned people who don't agree–like myself and Ryan, who were both for negotiation–and wondering whether we weren't in sympathy with the F.L.Q." But at the very least, Lévesque had left himself open to suspicion, during the week of Laporte's abduction, when he appeared to leave himself open to almost any eventuality.

"I don't think he ever would have formulated it in an explicit way, even to himself," recalled a member of the Holiday Inn Lévesque-Ryan group, "but he must have felt in the very bottom of his mind that something was in the wind that was hard to define, and that he must be prepared for the unexpected."

If Lévesque in fact was holding himself in readiness for a larger role, there is no evidence that the public was aware of this or desired it; nor is there any real indication, apart from his Friday statement in reaction to the War Measures Act, that Lévesque encouraged people to see him in this light. It is difficult to accuse Lévesque of hungering for power during the crisis when the public itself has no recollection that this had ever been an important aspect of the whole affair. An indication of his own unimportance in the "provisional government" scare lies in the fact that it never subsequently became a political issue.

Lévesque was not a major, visible protagonist during the crisis, on a level with Trudeau, Bourassa or even Ryan. It was Ryan, somewhat to his own surprise and horror, who became identified eventually as the main "villain" of the provisional government conspiracy, despite the fact that he had gone to the Holiday Inn meeting at Lévesque's invitation to discuss a statement that had already been prepared by Lévesque and others.

In the long run, the "October Crisis" helped the Parti Québécois by eliminating terrorism as a factor in Quebec's political life, but its short-term effect on the party was disastrous.

Interviewed the following December for the Paris weekly *Nouvel Observateur*, Lévesque admitted that a Quebec election at that time would result in a serious setback for his party because of the "hero mentality" generated by the events of October. In the following September, he revealed that membership in the party had decreased from 80,000 at the time of the April 1970 election to 30,000. In the twelve months ending July, 1971, the party had received only $200,000 in membership dues and donations while expenses had amounted to $260,000.

Lévesque claimed that the decline in membership and donations was a normal sequel to the 1970 electoral period but the editorial vultures were hovering over the Parti Québécois. The *Gazette* speculated in an editorial that "as a separatist political force, the P.Q. reached its peak just before last year's election and is inexorably on the decline."

XXIII
The 1973 Election:
The Battle of the Budgets

The "October Crisis" of 1970 polarized public opinion in Quebec and pruned back the Parti Québécois to its core of committed separatists. Some observers saw this as the beginning of the end for the party. In fact, the crisis helped it in the long run.

While the vast majority of Canadians supported the Trudeau government's swift and forceful response to the terrorists, many of these same people worried about this authoritarian suspension of basic freedoms that affected, for all practical purposes, only one group in a single region of the country. In English Canada, the New Democratic Party opposed the War Measures Act without suffering any significant loss of support in the long run. In Quebec, similar opposition was not only a matter of principle for many, as it was in English Canada, but also the result of personally experiencing life in a police state, albeit in a relatively mild form and for a short period of time.

The Westmount home of Secretary of State Gérard Pelletier, where Trudeau and Lévesque had argued about democratic freedom and responsibility, was one of the first to experience a midnight raid, as a result of police error.

For several days after the War Measures Act was promulgated, people were pulled off the street or taken from their homes and offices to join hundreds of others being questioned at Quebec Provincial Police headquarters in Montreal. Most were held without being charged and without being able to call their lawyers. And all was not forgotten after they were released. In 1976, Quebec authorities admitted that they were referring to their 1970 lists of suspects as they tightened security in Montreal in preparation for the Olympic Games.

In the face of the terrorist challenge, Prime Minister Trudeau acted decisively; Premier Robert Bourassa played for time, seeking an opening to negotiate for the life of Pierre Laporte, keenly aware that there was some sympathy for the terrorists among the confused Quebec population in the early stages of the crisis. Holed up in Montreal's Queen Elizabeth Hotel under police protection while Trudeau commanded events from the House of Commons in Ottawa, the new Quebec Premier was totally eclipsed by the federal authority. It was years before he recovered from this humiliating subordination, before his reedy frame and receding chin began to fill out in the public mind with the weight of experience and authority.

The crisis had the opposite effect on Lévesque. It snapped him out of the personal depression that he always suffered after an electoral defeat. In any crisis, it was quickly evident to everyone in the Parti Québécois that only Lévesque could hold them together and speak effectively for them. He now had to steer a difficult course, advocating negotiation with the kidnappers while condemning violence, but he emerged from the ordeal with his own integrity and authority intact, and a unified party.

As political life quickly returned to normal, the P.Q. began to turn its attention to the next election.

The 1973 election was a transitional election for the Parti Québécois. In some respects, it seemed to be a repeat of the 1970 contest, with Lévesque personally losing his second election attempt since he became leader, although this time by only a few hundred votes, and with the party increasing its popular vote considerably while actually losing one of its seats in the Assembly. The P.Q. polled 30 per cent of the vote, compared with 23 per cent in 1970, but retained only six of the 110 seats in the Assembly. In terms of elected members, Bourassa's victory was the most lopsided in the history of Quebec.

The most obvious change after the 1973 election was that the Parti Québécois became Her Majesty's Loyal Opposition in the National Assembly. Both the Union Nationale and the Créditiste parties slipped almost into insignificance as the Quebec Liberals and the Parti Québécois waged a two-party contest, with the Liberals always decisively in the lead.

If the result of the election seemed to be almost a replay of 1970, the campaign itself was a preview of future electoral battles. As the Parti Québécois and its leader became more familiar features of the political scene, voters began to pay serious attention to the content of their campaign. The party's position on independence and its social program came under close study.

In retrospect, the 1973 election was only an episode in this deeper and longer process of mutual examination. The voters of Quebec had started to look closely at Lévesque and his party as an alternative to the government; and that scrutiny began to have an effect on the party.

There was a superficial change in Lévesque's own style.

"Gone is the rumpled look," wrote Richard Daignault in the Montreal *Star*. "In its place, a rather conservative blue suit, well tailored, topping shiny black shoes. The famous cigarette that dangled from his mouth has gone..."

Lévesque arrived on time for press conferences and public meetings. When he rambled during his speeches, his secretary would give him a sign from the front row of the audience and Lévesque would wind things up within a few minutes.

Other changes were more significant. In particular, there was a softening of the party's position on independence.

Only the previous February, militant delegates at the party's annual convention had reaffirmed the position that Lévesque himself had taken in the early days of the party: that a vote for the P.Q. was to be taken as a vote for immediate independence. When the campaign opened little more than six months later, Lévesque simply set aside the decision of the convention.

"A Parti Québécois government," he said, "is committed in advance to consider that its mandate is one of preparing and carefully explaining stage by stage this accession to sovereignty, and to achieve it constitutionally at the decisive moment with a consultation of all citizens by means of a referendum."

Dominique Clift, the Montreal *Star's* Quebec editor, detected an increasing tendency "for the party leadership to avoid giving the impression that independence means a dramatic break with the past or an unpredictable political convulsion.

"It is conceivable that by the time the next general elections are due in 1977," he wrote, "they will be talking of independence simply as a redrafting of Quebec's links with the rest of the country, in the same sense that Confederation achieved this in 1867 or the Act of Union in 1841."

The decision of the Parti Québécois to "tone down the independentist theme and put the emphasis on economic and social reform" impressed an academic observer sufficiently to make him speculate about the traditional loyalty of English-speaking Quebec voters to the Liberal party.

"There are not the same tensions and fear of separatism in 1973 as there was in 1970," wrote Herbert F. Quinn, professor of political science at Sir George Williams University and the author of a history of the Union Nationale. "As a consequence, the Liberals would be wise not to take the English voter for granted."

When a cautious political historian such as Quinn ventured to speculate about an English-Quebec vote for the Parti Québécois, it showed how deeply the political scene in Quebec had altered since the formation of the P.Q. in 1968.

"I have no illusions about the English vote," Lévesque said during the campaign, "but I feel that many English Quebecers are now getting closer to us." He estimated that 2 to 3 per cent of the English-speaking voters had sided with the P.Q. in 1970 and guessed, optimistically, that perhaps 10 per cent might vote for the party this time.

The attitude of the Parti Québécois toward labour also showed how far the independence movement had travelled in the Seventies, and in which direction it was headed. Most Quebecers had been thoroughly alarmed in March, 1972, when more than 200,000 public service employees staged a twenty-four-hour general strike, the first in Canadian history. Certain of public support, the Bourassa government pressed charges against the two leaders of Quebec's rival union federations and the head of the province's teachers' union. There were threats of more general strikes when the three union leaders were sentenced to one year in jail but the province remained calm as they served about three months in a minimum security institution.

Once again, the vast majority of Quebecers had adopted a conservative position when radical forces in the province directly challenged authority.

Lévesque kept the unions at arm's length during the 1973 campaign; the unions responded by urging their members rather vaguely to vote for whatever party they considered to be "closest" to the labour movement. This also showed the direction of Lévesque's development in the fifteen years since the producers' strike at Radio Canada had propelled him into politics, and the direction that the separatists had taken since members of the R.I.N. had routinely marched in the Sixties on every picket line where they had been welcome.

At the outset of the campaign, a public opinion poll gave the Liberals 37.5 per cent and the Parti Québécois 18.7 per cent. Another poll commissioned by *Le Devoir* in Montreal and *Le Soleil* in Quebec City, halfway through the campaign, showed only slight movement away from the Liberals and toward the P.Q.

Early in October, Paul Desrochers, one of Premier Bourassa's closest advisors and the director of the Liberal election effort, forecast that the campaign would be dirty–"*une campagne de cochon.*" It wasn't long before the smaller parties were snarling desperately at the leaders, particularly at the upstart separatists who were challenging the government for the first time. Gabriel Loubier, the leader of the Union Nationale, at one point tried to compare Lévesque to Adolf Hitler.

"Corporal René Lévesque," he said in a speech to a rural audience, "will continue his Hitlerian invasion of half-truths, his psychological brainwashing operation and his intellectual guerrilla tactics to capture the vote of separatists, socialists and extremists of every stripe."

Both major parties accused one another of racism during the campaign, claiming that voters were being screened on ethnic grounds. Liberals charged the Parti Québécois with challenging and striking from the voters list 1,200 names that obviously were not French-Canadian; the P.Q. replied that the lists contained the names of many immigrants who were not Canadian citizens while 100,000 qualified voters had been omitted.

On October 9, the Parti Québécois altered the course of the campaign dramatically by releasing a "budget" showing the spending and revenue of a P.Q. government during the first year of independence. This was the brainchild of economist Jacques Parizeau. Claude Ryan said that the project was "debatable but eminently respectable." Within the party, however, the "budget" took some members of the rank-and-file by surprise. They worried about its effect on the campaign and criticized Lévesque and Parizeau for releasing it without consulting the full membership.

The "budget" bogged down the Parti Québécois campaign in a morass of conflicting statistics. Bourassa already had claimed that the P.Q. program would raise taxes to such a level that international companies would leave the province and "thousands of young workers" would have to follow them. Gabriel Loubier had predicted that the dollar of an independent Quebec would be worth about 50 cents compared to the Canadian dollar. In its "budget," the P.Q. showed a surplus of more than $180,000,000 despite a social affairs program that would cost as much as the current total annual budget of the province. It also provided for large increases in state funds to aid industrial development in a mixed economy.

Lévesque's former comrade-in-controversy in the Quebec cabinet, Eric Kierans, back teaching economics at McGill University, said that the "budget" had been balanced by superimposing democratic socialism on an unchanged capitalist system of production.

"This is a neat trick," he conceded, "but it cannot be done."

When Kierans shifted his attention from the revenue to the spending side of the "budget," he saw the same philosophy at work that had influenced Lévesque when they were both in the Lesage cabinet.

"He believes that spending should be for people, not projects," wrote Kierans in the *Gazette*. "Both the Bourassa and Trudeau governments, and indeed every provincial government, could learn a great deal by analyzing the social objectives outlined in this budget."

Premier Bourassa responded by defending his policy of "profitable federalism" and by claiming that the federal government spent $653,100,000 more in Quebec in 1971-72 than it received from taxpayers in the province. The Parti Québécois economists said that exactly the opposite was true, that Ottawa collected an average of $238,000,000 more a year in Quebec than it spent in the province in the 1961-71 period.

This inconclusive debate probably had little effect on voters. What the Parti Québécois gained in credibility as a serious alternative to the government it lost in terms of campaign momentum.

The Bourassa government was never seriously threatened during the campaign, as the public opinion polls showed, but its sweeping victory could hardly be regarded as a massive vote of confidence.

La Presse had deliberately refrained from publishing polls before the election. Three weeks after, it released the results of a poll taken during the campaign. This showed that five out of six voters regarded the election as a constitutional referendum rather than a test of the government's performance.

In such a contest, the P.Q. had been doomed to defeat. Half the voters, according to the *La Presse* poll, were favourable to federalism while only 28 per cent favoured separatism.

Among French-speaking Quebecers, the difference was less decisive: two separatists for every three federalists. And a portent for the future: there were twice as many separatists in the group under thirty-five years of age than in the older group.

The Liberal victory in 1973 forced the Parti Québécois to confront the same questions that it had struggled to answer after the 1970 election. Once again, Lévesque's leadership came into question, and serious thought was given to replacing him in 1974. Linked to this, to a certain extent, was renewed debate within the party about its position on independence.

Two days after the 1970 election, *Le Devoir* gave special prominence to a letter from André Normandeau, a criminology professor at the University of Montreal who had unsuccessfully contested a Montreal riding for the Parti Québécois. It was high time, wrote Professor Normandeau, for the party to consider the option of "social democracy in Quebec, culturally more independent than ever but joined in a Canadian economic federalism."

On the far side of English Canada, the following week, Premier Dave Barrett of British Columbia repeated the same idea when he told a New Democratic Party convention in Vancouver that he had invited Lévesque and the Parti Québécois to forget separatism and "to build a socialist Quebec within Confederation."

XXIV
The Discipline of Power

By the end of the Seventies, the final meaning of René Lévesque's political career, and the separatist wave that has coincided with it, will be much clearer than it is now.

Lévesque has said that the next Quebec election is crucial, that he'll "hang up his skates" as leader of the party if it fails to make substantial progress and if he fails to win his own riding. Lévesque is noted for dramatic now-or-never pronouncements about elections but this time, the ultimatum isn't only his. It's doubtful that the party would tolerate another defeat.

It came closer than ever before to dumping him after the 1973 election. As Lévesque went into one of his deepest post-election slumps, opposition to his leadership mounted within the party's six-man caucus in the Assembly. By the fall of 1974, four of the six members were letting it be known that they were dissatisfied with Lévesque's performance since the election. They accused him of abdicating his leadership role within the caucus and of not working hard enough for the party outside the Assembly.

The four men identified with this criticism lead what is generally regarded as the left wing of the party. Robert Burns, the Montreal lawyer who led the caucus from 1970 to 1973, is at their head, followed by Claude Charron, the youngest member of the caucus, Marcel Léger, another Montreal member who was the party's chief organizer in 1974, and Lucien Lessard, from Saguenay riding on the North Shore of the St. Lawrence River below Quebec City. All these men have been in the Assembly since 1970. In some of the breakdowns given by party insiders, Léger and Lessard are classified as a central "bloc" between the left and right wings.

When the six-man caucus gathered after the 1973 election to choose a new House leader, there was a tie for the job between Burns and a new Montreal member, Jacques-Yvan Morin, a prominent academic who had been the guiding spirit in the Sixties of a huge nationalist lobby called the "Estates General." Lévesque and three other members of the party executive cast the deciding vote in favour of Morin, who developed into a remarkably capable leader in the Assembly as well as a strong supporter of Lévesque in the party. Recent public opinion polls have shown that Morin is generally regarded as Lévesque's likeliest successor. The other member of the right wing of the caucus is Marc-André Bédard, first elected in 1973 in Chicoutimi, an industrial region northeast of Quebec City.

Under Burns and Morin, the small P.Q. opposition in the Assembly has been both vocal and effective.

"The best opposition in the country," was the rueful judgement of a prominent Montreal Liberal. "With a lot of help from their friends in the civil service, they've been ahead of the government on most issues.

"And Morin knows more about parliamentary procedure than anyone in Quebec and most people in Ottawa. When he was a student at Oxford, he used to spend hours in the House of Commons."

The issues that distinguish right from left in the Parti Québécois are, roughly, whether or not to have a referendum on independence after a P.Q. victory, the role of labour unions in Quebec, and Lévesque's leadership.

Burns led the attack on Lévesque in the summer of 1974 after an unsuccessful P.Q. campaign to persuade voters to spoil their ballots in the July 8 federal election, when Quebec gave massive support to Trudeau, and after a P.Q. candidate ran third in a by-election. Burns said publicly that Lévesque should either win a seat in the Assembly or step aside as leader before the next election. Party organizer Marcel Léger joined in the attack by writing a newspaper article that said the party was "stagnating" under Lévesque's leadership.

Lévesque publicly challenged his critics to take the job away from him if they could; and at a closed meeting of the party hierarchy at the end of September, 1974, he brought his critics to heel. Since then, his leadership of the party has been secure, with the left wing biding its time until after the next election. In private, some of them remain strongly critical of Lévesque.

"I've always admired Lévesque," said one. "He's a little French-Canadian, not elegant, and he's shown them what a little guy can do.

"But his authority as a moral leader of Quebec is much less than it used to be. He's not sought out and quoted the way he used to be."

The critics claim that their case has been strengthened by the evidence of recent public opinion polls. In April, 1976, a survey by the *Centre de*

Recherche sur l'Opinion Publique (CROP), one of the two leading opinion sampling firms in Quebec, showed that 18.3 per cent of the respondents chose Premier Bourassa as the leader they wanted to see leading Quebec, while 23.7 per cent chose Lévesque. It was the first time that Lévesque outranked Bourassa in this type of poll–the two had been tied at 25 per cent the previous October–but the poll also showed that Lévesque had dropped slightly in public esteem and that he was running more than six percentage points behind his party.

"In any kind of normal political organization with a bit of objectivity," said one of his critics, "you'd look at those figures and say, Jesus, we've got a problem. But that's where the almost religious atmosphere of the P.Q. comes in. You can talk against Lévesque, but not too openly."

Lévesque also has his critics today in the Press Gallery of the National Assembly, which functioned as his private fan club in the Sixties.

"When people in the rural areas hold kitchen meetings with P.Q. candidates," said one journalist, "they always ask now about two things– unions and Lévesque. I used to think that Lévesque was popular in the country because he comes from the Gaspé. But he really isn't. He's just another urban intellectual as far as they're concerned."

"If I write something critical about him, I hear from him the next day," complained another reporter, not at all pleased about this development of the *camaraderie* that once linked Lévesque with the press.

"He sounds tired, as if he's said it all before," said another journalist. "On television these days, he often just sounds impatient, irritated."

"Many Quebecers are afraid of him," claimed one of the other party leaders. "He has a bilious temperament."

Despite evidence of some dissatisfaction with Lévesque in his own party, and among the press and public, opinion polls also show that the Parti Québécois has steadily progressed under his leadership. In November, 1974, a poll for *La Presse* by *l'Institut Québecois d'Opinion Publique* (IQOP) showed that 28 per cent of the respondents were in favour of separatism, almost twice the percentage shown by most polls in the Sixties. In May, 1976, a Gallup poll in Quebec showed that 30 per cent of the respondents favoured the Parti Québécois compared with 23 per cent in favour of the Liberals.

This was the first time that an important poll gave the P.Q. an edge over the government, perhaps enough to defeat the government if an election had been held at that time.

Dissatisfaction with the Bourassa government appeared to be the major factor in the rising popularity of the Parti Québécois. More than two out of three respondents said that they were dissatisfied with the government. Half the respondents who had voted Liberal in 1973 said that they no longer supported the party, with the largest proportion of them going over to the Parti Québécois.

The government of Premier Robert Bourassa seemed to be going the way of all governments with unmanageably large parliamentary majorities. Bourassa himself, having overcome the weak, vacillating image of his early years as Premier, now was an aloof figure who managed to appear both authoritarian and ineffective to many Quebecers.

Quebecers blamed him for the deteriorating labour relations with a "common front" of public service employees that resulted in one work stoppage after another in the first half of 1976, closing schools and hospitals and interrupting the power supply. They were horrified by the revelations of various official inquiries that showed widespread corruption among Quebec construction unions, and exposed a tainted meat scandal of nauseating proportions, with dealers making under-the-counter sales of meat unfit for human consumption to butchers and institutions, often with the connivance of health inspectors.

What little credit Bourassa gained for appointing the inquiries was lost in the public outcry about corruption apparently tolerated under his regime. Even Bourassa's closest advisor for many years, Paul Desrochers, the architect of his stunning 1973 victory, was cited by one of the inquiries for "imprudence" in his dealings with unions working at the huge hydro-electric site in James Bay. Desrochers had asked one of the province's labour federations for electoral help on the same day that he had awarded it a virtual monopoly on organizing workers at James Bay.

"Part of the problem stems from Bourassa's own devious style," said a Montreal journalist. "He reminds me of Nixon at times. He always tries to move around an issue rather than face up to it."

One issue that no Quebec Premier has been able to dodge indefinitely is the language issue. Bourassa took the bull by the horns in the spring of 1974 and introduced Bill 22. The heart of this legislation was the repeal of parental freedom to choose the language of education of their children, a custom that had existed for so long in Quebec, although not in all other parts of Canada, that many English-speaking Quebecers were surprised to discover that it was not a constitutional right.

Bill 22 had no effect on the English-speaking children of Canadian parents, or on the children of English-speaking immigrants; but its provision to test all immigrant children trying to enter English-language elementary schools for "sufficient" knowledge of English outraged Quebec's English-speaking community. Without the constant recruitment of immigrant children, the size of English-language schools in Quebec, and ultimately of the English-language community, would be stabilized and perhaps even reduced.

On the other side of the question, Quebec nationalists were upset by the bill because they felt that it would guarantee the survival of the English-language school system in Quebec.

In the summer of 1975, Education Minister Jérôme Choquette resigned, claiming that the bill that he had been given to administer was "unworkable." An English-language radio station in Montreal collected 599,000 signatures on a petition to Bourassa and Prime Minister Trudeau against the bill. Protestant school boards began the first of a series of tests of the bill's constitutionality, with the initial ruling by the Quebec Supreme Court upholding the government.

By the spring of 1976, two trends were apparent. It had looked for some time as if the Bourassa government was well on the way to defeating itself, and the prospect of power was having a sobering effect on the Parti Québécois.   In November, 1974, the fifth convention of the Parti Québécois dealt again with the referendum issue, deciding finally that a referendum on independence would be an essential step between the election of a Parti Québécois government and a declaration of Quebec independence. The editor of the *Gazette*, Tim Creery, reported that the resolution was steered through the convention by a "Lévesque machine" that operated "with the efficiency of a pop-up toaster."

"In fact" Creery wrote, "the P.Q. in Quebec City sounded just like one of those old political parties with which we are familiar. The kind that take power."

The referendum plank is undoubtedly a popular one for the Parti Québécois. The same 1974 poll that showed 28 per cent of its respondents in favour of separatism also indicated that 83 per cent thought that a referendum should precede a declaration of independence by a Parti Québécois government, and 65 per cent said that more than four years should elapse between the election of a P.Q. government and a referendum.

Within the left wing of the party, opposition to the referendum is still strong.

"First, Lévesque says it's going to take six months to organize a referendum," said one of his critics.

> Then, a few weeks later, he says, 'What's a year in the life of a nation?' Then, a few weeks later, it's–'Well, two or three years is a normal period for setting up...'
>
> And now you're up to four or five years, and it's going to take two elections. The nervousness now is not about the principle of a referendum but about how many people in the party just want to get into office, period! We don't want government for the sake of government.

Lévesque himself has warned Quebecers against jumping to the conclusion that "separatism is dead," as the Prime Minister stated in the spring of 1976. In a radio interview shortly before Trudeau's statement, Lévesque said that anyone who thinks that his party will give up independence as its ultimate objective is "daydreaming."

"We won't try to buy votes with hypocrisy," he said.

Despite Lévesque's adherence to independence as a basic policy, the question of referendum has confused the electoral picture in Quebec.

"Should the P.Q. ever be brought to power with a minority," said a respected Montreal journalist, "I'm not sure they wouldn't be open to the idea of governing without effecting separation.

"The referendum hasn't attracted people to the party who would not otherwise be attracted but it might attract people at an election. There's a real possibility that the P.Q. would get a lot of non-separatist votes, and some of these voters might be persuaded to join the party after the election."

A journalist in the Quebec Press Gallery went even further when he speculated that "the Parti Québécois could end up with thirty-five members after the next election, and many of them may not be separatists at all."

There was a curious parallel in the spring of 1976 between the Quebec situation and the general election in Italy, where the Communists under an attractive and experienced leader threatened for the first time to move into a position of power. Like the Parti Québécois, the Italian Communists appeared almost to forget about their basic philosophy as they campaigned on a promise of good government. The "Italian" technique is clearly the electoral direction in which the Parti Québécois is heading: separatists in government but not necessarily separatism.

"If we have an intermediary phase, with the P.Q. as a strong opposition, perhaps in a minority government situation, it becomes a very open game," said a Montreal journalist.

> The labour unions would have to think twice. The P.Q. might affect a greater rapprochement with the unions in exchange for more responsibility on their part.
>
> If this was achieved, then they would be ripe for power, not necessarily on a platform of separation...well, perhaps on a separatist platform, but if the idea of responsible behaviour was solidly implanted, even that prospect would be much less disturbing.
>
> Lévesque might be the man to steer them through that very difficult course.

This prospect raised another "Italian" question in the minds of some Quebecers.

"Lévesque is too dictatorial," said the leader of another Quebec party. "There's no commitment to democracy.

"If the P.Q. got in, there's real uncertainty as to whether they would respect democratic forms."

In the volatile Quebec political situation in the spring of 1976, two constants tempered speculation about the future of the Parti Québécois: the conservatism of the majority of Quebec voters, and the recuperative powers of the formidable Liberal machine in Quebec. Despite this, many informed people in Canada were looking seriously at the possibility of political changes in Quebec.

Thomas Enders, the new and somewhat unconventional U.S. ambassador in Ottawa, travelled quietly to Quebec City for long conversations with Claude Morin and Jacques-Yvan Morin, discovering in the P.Q. House leader someone he could reminisce with about student days at Harvard.

In the Parliamentary Restaurant in Ottawa, an Ontario member of the Trudeau cabinet thoughtfully chewed over the possibility of an electoral victory for the Quebec separatists.

"It wouldn't be the end of the world," he said smoothly. "We've had this Sword of Damocles hanging over our heads since 1960. A victory for Lévesque might be the catharsis we all need. Then we could sit down and have a real negotiation with Quebec."

The situation is filled with contradictions and ironies. If the Quebec Liberals continue to lose support, it will be in part because they have had to absorb and implement the strong nationalist spirit of the Sixties. Now, in a more conservative period, Lévesque begins to appeal to Quebecers as a leader who might restore efficiency and stability to the province.

For Lévesque and his party, the political world has turned upside-down since the brave early days when independence was a challenge that seemed to require a relatively simple response. The final assessment of the movement, and of Lévesque's contribution to Quebec, will be a complex matter even for historians who will know results that are still hidden from us.

Whatever the outcome, Lévesque will always be a public figure and private individual whose life is almost infinitely revealing about Canadians and their country.

He has always talked about political leadership as a job, neither an arcane art nor a mystical vocation. By that definition, he has been an unconventional but useful craftsman.

Note on Sources

The basic source of this book is my experience as a political journalist in Montreal from 1960 until 1971, first as a reporter with the Montreal *Star* and later as a freelance journalist working primarily on television for the Canadian Broadcasting Corporation. For specific information, I relied on two main sources. The first was a thorough search of the journalistic record of Lévesque's political career, concentrating on articles published by *La Presse* and *Le Devoir* but also including other French-language newspapers in Quebec and the English-language press in Montreal and outside Quebec. The second source was thirty-four lengthy interviews with people whose recollections of Lévesque went back to his student days. These interviews were done on the understanding that quotations would not be directly attributed. In all but a few cases, though, they were recorded on tape. It is material from these tapes, and my own notes of interviews, that give this book vitality and some special interest.

René Lévesque talked with me about himself in a series of interviews in 1973, when I commenced work on this book, and in 1976. In 1973, I travelled with him on a political tour of the Gaspé, when we visited his home town.

As this is a journalist's book, and the source of almost all the material has been indicated in the text, I saw no need to publish the reference notes that are in my original manuscript, or to include a version of the standard Quebec bibliography that has appeared in many other books in recent years.

Appendix

In 1969, when I was a freelance journalist in Montreal under contract to the Canadian Broadcasting Corporation, *The Canadian* magazine in Toronto asked me to write a scenario for the separation of Quebec. This wasn't the first such request from Toronto and by 1969, I was bored with writing this kind of political science fiction, so I suggested asking René Lévesque to do it in the form of an interview.

The editors at *The Canadian* were enthusiastic; and Lévesque, for his own political reasons, was interested in the project. He was also the only politician I had ever met with the journalistic talent to accomplish it with wit and style.

And he did just that, although it took time and perseverance, as usual, to drag it out of him. I don't recall how many missed appointments there were, but I remember waiting for him in his Montreal office one morning when the phone rang and his secretary handed it to me. It was Lévesque, apologizing from somewhere in rural Quebec.

Finally, on a Saturday afternoon, hours late, when I had almost given up once again, he trudged up the stairs to my office in Montreal ready to tape the interview. He had told me previously that he had been working on the list of questions that I had given to him and, much to my surprise, he actually had. He dumped a messy bundle of handwritten notes on my desk, I started the tape recorder and we placed ourselves mentally in the year 1977 in an independent Quebec.

The interview was even more successful than I had expected. When the transcript reached Toronto, the editors of *The Canadian* had the same reaction. They immediately decided to publish the entire transcript in two instalments.

It never appeared.

Some weeks later, *The Canadian* informed me that the interview had been checked with the editors of *The Gazette* in Montreal, one of the newspapers that included *The Canadian* as a supplement in Saturday editions. That was normal procedure for *The Canadian* at a time when many people saw Quebec separatism as a threat to Canada's future. The editors of *The Canadian* sought *The Gazette's* advice, as they later explained, because they felt that the Montreal newspaper was closer to the situation and had more intimate knowledge of it.

After reading the transcript, *The Gazette's* editors warned *The Canadian* that the interview, in their estimation, gave a credibility to Quebec's secession that was unjustified and, given the magazine's 2,000,-000 readers across the country, could create a widespread impression that secession was much more feasible than *The Gazette's* editors considered it to be. In their view the article would be needlessly divisive for Canada. *The Canadian* agreed that, in that light, it would be irresponsible to publish it at that time.

The Canadian paid me for the interview and until now, it has remained unpublished. Now, with the kind permission of *The Canadian*, here it is – René Lévesque's 1969 vision of what our own time might have looked like.

Peter Desbarats

DESBARATS: This is now 1977 and I wonder if you could look back six years – to the year 1971 – and tell me something of the initial reaction to your party's victory?

LÉVESQUE: First of all, the election was no great surprise. Our victory was expected. More or less everything had been building up to it after the first great breakthrough in the 1969 election when we won thirty-three seats in the Quebec provincial house and became the official opposition in Quebec. As far as reaction to the 1971 election – when we won a majority – for us as newsmen (well, I'm a former newsman) the simplest thing is for us to look back at the headlines. They give you a sort of bird's eye view of reaction.

In Quebec, for instance, *Le Devoir* had the solemn headline the day after the election: *La Fin d'un Régime – l'Histoire de Québec Recommence* (End of an Era – The History of Quebec Begins Again). And Claude Ryan had an editorial on page four – *Où Allons-Nous?* , You know – Whither Quebec? In the *Journal de Montréal* and the *Journal de Québec* – they were pretty close to our way of seeing things– it was: *Enfin!* At last! Here We Go! In the Montreal *Gazette* it was: *Québec Libre?*

In the rest of Canada there were two that gave you a pretty good idea of the mixed reactions. The Toronto *Star* had: Quebec Opts Out – Now What? But the Vancouver *Province* had: Quebec Opts Out – So What! In the United States, the *Daily News* in New York, at the bottom of the page: Quebec Election – Separatists In, Canada Out.

DESBARATS: At the bottom of the page?

LÉVESQUE: Oh yes, it wasn't top news. Not that much. In the *New York Times*, they had: Québécois Party Runaway Winner In Crucial Quebec Vote. So it wasn't a great surprise as you can see from the headlines.

DESBARATS: What was your first concern in the first few days after this victory?

LÉVESQUE: Well, it was two-fold. First of all, to get a cabinet together and get it down to work, with no waste of time, readying our first session, which would be all-important, the session in the fall of '71. We had to prepare legislation and also keep the store going under normal provincial government – don't forget, we were a provincial government to start with – and also to get the store ready for major alterations.

The second concern was negotiations with Canada – very few speeches but a tone of quiet but total determination, announcing that we were ready for negotiations and that time was of the essence.

In other words, on both sides, we had much to lose. To avoid driving Quebec to a unilateral declaration, independence had to be before June '72. We set a limit.

Our negotiating team, at least the political end of it, was ready when we got elected; and, to flesh out that political team, we gathered a team of civil servants. Quebec had built, over the previous few years, a pretty non-partisan civil service and they were ready to work immediately.

DESBARATS: Could you tell me what happened between 1969, when your Parti Québécois became the official opposition, and 1971, when you won a majority?

LÉVESQUE: Well, if you remember the Quebec election of November, 1969, that was the major shock, I think. That was the one that decided everything – when the result gave us thirty-three seats out of 108.

After that, as you may recall, both old parties in Quebec – the National Union and the Liberals – were wracked with continual division because there was no majority in the Provincial House. The National Union first tried to go it alone. They had to count more and more heavily on the support of the Liberals, including a group of about twenty Liberals who were pushing more and more toward accommodation with Ottawa. Three other Liberal members – who didn't like this accommodation with Ottawa – joined our Parti Québécois and they were followed by a handful of National Union members. This brought up our strength – six months after the election – to forty-three members.

So in June of 1970, at a special convention of the Quebec Liberal party, they managed to vote a sort of common front with the National Union and there was a coalition cabinet formed under Mr. Bertrand (the late Quebec Premier Jean-Jacques Bertrand.*) And finally – I'm sure no one has forgotten this – after a joint convention in January 1971, where there was a drafting of Jean-Luc Pepin as the new coalition leader in Quebec. (In 1975, Pepin was named chairman of the Anti-Inflation Board in Ottawa.*) A general election was called for June 28 of 1971. And that was it!

That's when we got sixty-three seats and 56.5 per cent of the vote.

DESBARATS: What was the decisive issue in Quebec's decision to vote for your party?

LÉVESQUE: Well, there were so many things that counted, it's very hard to tell what part each ingredient played in the eventual result. Mostly, I think, it was the normal result of the process of self-affirmation and self-discovery that Quebec had been going through for the previous ten years.

More immediately, it was the result of the general economic slump during most of '69 and of '70 that North America was going through, all that post-Viet Nam reconversion in the United States, that was pretty tough during the first couple of years...

DESBARATS: Gave Mr. Nixon a lot of trouble?

LÉVESQUE: That's right. Now, of course, in '77, we've got a New England president. (Lévesque was thinking, in 1969, of Edmund Muskie, of Maine, or Edward Kennedy, from Massachusetts.*) This helps a lot, too. Keeps us on good-neighbour terms, and all that. Anyway, that economic slump had a lot to do with it.

I think one shock that was pretty decisive in Quebec, in a symbolic way, was when we officially learned in 1971 that Canada had slipped right down to ninth rating in the Western world in its standard of living. After the U.S., Sweden and Iceland, who already had passed us in 1968, Denmark and Switzerland went ahead in '69, West Germany, Holland and France in late '70 or '71. Needless to say, Quebec knew it was fourteenth or fifteenth, on that basis.

But the most decisive factor that emerged, was the point of no-return that was reached in the federal-provincial confusion, and the accompanying political panic tactics that came out of that. There was an incredible number of what you might call "standing committees" trying to sort out the Ottawa-Quebec field – the number had risen from 151 in 1968 to 240 or more in 1971. There was a great deal of mutual frustration.

Nobody knew whether they were coming or going anymore. And then you had that incredibly dense political tactic of plunging us first into a federal election in early June of 1971, in the hope that a few weeks later a majority could ride in on what was left of the coattails of the Trudeau government.

*author's note

210

DESBARATS: The Trudeau government – I'm sorry, I can't remember – did they win that election in 1971?

LÉVESQUE: No, I guess Quebec voters finally got disgusted with the whole thing. Anyway, the Trudeau government was kicked out and Quebec was decisive in kicking it out. Then, a few weeks later, it was almost an anti-climax when Québécois agreed with our slogan, which was, "*D'abord, il faut que ça finisse*" – "First of All, It's Got to Finish."

DESBARATS: By that time, the Conservatives were back in Ottawa? With Stanfield?

LÉVESQUE: Uh-huh. A minority government.

DESBARATS: Did the Trudeau government lose support mainly in Quebec or were they losing ground in English Canada at that time?

LÉVESQUE: Mostly in Quebec but the basic ambiguity of the whole Trudeau position caught up with them, especially in the Maritimes where Mr. Stanfield still had his strength and in parts of Ontario and the West. Anyway, they went out.

DESBARATS: Where did your financial support come from during this period?

LÉVESQUE: In both campaigns, most of it came from popular sources. In the '71 campaign, the one that decided the thing, of course we got much more substantial support from some elements of the business community because obviously we were closer to power. Nothing attracts them like that. You can go back and check on the official report on the Parti Québécois' electoral fund in '71, if you want. If my memory serves me right, we spent something like $300,000 on a party basis, as opposed to $750,000 by the coalition party.

DESBARATS: Were terrorist activities in Quebec at that time a help or a hindrance?

LÉVESQUE: That, I think, only history can assess, and it will take some time yet. Whatever the final evaluation may be, there's one thing we can be thankful for – as soon as election results proved that we were going places in 1969 and we got that pretty wonderful channelling of youth power in our political action – in a democratic action – there were practically no terrorist outbursts, except for the odd nut that you'll get in any uncertain climate.

All told, I think the '70 and '71 figures on bombing incidents came pretty close to zero. About five or six, I think, in each year.

DESBARATS: There was never any attempt by the English to resort to this kind of activity as they began to lose ground?

LÉVESQUE: Some of those odd cases could have been English, but we never got proof.

DESBARATS: What was the position of Quebec's English-speaking minority during this period?

LÉVESQUE: As you know, I think the best word to describe their position as a group during most of those decisive years would be "painful." It was painful for many of the English-speaking people, particularly the older generation, it was like... well, at first, in the Sixties, the writing on the wall, becoming clearer all the time, and then something like the end of the world when they saw what was really happening.

We sure felt it in the election of '69. We had candidates everywhere – we had to – but the most that can be said is that they didn't do very well in any English-speaking riding.

DESBARATS: English-speaking candidates in these ridings?

LÉVESQUE: We had a few, among the younger, radical generation, especially after we got our first campus association, at McGill, things changed quite a bit. In fact, they changed a lot more than we thought possible. And I'm still a bit flabbergasted, when I think of it now, that our candidates got elected in '71 in Notre-Dame-de-Grace and St. Anne's. And I'm especially proud of them, Jones in St. Anne's and Smith in N.D.G. They are brilliant young bilingual English Québécois. I think that that, especially, helped keep problems to a minimum when the transition period really came, before independence, in the 1971-1972 negotiation period.

After all, we managed to keep the flight of people from Quebec to a real low. Less than 25,000 people, or thereabouts, left during the first three years. We thought it would be a hell of a lot more than that. And the proudest thing of all, I guess, is that out of those few, many already have moved back in or at least are actively thinking about it.

DESBARATS: These 25,000 people who left in the early Seventies...some of those were French-speaking Québécois?

LÉVESQUE: Some of our moneyed people, especially, moved out. Some haven't come back. You find that kind everywhere. I don't think you can call it a loss.

DESBARATS: Where did most of the people go? Did they go to other parts of Canada or the States?

LÉVESQUE: Both. The French-speaking ones that did leave with their money went mostly to the States.

DESBARATS: What segments of the population were most resistant to your party's appeal?

LÉVESQUE: Apart from the English-speaking community, the most resistant groups in the '69 election generally were those rural ridings where you had this rather sick combination of being truly rural and an above-average elderly population.

Even in those districts, relatively, it was much better for us in '71 when we took power. They were caught up in the bandwagon atmosphere that was created by three major pillars: workers, both white and blue collar (in fact more white than blue); young people, a lot of whom were literally mobilized by student leaders; and professional people, taking in everything from university professors and public school teachers to some business people and civil servants, doctors, lawyers, mostly all in the twenty-five to forty or forty-five age bracket–in other words, the ones with an immediate stake in the decision.

DESBARATS: Could you tell me something about the actual process of achieving independence?

LÉVESQUE: We were sworn in as a new provincial government on July 15, 1971. On July 31, the make-up of our negotiating team was announced, made up of the Ministers of Finance, Economic Affairs, Inter-Governmental Affairs (which would be the Foreign Office eventually) and yours truly, and we also announced that we were ready to start substantial talks as soon as possible.

Now the minority Conservative government in Ottawa was brand-new, as you recall; Stanfield had been elected with a minority in June of 1971 and the government was still pretty shaky. They had gotten in touch with us on July 16, as is well known now, through Mr. Valade, the Honourable Monsieur Valade (In 1969, the Member of Parliament for Montreal-Ste. Marie*) and asked us for a brief moratorium of a few weeks because they had to pick up the pieces and also, I guess, they had to assess reaction throughout the country.

Because, instantaneously, more or less, Ottawa became a sort of power vacuum and had to know whether it had any kind of popular mandate to do anything–either refuse or accept negotiations.

What they found out during those few tense weeks, about reaction in the country, was basically this: reaction was divided into three parts.

In the Maritimes, most people were for a negotiated way out. Even elder statesman Joey Smallwood (Premier of Newfoundland in 1969; in 1976, still a member of the Newfoundland legislature*), who was then visiting with the Nixons in southern Florida called for a friendly settlement, which gave us an additional lead on official U.S. attitudes, because normally Joey wouldn't have reacted that way.

In Ontario, generally, they were also for negotiations. The theme was something like this: "That's the way it is. That's the way it has to be. Let's make the best of it."

In the West, it was different. It was either cold or hot hostility in many circles, especially Alberta and British Columbia. You even had quite a few prominent people, including government members in British Columbia, throwing out very confused calls both for annexation to the United States and for a fight to the finish. It was a real mix-up.

But pretty soon (as far as I recall, by August 15, when the preliminary talks had opened in the Ottawa-Hull area) the federal people had recei-
*author's note

213

ved reports that were comprehensive and pretty convincing on the consensus that was shaping up: that Canada was to go on and should do it by some sort of peaceful arrangement with a free Quebec.

This consensus, in fact, when you look back, was the deciding factor because from then on, until the so-called "Ottawa Protocols" were finalized in March, 1972, everyone was mostly working like hell to get the old set-up out of the way and the new one ready. Now some extremists–marginal groups of hot heads, mostly in various Maritime and Western areas–still called for a march on Quebec and we had our own kooks calling for a takeover in northern New Brunswick and Northern Ontario... even some volunteering for a sort of polar expedition to take over Baffin Island.

You remember also that the Labrador Liberation Front, which wanted us to "liberate" Labrador from Newfoundland, cropped up at that time, too. I hope to God we can eventually settle that cancer but it's not settled yet.

But apart from such small-scale, inevitable eruptions, as of mid-August, 1971, the main effort was both constructive and looking toward a peaceful agreement on both sides.

What helped a lot was the immediate positive attitude in Washington. It was both absolutely calm–they didn't have any kind of nervousness about it–and unobtrusively helpful. We know it was from our side and I guess they put the same pressure on the other side.

Soon after the 1969 election, there was that vicious anti-Quebec campaign by some English Canadian groups who tried to reach U.S. administration and business circles. As a result, you remember, we set up representation of our party both at New York and the U.N., in Washington and in Boston, and we established pretty close and fruitful relations eventually with Franco-American groups in the New England states; and we got the dividends of having that representation during the crucial 1971-72 period, because there was more understanding than anyone had hoped for on the American side.

There were some people in the States who were camouflaged English-Canadians–you have a lot of English-Canadian people who have moved there and, after a few years, nobody knows they are not native-born Americans–and we had some of them in the Wall Street area who were trying like hell, with Toronto and Montreal accomplices, to do a job on us. Using the Castro smear and everything else.

But there was one thing that was basic. On account of their very important investment in Quebec, and the strategic importance of Quebec–just think about the Seaway–Americans were much better posted on what was really going on in Quebec than some of those rather naive anti-Quebec Canadians. And so eventually, the truth came out in the wash.

DESBARATS: How long did this intermediary stage last? Was there a specific day on which Quebec proclaimed its independence ?

LÉVESQUE: It depends what you call intermediary, because in many respects...here we are on June 24, 1977, five years after the official proclamation of the Quebec republic, and we're still in an intermediary period... things are still tentative in many fields and we're still groping on many problems...but all in all, I think it's been a magnificent achievement of civilized negotiation.

In fact, it's been a lesson for other countries; and also, it's an incredibly promising new arrangement. Here again, we've made some pioneering steps. For instance, our monetary union and the common market and labour market treaties, and the related agreements on citizenship and the Seaway and transport and communications. Well, that monetary union in a way was a pilot project for the European monetary union which they finally agreed on and which, in fact, saved the European community from flying apart.

DESBARATS: Did monetary union mean that the Canadian currency...

LÉVESQUE: That was the benefit of not waiting too long in the summer of 1971, to initiate negotiations, because we could keep the former currency going until an agreement had been made–and we finally got an agreement, as you know – on a common monetary unit and a common central bank.

Without going into all the intricacies (a lot of people still talk about monetary policy–the less they know, the more they talk) it was an expert agreement and it worked. One thing that has to be said: it was a lot simpler for us than it was for the Europeans because we had an easier starting point.

DESBARATS: What was the first country, five years ago, to recognize Quebec?

LÉVESQUE: That's one thing nobody will ever forget: the complete, utter astonishment in so many quarters when Great Britain was the first informally to recognize Quebec's new status. In fact, just one day after the preliminary talks began on August 15, 1971, you remember the British Prime Minister made that great speech in which he made Britain's final bid for entry into the Common Market, the one that was successful, and he threw in that celebrated sentence about "this changing world" where such formerly unthinkable events as "*le Québec libre*"–and he said it in French–were now coming to pass peacefully.

You remember this was taken up in Paris immediately, quite favourably, and I guess in a modest way you can say that Quebec's independence helped to finalize the passage to Europe of old Britain.

I suppose when some documents that aren't published yet become public, we'll also find out that this first real recognition was probably pre-arranged with Ottawa because, as you know, those were the weeks when Ottawa was wondering if it had any kind of mandate left; and I suppose, to keep a cool climate as much as possible, they arranged things with the British in London because they felt that some sort of semi-recognition would have a good psychological effect.

And the reaction was pretty good. As far as formal recognition goes, in the spring of 1972, the Canadian signing of the protocol in essence constituted Canadian recognition of Quebec and as soon as that was finalized, recognition from the United States and France came practically at the same time. The U.S.S.R. was close behind and then, well, normally, Gabon, Belgium and Biafra and Tunisia and the whole bunch.

But the day of days, of course, was the formal proclamation of the republic in Quebec and that came in a one-two sequence: on June 17, there was the referendum on the new constitution, and it was overwhelmingly approved.

And then, on June 24, 1972, there was the first *"jour de l'indépendance."*

DESBARATS: St Jean Baptiste Day, of course.

LÉVESQUE: Yes, and that was a good thing too, because it kind of renewed the old, antiquated St. Jean Baptiste climate, and made it really mean something.

But that first day was mostly a day of fulfilment, rather quiet in a way, because we didn't have the old folkloric parade and all those speeches; the proclamation spoke for itself. I think people knew in Quebec really who they were as a group and it helped them as individuals. They were standing, not so much taller as a lot straighter than they had been.

Among other things, the proclamation set the date for the next election–that was part of the constitution–the first under the republican regime, with a statutory date of the last Sunday in October in that year of 1972. The election was both for the president and the vice-president and for the new National Assembly.

On that Independence Day, the whole of downtown Montreal became the scene of spontaneous, all-night, open-air celebration and a new tradition was born. Now that's the way it's done every June 24. Instead of the rather dull spectator sport of lining a parade route, it's the people's day to participate and they just take over–in the downtown areas, in most places–which I think is a hell of a good way of celebrating.

DESBARATS: Did Quebec City automatically become the capital of the new state or was there an attempt to transfer it to Montreal? And did Ottawa remain the capital of Canada?

LÉVESQUE: Quebec was kept as the capital. There wasn't even any serious thought of changing it. And now it's grown, as of the 1976 census, to about a million people. After the referendum that Canada held in 1973, they decided to move the capital to Winnipeg and to leave Ottawa and Hull as the administrative centre for the common market and the monetary union commission and the secretariat.

As you remember, the '73 referendum revamped a lot of Canadian structures. There was this grouping of the former prairie provinces into a single prairie state with a common state capital in Regina. So now you have British Columbia, the prairie state, Ontario and Eastern Canada ... well, at least three of the Maritime provinces are together now, and if the second referendum in Newfoundland works out right this year, Newfoundland will probably join them, because they can't go it alone.

You know, in a way, the whole thing–the settling of the Quebec problem–was a godsend for Canada. There was a lot of initial uncertainty in 1971–talk in Alberta of joining the U.S. and the growth of the go-it-alone party in British Columbia. Canada had to face the big question of whether to try a unitary government or a new federalism with a better balance.

And the ironic thing, mostly on account of the Maritime region, is that they've opted for a new federalism which has many elements of that "special status" everyone was talking about for Quebec back in the Sixties but which had seemed unthinkable then. And now it's working out pretty well for the *rest* of Canada.

DESBARATS: Did Quebec immediately establish an embassy in the capital of Canada?

LÉVESQUE: Yes. That was part of the initial agreement, the protocol in the spring of '72. The first exchange of ambassadors was with Canada. Since then, we've kept the development of our embassies to a minimum. We've done it as slowly and as rationally as possible. We've got barely a few dozen real old-type embassies because we try to work mostly through legations and also through joint deals, mainly with Canada.

We've got the usual embassies at the U.N. and Washington, Paris, London and Rome (which is also tied to the Vatican; we don't have a special one for the Vatican), Brussels, Moscow, Prague...

DESBARATS: You decided not to have one for the Vatican ?

LÉVESQUE: Politically it wasn't necessary and the Rome one could handle the Vatican–and does. Where were we?...Prague, Mexico, Buenos Aires, Stockholm, Tel Aviv and Beirut–for obvious reasons, we have one on the Arab side and one on the Israeli...Algiers and Dakar, Tokyo and Peking.

The Peking thing was very simple, of course, because we just followed the trend after the U.N. breakthrough on the China question in 1971.

We're out of the Commonwealth, as everyone knows but, on the other hand, in most Commonwealth countries we've got joint representation with Canada and the same applies in reverse in the French "Francophonie"–the culturally and economically important commonwealth of French-speaking nations.

The best example of the set-up would be the fact that we use services from the Canadian side for Pakistan, India and Ceylon, while they, the Canadians, use our services in the Quebec embassies in Hue, in Viet Nam, and Phnom Penh, capital of Cambodia. Hue, as you know, is now the capital of a united Viet Nam.

DESBARATS: What happened to all the federal buildings in Quebec? The Seaway and railway head offices and airports, for example?

LÉVESQUE: Well, there was an artificial mountain of problems, as you remember. People were inventing difficulties, making elaborate calculations about how much Quebec should pay or not pay, and what Quebec's share should be of this or that or the other thing...in fact, some people were practically inventing new mathematics in all that confusion.

But finally, in the 1972 agreement, it was relatively simple, and common sense prevailed. For instance, federal assets fixed in Quebec became simply Quebec property because Quebec taxpayers had never received more than their share of tax money. So everybody agreed that they had already paid for the federal property in Quebec.

The 28 per cent rule of thumb, based on population, was accepted for moveable stock–you know, railway cars and things like that–so, finally, there wasn't much problem on that score.

The Canadian federal head offices, such as CN and Air Canada, obviously had to move to Ottawa in the first few months. After, there was the second transition to Winnipeg and that made Winnipeg feel pretty good after those old disputes with Montreal over Air Canada facilities.

Then the tripartite Seaway administration–U.S., Canada and Quebec–was set up as a natural thing because it was just adding a third party to the two that were there before.

DESBARATS: Did Quebec form its own national airline?

LÉVESQUE: As you know, Air Québec is growing healthily. It covers all of our internal routes and gives better service to remote parts because it has the paying lines to supplement things. Of course, we have the agreement with Canada on route-sharing, and we have the joint venture on the so-called "air lifeline"–you know, the one that goes from the Canadian capital at Winnipeg to Halifax but also takes in Toronto, Ottawa, Montreal, Quebec and Moncton. We share this on an equal basis.

The Air Québec and Air Canada lines complement each other and they give one of the most efficient and sensible services ever devised between two friendly countries. Pretty soon (from what I hear, because I'm not in government anymore –I haven't been for a few years) we should be ready for an international joint venture between Air Québec and Air

Canada. Air Québec, you know, didn't want to go into all this business of costly sovereignty and prestige flying, so our only foreign connections for our Quebec airline are the link between the eastern United States and Mexico, and the circuit that covers Montreal-Quebec-Paris-London.

But now we have a good chance of having a joint international venture with Air Canada, more or less on the Scandinavian model. The only major hurdle seems to be what name the joint public corporation should have–which is crazy…but you know we're not so far from our crazy past; we still have remnants of that kind of hassle.

DESBARATS: Did Quebec have to set up its own customs service?

LÉVESQUE: No. Thank God, that was settled with our common market treaty of 1972 and with the agreement on common tariffs with outside countries, and the sharing of customs revenue between the two countries. That's one sector where European community experience was invaluable and we've bettered it in many ways through our own agreements.

DESBARATS: What happened to the CBC facilities in Quebec?

LÉVESQUE: Well, that was a welcome finish to a growing and rather stupid pain in the neck on both sides. You just have to think back to that crazy mix-up which came to a boil in 1969 about educational TV and the satellite problem.

Now what we have is a Quebec radio and TV network based on the former CBC French-service headquarters in Montreal, and there is the CBC on the Canadian side. There are exchange agreements on programs for minorities. We also have the bonus of joint technical facilities, particularly our joint public satellite corporation, which we both use, and a lot of joint research that came out of that.

And one thing we're very proud of is that Quebec's part in the "Francophone" satellite corporation is now stimulating the Commonwealth project which, from what we hear, may eventually be realized.

DESBARATS: What about other sectors in the whole field of communications? Bell Telephone? Press communications?

LÉVESQUE: Well, Bell Québec is now, and has been for two or three years, as you know, a mixed enterprise – fifty-fifty private and public. The whole of Quebec now is getting decent service at properly determined rates.

The Quebec news agency, which is state-supported but is pretty well protected against government interference (it's more or less on the lines of the BBC or CBC), is doing a pretty good job of internal coverage, which we never had in Quebec, and it's slowly developing a corps of foreign correspondents. Its working agreements with Canadian Press are also a good example of cost sharing for better international coverage.

DESBARATS: What happened to French-speaking Québécois who had

219

been serving in the Canadian Army or the RCMP or the federal–the *old* federal civil service?

LÉVESQUE: On that score, we found out that our Quebec people in these jobs–most of whom elected to serve the new Quebec state when they were called upon in 1972 (they obviously had a choice)–well, we found out that those poeple were far from numerous enough to answer our needs. We sure found out that our suspicions were correct, that we really had *not* had our normal share of that sector of employment. Especially in the middle and top ranges of management.

Anyway, even though they all more or less joined us, we didn't have enough. That was a bitter discovery but we decided. . .let's forget it. Bygones are bygones. On our side, we didn't have any trouble assimilating these people but there were too few.

There was also a problem on the Canadian side: there were quite a few people who went back to the Canadians from federal administrative jobs in Quebec, or Quebec-oriented civil service in Ottawa, and some of them were hard to re-integrate at first because the Canadians found they had a surplus of civil servants. But now the problem seems to be pretty well settled.

DESBARATS: How did Quebec tackle the problem of its own military defences?

LÉVESQUE: We didn't have a big problem. The main scare, or the main nervousness was that the Americans would be hard to convince, because we had decided to leave NATO and we didn't accept the NORAD thing...

DESBARATS: That took out the Bomarc base in northern Quebec right away?

LÉVESQUE: Yes, that settled that. There was some reaction in the U.S. about our "neutralist" attitude but thank God, the U.S. has ever since the Viet Nam settlement in 1970-71, largely given up its policeman's role. Especially since the '76 election, with the Bicentennial year in the U.S., and this new dedication to development of their own society which had so much trouble in the late Sixties and early Seventies. And urban problems and racial problems. . .now the U.S. is really moving on that, so they've lost this morbid fixation they had on military things, which helped Quebec make its own role acceptable. Because, as you know, we don't have any military defence force of any kind except a simple group to help young people. . .this mixed peace corps-labour corps thing we have for young people instead of military service.

DESBARATS: Is that voluntary or is there some sort of conscription for that?

LÉVESQUE: There's semi-conscription. In other words, there are a lot of exemptions for post-graduate students, and people in essential jobs, or young married couples with kids. But anyway, with a lot of exemptions, it is conscription, especially for drop-outs. If you want to drop out, well and good, but you'll have to give at least one year of service. It gives us a chance to at least give them a trade and get them ready in a better fashion for earning a living.

DESBARATS: Was there any move, at any time, to withdraw foreign capital from Quebec?

LÉVESQUE: There was no problem as far as American investments were concerned. There *was* a problem, but it was exactly the opposite of the one that people had predicted in the late Sixties. There was not so much a flight of capital but rather an American rush leading to too many takeovers.

As far as English-Canadian capital was concerned, based in Montreal and Toronto, substantial amounts of it had gone out in stages long before 1972. That's unfortunate but there's never been any logic or reasoning in that kind of thing. When things are uncertain and people don't know where the hell they're going, and they're used to a dominant position and they see themselves losing it, well, that's the inevitable reaction.

So the problem was to avoid being swamped by American investment. But at least with the setting up of our economic community–the common market and monetary agreements – when the uncertainty was over and the horizon was clear, quite a bit of that money came back from Canada.

DESBARATS: What about the new state's access to Quebec's traditional sources of capital in the United States?

LÉVESQUE: As I've said before, there were some vicious efforts to distort Quebec's image in the United States in the late Sixties and early Seventies, but the Americans, as I was reminding you, have a pretty solid knowledge of what's going on in Quebec.

So it didn't hurt, really, on the American side and, as you know, we worked like hell to keep their picture of Quebec clear. And we were lucky, too, in this way: Quebec came in with the beginning of the new economic expansion which started in '71 and which is still going on. So there's no problem about the money markets except that we do work to diversify our sources of outside money and Europe is, increasingly, an alternate source.

DESBARATS: Did unemployment remain a major problem in Quebec during the first years of independence? Did the new state make any new departures in social welfare?

LÉVESQUE: In all those fields, we still have problems, and we're finding them tough problems. But at least instead of the old and rather sterile attitude of waiting for miracles, mostly from outside, we're tackling them as we never did before. One thing there is, as never before, is participation.

221

People themselves are involved as they never were in Quebec. And there's a growing feeling that the whole of Quebec is basically a great community-building project–better production, better distribution, more efficiency, but also better justice.

Now that doesn't mean we're close to utopia, but that's the point: we've become responsible, and now we realize that utopia, or instant paradise, is out! But at least we're beating our problems on a pretty wide front and we're making more progress than we ever dreamed was possible. And that's the essential thing.

You see, Quebec independence was never an end in itself. Basically, it had to be a means to a more active and self-developing society. And the first tool to do that job – we're being proved right every year–is self-government because that means responsibility and dignity.

DESBARATS: How about your own career these days? Do you miss political life?

LÉVESQUE: No...the year of independence, 1972, just happened to coincide with my twelfth year in public life and I decided that I had had it! Twelve years was enough.

So, as you know, I was fortunate enough to be appointed Quebec's first ambassador in Washington. I love Washington. So I've had a great time of it. And looking at Quebec from the standpoint of Washington explains why some of my answers might have had a more "American" flavour than you might have expected.

DESBARATS: In that first election in the Quebec republic that was held in '72...do you remember the parties that contested it?

LÉVESQUE: Well, let's forget names. The first election was very simple. It was almost dangerous. We came very close to a one-party state. The Parti Québécois, which hadn't changed it's name, literally...well, I think for a while there were only about ten opposition people in the National Assembly.

The "crunch" election, the one that decided whether we should go on or not, was in '76, just last year. And then you had three parties, as you know: the Parti Québécois had broken up for the election into what you might call its right and left wings, and you also had the know-nothing group, the last remnants of the old rural Quebec, the bad part of rural Quebec.

The social democratic wing of the Parti Québécois came to power with a normal majority and a healthy opposition and now this means we're all right, I think.

DESBARATS: How did you manage the little, picayune things that used to give the old Canadian federation so much trouble, such as–whose picture was going to be on the currency ? And the Quebec national anthem? And what flag would be used, and so forth?

LÉVESQUE: That was easily solved because, as you remember, when Canada reorganized itself on that new state basis, and decided at the same time that even though it was staying in the Commonwealth, it was moving away from the royal tradition (although they still have great respect for the head of the Commonwealth) . . . well, almost as a by-product, there was no fighting on the issue of money, because some of our common founders such as Champlain and Cartier and d'Arcy McGee and Macdonald were put on the currency on the same basis as Americans used former presidents. With a logical balance of French and English figures, this has made the currency acceptable to everyone.

DESBARATS: And the flag . . . was it just a matter of adopting the old Quebec flag?

LÉVESQUE: That was it.

DESBARATS: And the anthem?

LÉVESQUE: Oh well, as you know, Gilles Vigneault came up with a stroke of genius with that song of his in '71, and that's the anthem now.

DESBARATS: What is the position of the English minority in Quebec today, in 1977?

LÉVESQUE: The frustration and hostility virtually disappeared as soon as Quebec made up its mind to be independent, at least on our side. There was no longer any danger of being swamped by English culture because we knew that it was up to us to decide things, on a majority basis. Especially since we controlled immigration completely and immigrants were–there were no two ways about it–immigrants were oriented to the French school system.

So we left the English school system pretty well on its own, tax-supported, and basically what's going on is, I guess, the normal thing. . .it will take a while for younger people, while keeping their English set-up from elementary school to McGill, to learn French. But they will have to learn. It's a French-oriented society!

And some every year (as used to happen) are leaving because it's not the kind of society they want. The others, the majority, are staying and making careers in Quebec. I think that eventually everyone will be assimilated.

DESBARATS: I keep thinking of an interview we did back in 1969–where you were doing some forecasting that has since turned out to be pretty accurate. Did you really believe, back then, that it would actually turn out as you were predicting?

LÉVESQUE: At that time, of course, I was trying to choose between quite a number of future happenings. And trying to build something like a logical half-way forecast–some people would say I made it too optimistic. Many things have happened a bit differently but I think that it wasn't too far off.